Raising a Handicapped Child

Raising a Handicapped Child

A Helpful Guide for Parents
of the Physically Disabled

CHARLOTTE E. THOMPSON, M.D.

Ballantine Books • New York

To Jennifer, Geoffrey, and Margaret,
whose unwavering love and support
have made it all possible

Library of Congress Catalog Card Number: 87-91167

ISBN: 0-345-34819-2

This edition published by arrangement with William Morrow and Company, Inc.

Cover design by Dale Fiurillo

Manufactured in the United States of America

First Ballantine Books Edition: November 1987
10 9 8 7 6 5 4 3 2 1

Acknowledgments

I would particularly like to thank Lisa Drew, Senior Editor of William Morrow, for her vision and support in selecting and preparing this book for publication. Also, the editorial assistance of Jay Stewart has been invaluable, as has the manuscript review and criticism by Dr. Esmond Smith, Chief of California Children's Services (CCS).

I would like also to express my gratitude to Dr. Kathleen Peters and Dr. June Bigge for their suggestions and review of the chapter on education; my daughter-in-law, Margaret Thompson, for acting as my art consultant; Joy Tassi for all she has taught me over the years about having a child with a progressive neuromuscular disease; Lanie Carter for her insistence that the book must be published; Dr. Harry Allen; Dr. John Petroni; Dr. Betty Bernard; Jennifer Thompson; Nancy Brose; Amy Cluck, RPT; Wally Motloch; Ann Hallum, RPT; Victor Alterescu, RN, ET, and the many parents and patients—those who wished their names used and those who made anonymous contributions. Also, a special thanks to my agent, Sandra Dijkstra.

Many agencies and others have kindly sent literature and offered assistance, and to all I wish to express a very deep appreciation and a hope that the completed book will be more than any of us could have envisioned.

Contents

Introduction

As a practicing pediatrician for thirty years and a mother of two children, I know both the medical and practical sides of raising children. It is hard enough in these unsettled times to raise any child well, yet many books and courses help with the parenting of nonhandicapped children. When I have looked for resources or reading material for the parents of my handicapped patients, I have found very little available. So to fill this void I have written this book to try to make life a little easier for those of you who have a child with a handicap.

One of the many hardships that comes with parenting a handicapped child is the loneliness, the isolation from other parents, who all seem to have "normal" children. Yet 12 percent of all schoolchildren are handicapped from birth defects, accidents, illnesses, or other causes. Another 6 percent of all children in this country from birth to age five are also handicapped, and 255,500 infants are born each year in this country with some defect. This means 700 infants a day, and the number appears to be growing.

Certainly, then, you are not alone. Many parents face the same problems and questions. Many others have already faced them successfully. I have been able to help a number of parents find answers, and many have taught me skills and provided me with survival tools that I would like to pass along to you.

I think parenting is probably the hardest job there is, if it is done well, and parenting a handicapped child takes immense dedication, energy, and self-knowledge. If even one of my suggestions makes your life easier or helps the quality of life for your handicapped child, then the time and energy I have put into this book will be rewarded many times over. Most of the parents of handicapped children seem to me to be extraordinary people, and the care and love they show their children are among the highest tributes to the human spirit.

Chapter 1

How to Cope with a Devastating Diagnosis

Time heals what reason cannot.

—SENECA

As the parent of a handicapped child, you have already survived the terrible blow of being told your child is not normal. Whether you learned this at birth, after an accident or an illness, or when a condition was diagnosed later on, the experience, no doubt, brought intense pain and grief. Soon you probably found yourself on a roller coaster of emotions that has exhausted you and often makes you wonder how you will survive. You may have reacted right away by becoming hysterical or angry, or you just may have become quiet and kept everything deep inside. All parents react differently.

Some parents feel they cannot stay still; they must do something, find some help somewhere. I would like to try to help you through this ordeal, as I have tried in person to help hundreds of other parents. You are not alone.

Getting through this initial period will be easier if you understand more about what is happening to you, so responses that are specific to your particular situation are covered later in the chapter.

The first step in surviving successfully with a handicapped child is learning to acknowledge and accept the unfamiliar and painful feelings that may overwhelm you many times during each day after you receive your child's diagnosis.

The First Emotional Storms

Anger, grief, numbness, denial, hysteria, rejection, and guilt are all normal reactions, but the most immediate response to hearing the diagnosis of a handicap is one of shock. Shock is like a direct assault, which quickly turns to an overall numbness. After a varying period of time many or all of the other feelings will erupt.

Numbness is nature's way of giving us time to withdraw and develop our individual coping mechanisms. We all need this psychic anesthesia to survive any terrible, painful experience. For you, hearing your child's diagnosis may be the very worst thing that has ever happened. In moments like this—so painful you feel as if it could not really be happening—numbness gives you time to adjust and to handle the news you have just received.

This first response to the pain and shock of a handicapping condition is healthy, and it is actually the first stage of healing. Only if you find numbness persisting for too long should you be concerned. Sometimes parents cling to numbness as a way of walling themselves off from the flood of grief they can feel pushing to get out. It may seem natural to try holding off this wave of painful feelings, to keep it buried, so there is no danger of its washing over you. Most of us fear pain and emotional intensity, but the only way out of grief is to go through it. You will never get beyond grief until you let it in and allow yourself to feel it.

No specific time limit for handling a stressful diagnosis is right for everyone. The practice of working out feelings—especially ones that are intense and frightening—depends on many factors in each person's life. If you don't begin to develop some acceptance of the diagnosis or start making an adjustment to it after weeks or months, you might need some counseling or guidance to help move you on to the next stage of the healing process. Seeking professional help can make an immense difference to you if you have become rooted in a place you know is not right or healthy, and you will know if this is true for you. Never hesitate to seek counseling. I would recommend it for all parents of a handicapped child, particularly when they first receive the diagnosis of a handicap. It helps start the healing process.

Grief

Because we are human and caring, grief is unavoidable. Each of us will grieve at some time in our life. It is an inevitable part of the life cycle and is a natural and healthy response to the pain we feel because of loss, illness, or death. Grieving is a powerful process that has its own stages. It has the power to heal us and move us on to a new view. Dr. Elisabeth Kübler-Ross and other professionals have spent years studying the phenomenon of grief. Because of their work, we now know the various stages of grieving and its ability to heal our pain.

The grief that engulfs you at this time must be honored and allowed to surface. Grief that is not acknowledged, that is just pushed deeper down inside, works away at us whether we admit its existence or not. Not allowing your feelings an outlet now can lead to problems such as tension headaches, nightmares, inability to sleep, anxiety reactions, or some kind of strong generalized stress reaction later on. Also, refusing to acknowledge your pain and grief can make full acceptance of or adjustment to your child's handicap difficult. This is a double tragedy for your child.

Parents who close themselves off from the pain of grieving often cannot go on to have a close, wonderful relationship with their child, and this is one of the beautiful things that is possible with a child who has a handicap. Many of the parents I work with tell me that having a handicapped child in their family has brought everyone in the family closer together and made them see how important human relationships can be.

Each person has his or her own way to handle grief. It can be a hard task because often we have no previous experience to guide us. This is often true for parents who have just been told of a child's handicap. If this news is your first reason to grieve, let me try to help with some suggestions.

First, consciously set aside a specific time to let yourself feel the grief fully.

Second, allow yourself to share your grief with someone—a close friend, your minister, priest, rabbi, or counselor.

Third, give yourself permission to let things go for a while, to be less organized, less productive, even a little less compassionate for others.

Fourth, find a quiet place for yourself to feel the grief—a special corner in your house or garden, a chapel, church, park, or private place.

Fifth, avoid as much noise as possible during this time so you can tune in to what you feel. Let yourself really feel the grief. Don't just pay lip service to it.

Sixth, look for some records or tapes—especially "relaxation tapes," often found in record stores—to help you relax and unwind.

At first it is important to take a few minutes out of each hour to experience some of the grief you feel. You have to plan to do this, otherwise it is easy to get caught up in rushing around as a way of avoiding painful feelings. Later on, you may only need to set aside a short time each day to grieve, but even this is terribly important and should not be forgotten. Grieving, feeling your sadness and pain, is one of the first important things you must do for your child.

Parents who have strong religious ties often find comfort through their religion and in their place of worship. Other parents find that meditation or reflection, long walks or intense exercise, listening to music, reading something inspirational, or just spending quiet time alone helps them survive this hard first period. For me, the ocean has always brought a feeling of peace, a sense of wholeness, and a belief in the continuity of life, even when things have looked unbearably bleak. It also seems to give me strength. Others have told me they get similar feelings from being in the mountains or sitting by a lake, in the woods, or by a running stream. The earth helps us feel our pain and absorb some of it, so we are not harmed by it. It helps us heal.

Again, if your grieving goes on to span weeks, months, and possibly years, it is no longer healthy. Many parents grieve so endlessly about having an imperfect child that they are never able to enjoy the child they do have, to accept the present and find the richness it can offer.

There is a delicate balance between letting yourself feel grief and making grief into a life-style. At first it is necessary to feel the grief, but eventually you have to find ways to let the grief and pain go so you can start learning to live again. It is true that the future is unknown and may seem frightening, but if you can be open to it, you will reach new levels of communication, intimacy, and love that you did not know could exist in your life.

One measure of maturity is an ability to face the problems of daily living, even the most terrible ones, head-on. A sure mark of living effectively is to look at what is real, what is happening at the moment, and work with just that. Real problems require energy, attention, and intelligence to find solutions. When we can look at our own situation honestly—no matter how bad it is or how bad we feel—and can accept our children as they are rather than holding tight to what we wish they were, we can begin to have special, creative, extraordinary lives for ourselves and our children.

Guilt

It is normal for parents to experience guilt when they learn that their child is handicapped. It is natural to feel desolate, at fault, to believe that the handicap is somehow a sign of their own failure.

In many cultures, handicaps are considered a punishment for earlier misdeeds. Your ethnic background may cause some of this type of thinking. In more primitive cultures or in earlier societies, handicapped children either were not expected to survive or were not allowed to. In our country, some handicapped children are still kept away from the outside world by their parents because parents feel such anger and guilt.

Guilt is one of those feelings that can promote more and more pain. Even justifiable guilt, when it was a parent's carelessness that injured a child, has to be let go of after it has been acknowledged and experienced. Anyone who has lived for a while has regrets and guilts—some intensely painful. But if we choose to immerse ourselves in guilt, we shut everything else out, losing precious opportunities. Parents floundering in guilt can cause themselves unnecessary pain, harm their other children, and hurt their handicapped child even more.

An illustration of this is a family referred to me who had a son originally diagnosed as having Duchenne muscular dystrophy. This diagnosis meant the boy would only live until his late teens or early twenties. It is a type of dystrophy passed through mothers to their sons. This mother felt particularly guilty and accepted full responsibility for her son's illness.

When I first saw the boy I felt that the original diagnosis was not accurate, so we did a repeat muscle biopsy. We found that he had another form of dystrophy, one not inherited through the mother, and that he would be able to live another twenty or thirty years, instead of five or so. The family became so caught up in reassigning guilt that there was no rejoicing at this news, and they totally ignored the boy and his needs. Their unresolved conflicts, their need to place blame and assign guilt, still keep them from experiencing many special moments in their son's life.

Parents who find themselves caught up in a guilt/blame cycle need to take action to free themselves from this emotional web.

Rejection

Rejection is another normal stage in the grieving process. However, many parents never find a way to truly accept their handicapped child. They unconsciously use excessive denial, numbness, or grieving to separate themselves from their child, who can become emotionally starved. They *seem* to be acting the role of parents because they are providing food, clothing, medical care, and shelter, but they are only taking care of their child's physical needs, and such a child can easily become emotionally starved. Financial support is not emotional support or love, and life is pretty sterile and lonely without love. Parents who cannot make a welcome place for their "imperfect" child in their lives are really just token parents. Tensions in the home can get so bad that one parent leaves—or both do—and the child has to go to a foster home.

If you think your initial normal rejection is continuing, you may need to seek counseling. You could be seeing just the handicap in your child and be so overwhelmed by it that you miss the person. Without counseling and some attempt to gain a change in perspective, children can be hurt by parents who let them know in subtle ways that they are not loved as are the other children because of their deformity.

In her book *The Inner World of Childhood,* Frances Wickes says, "Whenever we make a relationship with a child on any basis other than that of his own individuality, we violate something in his soul." She tells the story of a boy who had been injured at birth so that he "walked awkwardly." As a baby his defects worked in his favor because they brought him special attention and care, but when he started in school these same defects "provoked ridicule" and "gave him a feeling of being inadequate to life's demands." The boy grew angry and fearful. He started lying, boasting, and fighting, becoming a behavior problem at home and school. It took Dr. Wickes and the boy's parents a lot of hard work to help him develop some well-grounded emotional security. (The chapters in her book on fear and rejection are valuable reading for parents, teachers, or anyone working with handicapped children.)

Entering counseling does not guarantee a change of perspective. The purpose of counseling is to help you explore and accept your genuine feelings and capacities and to help release some of your anger. If you do seek counseling with a professional or your family doctor and find you still cannot accept your child, viable alternatives exist. There are good foster homes, as well as other people who can step in to help.

I had one family who placed their child in a foster home with a loving foster mother. The biological mother and father, both busy professionals, eventually moved to the East Coast. Two or three times every year the child's mother comes out for a visit and has genuine concern about the child. However, since neither she nor her husband could handle the day-to-day care, they were wise and courageous enough to admit it.

It takes great maturity to accept a handicap in a child, to learn to cope with it and to continue as a loving, giving person. But it takes a special kind of courage to simply say, if you have to, that you cannot or do not want to handle the situation. If this is true of you, I strongly recommend that you make the decision to place your child in a foster home, in a group home, or up for adoption.

Some time ago I had a teenage boy as a patient who had spina bifida, a birth defect. His parents were wealthy and could amply provide for his care, but they could not accept him or his defect. The boy decided to try living on his own as an emancipated minor. His parents did not keep in touch with him, probably glad not to have to face their own discomfort and their failure as parents when he was present.

You could feel the loneliness and suffering in this young man with his twisted body. He had put up high protecting emotional walls and had never learned to trust, so befriending him was difficult. Isolation, mistrust, and loneliness were all he knew. Occasionally I see his prominent father's name in a newspaper and feel sad for both the parents and their son. I wonder if some early counseling would not have made a real difference in the lives of this family.

In the press, on television, and in the movies, we see heroism portrayed as acts of physical bravery. Rarely do we see examples of the emotional courage it takes to explore and acknowledge our own deepest—and sometimes darkest—feelings and to accept them along with accepting ourselves. Being the parent of a handicapped child forces many feelings to the surface. The maturity to open oneself to this challenge and grow with it does not merely come with the passage of time. Many people in their fifties and sixties are not mature, whole people. They have aged and experienced life but have not acquired wisdom, understanding, or compassion. Maturity is earned with much hard work. This inner work of the mind and heart is surely the hardest but the most rewarding work of all.

Anger

Probably the most common, most unsettling, and strongest response to hearing your child's diagnosis is profound anger. This normal and healthy response to the pain and hurt of learning your child is handicapped comes up forcefully and naturally, and yet anger can be the hardest of all emotions to handle. Anger frightens most people. They fear they will be overwhelmed and lose control and are afraid of what they might do.

One father told me that when he first heard about his handicapped newborn, he wished his child were dead. He then became so frightened that he could think such a terrible thing that he withdrew and would not talk to anyone. He was sure people would think him either crazy or a demon, so he suffered in isolation. He pulled away from his wife and his friends and tried to be the strong male he felt everyone expected him to be. Inside, though, he was numb from his silent suffering. He said it took him a long, long time to feel any spark of joy in life again, yet before this he had always been the first to start some fun.

I wish I could have been there to tell this man how normal and common his thoughts were, that all parents who are honest have had times of wishing they could be rid of their child and the nuisance of raising children altogether. Fortunately, when most of us have such a thought we sigh at our shortcomings or lack of patience and return to the task of parenting our children. No one is immune to intense wishes of wanting to get rid of troubles, and often our children seem like trouble. So long as we do not act on these thoughts or make decisions based on them, we can forgive ourselves.

The anger a parent feels on hearing of a child's handicap usually takes the form of questions such as, Why me? What did I do to deserve this? What does this mean? There are no good answers to these questions. Some people have normal, healthy children, and others have one, two, or more handicapped children. Nothing we see can explain why this happens, and the very senselessness of it frustrates us even more.

If you are a person who likes your life to be fun, orderly, and predictable and so far have been satisfied in these respects, you are likely to feel intensely angry at having a handicapped child. All parents feel some anger. It is completely normal to respond in this way, though you may still feel uncomfortable about your feelings.

Try reading a small book called *Whoever Said Life Was Fair,*

Anyway? by Sara Kay Cohen. She points out that no one knows why certain people are given terrible burdens to carry in their lives. Her theme is that we each have our own unique journey to make and that learning how to handle anger and life's unfairness is part of how we become mature, whole people. It is life's trials that deepen and mature us and make us strong in ways that pleasant experiences cannot. The parents of some handicapped children have unbelievable burdens, and yet live with dignity, strength, and love rather than bitterness and constant anger.

Working through your anger to acceptance is one way to help your child grow emotionally and have a satisfying life. More than this, transforming anger can also bring new depth and growth to your life, helping you uncover strengths you had not felt prior to the diagnosis of your child's handicap.

Some counseling sessions right at first for the father who felt such anger might have helped him accept the fact that his dark thoughts were normal and nothing to fear or be ashamed of. I think all parents of handicapped newborns could profit from even one or two counseling sessions soon after the birth to get them started on the right track and help them handle the initial grief, anger, and adjustment to an entirely new and demanding situation. It seems to me that technology has outstripped emotional concern in many of our medical institutions. Money is available for complicated, expensive new equipment, but not for counselors or social workers trained to counsel parents. And when there *are* social workers, they usually are busy contacting the right agencies, arranging funding, and taking care of discharge planning. These are all important functions, but every neonatal intensive-care nursery should have counselors to aid parents and support them. A small amount of helpful and positive intervention at this time would, I am convinced, save much pain, suffering, and costly waste of human potential in the years to come.

If your neonatal unit does not have any counselors available, consider seeking a professional outside the hospital to help you handle the many issues and emotions this event will cause you. Talking to someone who isn't personally involved will help immensely. I will talk about how to find a good counselor later in the chapter.

Both rejection and anger can sweep you into pain and confusion. Rejection is a real possibility, particularly if your baby is very malformed or small. Babies in the intensive-care nursery can be pretty awful to look at. With all those tubes and lifesaving equipment, they hardly seem human. You may well wonder how you can establish any bond or feel any love for something that doesn't look like a part of you or even a member of the same species.

The classic new-baby picture of the father and mother gazing through the nursery window at a beautiful, healthy baby is not there for you if you are the parents of a handicapped newborn. You have every right to feel both anger and rejection of your child. However, you cannot remain caught in this emotional web as a permanent state because it can hurt you as well as your baby. Early anger and rejection can develop into anxiety, shutting out everything and everyone else.

One favorite parent, who has a girl with almost insurmountable problems, once confided to me that before her little Kathy's birth she felt she had lived with "blinders on." Kathy's coming and the complex problems of day-to-day living with a handicapped child tore those blinders away, and she feels that she sees life with more depth and realism now and responds with greater intensity to the emotions and beauty in her life.

I have discussed some of the emotions all parents feel when they first receive the diagnosis of their child's handicap—anger, fear, denial, shock, numbness, pain, guilt, and sadness. All of these feelings are normal and are more or less intense, depending on your unique circumstances. The parents of a newborn baby who is handicapped have different problems handling the diagnosis than do the parents of a child who is hurt in an accident or diagnosed as handicapped later in life. I would like to look at this situation separately before discussing acceptance—of your handicapped child and yourself.

The Handicapped Newborn

So many dreams, so many expectations—all the planning, the baby showers, the preparations for the homecoming—and now all has been shattered by a reality that must feel unbearable. You have just been told your baby is handicapped, and also may have to stay in the hospital for several months. You have not even been allowed to touch or hold your own child. How can you handle such pain?

Nothing in the atmosphere of the intensive-care nursery makes it easy for you to accept what is happening. It is a busy, noisy glaring place filled with doctors, nurses, aides, social workers, and others, all intent on the work they do. It is likely that no one has taken any time to spend with you, and yet it is *your* baby they are working so hard to help. Your own parents may be so grief-stricken that, even if they live nearby, they have been no help. You and your mate may just be clinging together, the two of you isolated in your misery. But even your partner may have already withdrawn into a private sadness. Your friends, usually so supportive, may be afraid of hospitals and phobic about tragedy, which means they aren't there to help either. You want to scream from the bottom of your being, "Help, please, someone! Help us to survive all of this!"

Hold on a moment. Take a deep breath and scream all you need to. Let some of that pain surface and get out. Then insist that the doctors, nurses, and social workers talk to you. Do not be put off by subtle or not-so-subtle suggestions that you are being a nuisance. The baby is yours, and it's your right to find out what is happening to your child. Insist that one consistent— and if possible understandable and caring—person keeps you up to date on your baby's condition and lets both of you know about the day-to-day decisions and problems that must be met. In the case of a handicapped newborn, there are hourly changes possible in your baby's condition; blood transfusions, medications, and corrective surgeries may be needed. You are an important part of the team helping your baby survive. Speak up and let the others know that you must be included.

In their zeal to do a good job and their own anxiety to keep a baby alive, most doctors just go ahead and make the medical decisions about handicapped newborns. Many of the parents I have known whose children were handicapped newborns tell me they were never given any options or choices in their child's treatment, including major care issues, anticipated surgeries, or potentially harmful medications. Often the experts' medical presentation can suggest that no options exist and that there is only one way to handle the case. If a parent is persistent and asks good questions, it sometimes turns out that several medical routes do exist, each with its own risks and potential benefits. You must involve yourselves in these important decisions. Also, many of these early decisions have moral and ethical implications that may influence your life for years, whereas the doctor making them will not have to care for or live with the results of these decisions after the initial crisis has been weathered.

I know that what I am saying may be hard to accept, that you must confront difficult and complex decisions when you can barely keep going or eat a meal. Comfort yourself that once you have helped make the major care decisions, you can let down and take time to think, to feel, and to cry. And cry you must, for that is the beginning of adjusting to your tragedy.

One mother told me that she hardly touched food for the first few days after her baby was born with many abnormalities. She lost weight, her hair started coming out in bunches, and she felt disconnected from life, as if she were in a trance state. Slowly this strange numbness began to recede, though not pass entirely. Food no longer nauseated her, and she began to take some interest in her husband and other children. Nature had given her time to begin developing her coping mechanisms.

Another mother and father literally lived in the intensive-care unit after their handicapped premature infant was born. Gradually the father returned to work and the semblance of a normal life, but the mother stayed on and on. Friends and neighbors cared for her other child, and while the infant survived, the marriage did not.

Making Decisions When Devastated

The pressure and stress of making decisions at the same time they are enduring the intense sadness and pain of receiving a child's diagnosis places an extra burden on the parents of a handicapped newborn. The decisions you face about your child's treatment are not easy ones to make under the best of circumstances—and these may be the very worst circumstances you have ever been in. This is one of the reasons physicians and others give for making the important decisions for you.

Certainly it is necessary to listen to people who are not as emotionally involved as you are, both experts who have information and dispassionate others who might have some clear logical reasons for seeing things differently than you do. The essential fact, though, is that the infant is yours. You conceived and carried this child, and you will bear the responsibility in the future. For this reason, you should be involved in all major decisions about your infant. By the word *you* I mean both mother and father, because a father who cares for his child's mother during pregnancy plays a large part in helping bring that child to its birth. The very fact that you are intensely emotionally involved, that only you have this unique perspective on the child, is all the more reason for you to make or help make the major decisions. You care as no one else does, and the decisions will affect you as they will no one else.

Making Decisions Under Pressure. Because the decisions about your child's medical treatment may be life-and-death decisions, they will have a component of intensity that many everyday decisions do not have. We often respond to this intensity by thinking and moving quickly. Perhaps we assume unconsciously that if we move and act quickly we can outrun the feelings that threaten to overwhelm us. Whatever the reason, pressure can push us to panic.

Also, you may find yourself urged to decide difficult issues quickly. The doctors may know what they want to do and be impatient with you. Perhaps they themselves are uncomfortable with the difficulty of the situation and prefer action to reflection. You can ask, clearly and straightforwardly, if it will jeopardize anything if there is a short delay of five to fifteen minutes while you think things through.

Once you have created this space for yourself, you need to use it to do two things. The first is to clarify the facts. For this, you will probably want to have a doctor review the pros and cons of the suggested course of action. If the doctors are suggesting a particular corrective surgery, for example, you might ask them about the possible improvement and potential risks, the overall success rate of this surgery in other infants who are like yours in most respects (age, weight, degree of impairment, overall strength, and so on). Ask the doctor to project these pros and cons into the future. Can this same surgery be done later, when your baby has gained strength and added some weight? What will happen or could happen if the surgery is delayed?

After you have asked as many questions as you can think of, tell the people waiting for your decision that you need to be alone for a while. You might chose to discuss the situation with your spouse, but whether you are alone or with your spouse, take time to let some of the information, the emotional intensity, and the pressure just wash over you without letting it sweep you away. Think of yourself standing on solid ground with the ocean waves washing over your feet and knees. You can feel the ocean's strength and power, but it still cannot knock you over. The feelings, the maze of facts, the stress are all very powerful, but it will help you make a better decision if you can take them in and let them go again without letting them overwhelm you. This is difficult, but not impossible.

Some people achieve this instant perspective by imagining themselves to be a hundred years old and looking back on the very decision they are now facing. Some achieve the needed calm and distance by visiting with their imaginations places that have a powerful calming influence on them—the mountains, the ocean, a cool forest, a deep lake. Others think of a quiet church, and that gives them the kind of power they need to make a difficult decision.

If you cannot find any quiet in the hospital, go into a bathroom and run the water to shut out extraneous noises. Cry if you need to. Sometimes a short crying session is a wonderful release. It can clear your head and give you strength that a moment before you would never have suspected you had. Try to be kind to yourself and give yourself permission to be scared, weak, nervous, uncertain. Just do the best you can under the circumstances. That is all, really, any of us can do, and your circumstances are particularly demanding. At best we are not well prepared to make some of life's most difficult decisions. Where in a high school or college course list have you ever seen a course called Decision Making, but wouldn't it be helpful? We seem to leave these things to fate, chance, and random strategies that we work out for ourselves or learn from others. Go easy on yourself and do what you can.

If you are faced with decisions that do not have tremendous time pressure, you have more options for arriving at good decisions. Whenever it is safe and possible to do so, ask for time to think about major medical decisions. Even twenty-four hours can give you a lot of thinking and information-gathering opportunities. Another advantage of additional time is that you can invite others to help you reach a decision that feels comfortable to you.

You may have a spiritual adviser—minister, priest, rabbi, or personal confidant with whom you have discussed meaningful issues in your life. You might have a good trusted friend who can help you look at some of the options with more logic and less feeling than you can muster by yourself right now. Your friend or adviser cannot—and should not—make the decisions for you, but can help you explore the options fully, project the potential consequences so you have some idea of what you might be facing, and just think out the steps and series of decisions you will have to make. Your friend or adviser can help you with the areas of decisions about your child that affect the quality of the child's life and your own as a result of a chosen medical plan. The physicians can provide the technical information about what the plan entails, its chances for success, and its potential hazards. The issue is partly a technical one, and that is why you want excellent informed medical opinion. Ultimately it is more than a technological issue, so the decision must rest on more than just logic and expert testimony.

A doctor might be interested in a certain medical procedure because it is revolutionary and medically exciting, a new breakthrough at which he or she is trying to become adept. Your needs and concerns are very different and much more important. If a doctor strongly recommends a particular medical procedure, ask the usual questions about successes and risks, potential hazards, and so on, but then you might go on to explore the doctor's position by saying something like, "You seem quite convinced, Dr. _____. Could you briefly explain your reasoning?" If the answer sounds vague, righteous, or moralistic, you might want to ask the doctor if the decision would be the same if the child were his or hers and the consequences would be ones he or she would have to live with and indeed pay for. Be somewhat wary of the physician who answers such a question without any hesitation. Faced with a person who takes no time to reflect at this moment, I would recommend seeking a second opinion from another well-qualified physician.

Factors in Making a Good Decision. In making decisions about a handicapped newborn, the "quality of life" is an important factor to think about. This refers to the potential the child has for leading a life that has some capacity for joy, beauty, love, and personal relationships.

Some individuals feel that life is valuable just because it is life, and that pain and suffering should not be an issue. Others feel that life is worth living only when the pleasure outweighs the suffering. Each set of parents has to decide what is right for their child. However, there are now legal cases about the rights of the infants, and questions of what rights parents have to make the final decisions. Unfortunately, the courts and governmental agencies have intruded in some cases and the issues are very complex, particularly since the case called the Baby Doe case, where parents refused treatment of a handicapped infant and the government intervened.

More and more hospitals now have ethics rounds, where issues such as lifesaving measures in handicapped newborns are considered. Your pediatrician or family doctor and your priest or minister should both be involved to help you make the final decision.

In countries other than the United States many of the lifesaving measures that are so costly are simply not available, and thus money becomes a major issue in the lives of many handicapped infants. There are growing signs in our own country that soon the financial aspects will be a major factor in whether or not lifesaving measures can be used in handicapped infants.

The basic message in all this is to try not to feel guilty. Whether there is any basis in fact for feeling guilt doesn't matter. What does matter is your child and your own mental health, which is what will help your handicapped child the most. Guilt is an unhealthy emotion. It is particularly damaging because it motivates us to act in ways to make us feel less guilty. Generally, though, others are harmed, and indulging children just makes them unpleasant to be around.

As with other negative emotions, guilt needs to be acknowledged—and then shown out the door politely but firmly. There is no place for extended guilt in a healthy family. Guilt keeps a person from responding to the present because the past is too compelling. The secret of survival with a handicapped child is very much a matter of living in the present. Do not allow guilt to upset your present moments and destroy your future and your child's potential.

If you are the mother of a handicapped newborn, you are likely to worry that something you did during your pregnancy caused the handicap. So much news floods the media these days about the harmful effects of medication, drugs, alcohol, and smoking that even taking a few aspirins can make you believe that a birth defect was your "fault." Another source of guilt is the worry that an accident or illness early in the pregnancy could have caused the handicap. You may be haunted by the idea that had you done something differently—even though you may not be sure what—your baby would not have been born with birth defects.

Medical researchers have been unable to trace most birth defects to a single cause. The studies that have been done testing drugs on animals cannot be related directly to human pregnancies, though they are frequently reported that way in the news media. This type of frightening information can make pregnancy a fearful time for women instead of the relaxed and happy time it should be.

If you are a woman in her late thirties who waited to have a family, you may feel that the birth defect was caused by your older age, even if your doctor does not agree.

The Handicapped Child

If your child has been healthy for several years and then suddenly has an illness, an injury, or a newly diagnosed chronic condition, your reactions still probably follow the same constellation of numbness, denial, guilt, anger, and rejection—along with an immense grief for your loss. It is as though there has been a death in the family, and in reality a kind of death has taken place; it is the death of what once was and can never be again. One father described the experience as an earthquake with aftershocks for years to come. He and his wife had to change the very foundations of their life, just as if they had lived through a major earthquake. The fire, death, and destruction a massive earthquake brings are like the common emotional responses of parents who have been ravaged by hearing that a child has a disease that will take his life, is retarded, or has suffered irreparable brain damage from an accident.

Numbness and Denial

The possibility of parents remaining at the stage of numbness and denial is more likely with a child who has appeared normal or actually been normal until some tragic event or the diagnosis of a handicapping condition was made. Some parents will not let go of the past to deal with the present in a creative, realistic way.

Two parents came to me with their only son, who was getting weaker and having difficulty keeping up with his friends. After examining him and looking at his muscle biopsy, I had to tell them that their son had Duchenne muscular dystrophy. With our current knowledge this meant that the boy would die in his teens or twenties. The parents, who were both intelligent, well-educated people, did not want to hear or absorb what I had to say. Almost every visit after that first one, they would tell someone on our medical team that I had not discussed muscular dystrophy with them, although I went over and over the condition and gave them literature on it. During each visit they asked the same questions about the disease and yet never really heard my answers.

These parents never went beyond the stage of numbness and denial. Even as their son's death approaches, I suspect that they will not be able to look at the disease clearly. Instead they will continue to deny it right to the end. This is terribly sad for the child, who must feel that he can never be open about his feelings or ask questions about what is happening to him.

Sometimes one or several members of a family recover from their initial grief and channel their energies into working with the child and learning to live with the handicap. But other family members cannot accept the child as he or she is.

One mother whose son had muscular dystrophy told me in despair that she had to make sure her child's father and grandparents were not around when the boy had to walk. They could not stand the pain of seeing his weakness, and they would not accept the idea of a wheelchair for him.

The poor mother was caught between trying to help her son and avoid upsetting the rest of the family. And what about the child with muscular dystrophy who had to pretend he was not weak just to save his family from pain? What about his pain? He knew he was getting weaker and weaker and was going to die, yet he had to use the last of his energy to pretend it was not so.

Not acknowledging a child's newly discovered or acquired handicap is easy enough for a while. At first on hearing the news, such denial allows time for healing and a break from the overwhelming problems that do not have to be confronted right away. But if this denial goes on and on, it blocks a healthy acceptance of reality and creates new problems that are difficult to solve because they are based on this artificial but very solid denial system. Denial of a problem cancels any chance of finding acceptable answers; it denies the creative use of our intelligence and loving concern as well as our awareness of the problem itself.

If you find yourself unable to accept what you know is true, then you need to seek help. If you can accept the facts of your child's handicap but others around you cannot, talk to someone else, preferably a professional counselor, about how to work with this situation and to gain much-needed support for yourself. It can be very lonely if you are the only one in a family who is willing to face the truth. It is sometimes impossible to change the others without outside help or some intervention counseling. Often people can hear an important message from a person outside the family that they will ignore when it comes from a close family member. The essential point is to get the message across that the child needs people who can accept the situation as it is and go on from there. How this message gets conveyed is not important, and you may not be able to deliver it yourself. You can always reach out for help, though, and in the case of extended numbness or denial, I strongly recommend that you do.

Guilt

Any parents will feel intensely guilty if their child is injured so seriously in an accident that there is a permanent handicap. Even if a parent is responsible for the accident, where the guilt seems justifiable, the parent must relinquish it in order to accept and work with the child and his or her condition. Guilt brings only pain, and guilt that is held down or held on to can have far-reaching harmful consequences.

I once treated a postaccident child who had been hit by a car driven by his father as he was backing out of the driveway. The child was brain-damaged by the accident and ultimately died, but the mother never let her husband forget his responsibility for the accident and his guilt. He could not forget his guilt either, and the other children in the family were deeply hurt by the constant destructive interplay between their parents. In this family, guilt wreaked its havoc for years, causing deep psychological scars that may be passed on from generation to generation.

In another family, the parents left their two-year-old with a teenage sister as a babysitter while they went on vacation. The toddler nearly drowned in the family swimming pool during this time and eventually had to be institutionalized. Both parents were bright, professional people, but their marriage did not survive the aftershocks of this accident. Neither did the teenage girl, as she later took her own life.

If the family involved in this tragedy could have been helped to work through the guilt they all felt, there might have been some acceptance and adjustment. Instead the family experienced terrible emotional destruction. If we immerse ourselves in guilt, everything else in the world gets shut out. Guilt and pain become a prison, and a handicapped child is hurt even more. Parents can bring terrible suffering to themselves and deeply harm everyone around them.

Seek out professional help if you find that guilt has taken hold of your life so that you feel immobilized by it. You may never stop feeling the regret and sadness, but you can learn to live in the present again and even feel some pleasure in life.

Guilt and blaming can become a particular obstacle to adjustment in a family where the handicap has a genetic origin. Some defects are passed through the female. These are the so-called sex-linked disorders. Hemophilia and Duchenne muscular dystrophy are two examples of disorders that mothers do not have but pass on to their male offspring. Women who transmit these diseases can spend their lives lost in guilt, even though they probably didn't know they had the trait. Most of the time they do not even know they carry the gene until the child is diagnosed. Besides ruining the mother's life, this guilt often motivates the mother to spoil her child in order to lessen her guilt. This doesn't help the child or anyone else; it just spreads the pain further.

The same thing can happen if a genetic disease is an autosomal recessive disorder, which comes from a gene called a recessive in each parent combining in the child to cause a disorder. In this case, where the disorder comes from both parents, their combined guilt can make home life unbearable. Fathers can spoil children, too, because of guilty feelings about their contribution to the child's problems. In a situation like this, one parent has to become realistic and practical and shake off the guilt. If someone doesn't do this, the problems are magnified, destroying that child's chances of having any happy adaptation to life.

Acceptance

The parent of one of my patients told me one time that she felt mothers and fathers never truly accept the idea of having a handicapped child. Instead they merely adjust their lives to the idea somehow, and learn to live with that reality. Adjustment in itself is a real accomplishment and a healthy beginning. Parents who can find ways of facing their problems without emotionally starving their child and still meeting their own needs will already have achieved meaningful goals.

It may not be possible for you to truly accept your child's handicap without some outside help. It takes time, patience, and personal growth to handle such an overwhelming tragedy. Other family members or close friends, a specialist who is seeing your child, a nurse, social worker, or professional counselor, a parent support group or other parents who have already survived a similar blow—can all help. But you have to start by looking carefully at your own way of reacting to your child.

Let yourself really feel the grief, no matter how painful it seems to you. Look into all your dark corners and explore your worst fears and secrets. You need to acknowledge, understand, and accept the validity of your own feelings, no matter what they are. Once you have learned the art of doing this, then you can begin to make some peace with what has happened. This will help you move toward acceptance. Keep in mind, though, that acceptance comes slowly and may come only when you give up trying to find it.

It will help you reach the stage of acceptance if you are kind to yourself. Don't expect too much of yourself or others during this period, but just concentrate on getting through each day. Lower your expectations so that you feel it is an accomplishment even if all you have done is to survive another twenty-four hours. At first there is a lot to do. Be gentle with yourself and those around you. You have been deeply hurt, and you need time, nurturing, and support to heal. It is natural to strike out at others when you are in pain, but it is more helpful if you can reach out and ask for a hand, a hug, or a shoulder to cry on. Let yourself do what you need to in order to heal.

If you feel some outside professional counseling is needed to start handling your grief and accepting the situation, try to find someone who will counsel you wisely. Many professional counselors are well trained in a general sense, but are not trained to work with the parents of a handicapped child. Some simply haven't had enough experience with the devastation that occurs when parents find out that their child is handicapped. You will need a counselor who can do more than just pay lip service to your pain. What you need is someone who has had enough experience with tragedy to walk in your shoes. A wise counselor once told me that you can take people only as far as you yourself have gone, and I feel that this is true.

Finding a good counselor with these special qualities may not be easy. Some of your best recommendations will come from parents who have been where you are right now. The hospital staff or the people in your doctor's office might also be able to tell you about good counselors or help you get in touch with a local parent-support group. The hospital social worker is another source for good recommendations. But don't stop there. Make inquiries among your friends and people you know who work in the health-care field. Find a counselor you feel comfortable with and someone to whom you feel you can say anything and it will be okay.

Rx: Time Alone

One of the most essential things you can do to help yourself and your child right after you hear the diagnosis and for the many days, weeks, or even months that follow is to set aside time for yourself. Somewhere in the day carve out at least ten minutes once or twice for personal grieving or just time alone. You need this time to center yourself and to focus on the immediate catastrophe. These quiet periods will give your feelings a chance to surface and heal. Time spent alone like this will bring a certain depth, calmness, and maturity to your life. These times alone will promote your own healing process and will greatly benefit your ability to help your child.

Many of us handle any kind of emotional pain, including grief, by getting busier, running around more and faster, doing more and doing it more quickly to avoid the feelings. This strategy works for a while, but finally it creates a painful cycle. The more we run, the faster we *have* to run. The only way out of this is to stop all activity completely once or twice a day and just be with yourself and whatever comes up in that short space of time.

Right now nothing will make the pain go away for you, but time will bring moments of good feeling back into your life. Remember that wherever there is deep pain, tragedy, or a death of some kind—even the death of your dream about a perfect child—new life or a new way of seeing life will be born. With time and healing, even from these bitter ashes of despair you can rekindle the joy of life and find pleasure in your handicapped child.

Kahlil Gibran wrote, "The deeper that sorrow carves into your being the more joy you can contain." I hope that joy will some-day come again for you.

Chapter 2

What to Tell Well-Meaning Friends and Relatives

Caring can cost a lot, but not caring always costs more.

—MERLE SHAIN

When you first learn that your child will be handicapped, your friends and relatives can be a strong and much-needed support for you. Depending on their sensitivity and maturity or lack of maturity, they can also add to the guilt and pain you are carrying. Someone making an offhand remark about "God's will" or "God's punishment" can make you grit your teeth or blink back tears. Even the most well-intentioned people can hurt with their casual comments about a personal tragedy. Handling situations when this happens will take all of your coping mechanisms at first. With some experience, and the healing that time brings, you will learn to relax a bit and not take these comments to heart.

People Put Off by Handicaps

A fairly common situation arises when certain friends and relatives cannot accept handicaps in others. This can be traced to many reasons, but the effect is the same: They cannot handle the situation or accept the child. If people like this are close to you, they can be rejecting in subtle ways even while voicing sympathetic phrases, projecting a confusing and painful double message to you and your family. It is as if they were pulling you close and pushing you away at the same time. Troubled themselves by your child's handicap, these people resist letting your problems and discomfort into their lives, and so they compound the problems you are facing.

People who were once close may gradually start distancing themselves from you when they hear about your child. They may no longer ask you to visit or invite your children over to play. This is not only traumatic for you as a parent, it can also hurt your child or children deeply. Children sense when acceptance is either withdrawn or never given in the first place.

You might be able to open up communication with the people who seem to be rejecting you or your child by approaching the subject gently. For example, you might begin by saying how hard it was for you to accept the handicap at first and that you appreciate how uncomfortable this sudden event might make them.

People are understandably reluctant to admit to feelings that are rejecting. It may help if you introduce the topic by exploring with them how much trouble you had when you felt these same negative feelings come up in you. That may allow them to admit to the same or similar feelings. If you make several genuine attempts to reopen communication, and nothing seems to work, not much you can do will change the situation.

Advice from Others

Another potential problem area with close friends and relatives is the area of treatment decisions. Everyone suddenly seems to become an expert or has an acquaintance with a similar problem that they handled well in a specific way. Naturally people close to you want to help, so they make many well-intended suggestions. Often, though, their suggestions are different from the treatment plan that your physicians are following. Also your friends or parents might list new physicians or consultants that they think you should see right away.

Certainly you don't want to cut off their kindness and obvious concern. You will be able to handle this common dilemma more gracefully if you have found a physician you really trust and a reliable diagnosis (see Chapter 7 for how to do this). To hold firm against this wave of well-meant advice, you and your primary physician must take charge right from the start.

This is more easily said than done, especially when you are feeling off center and uncertain, rather than strong and determined. Keep in mind that you can be firm without being offensive, and that you need to be firm in order to conserve your energy and help your child. Try saying something like, "We have decided to follow this course for now. After considering all the factors, it looks like the best approach for us. But if it doesn't seem effective after a fair trial, we will try another course of action. Thanks so much for your concern and for thinking of us." You may want to take note of some of the suggestions to ask your doctor about or file them away for future reference and exploration in case some other course *is* necessary. People will soon grow to respect your taking a firm stand and possibly be more supportive of the course you have chosen.

Too Much Help

A very real possibility for you is that your friends and relatives can overwhelm you with genuine concern. They can be so caring that they smother you to the point that you find no time for your spouse, your other children, or even your own scattered thoughts.

It is up to you to establish right away how much involvement you want your friends and relatives to have in your life, even though talking clearly to your relatives and friends may not be something you have ever done comfortably.

But look at the situation from their perspective. They have no way of knowing what you need or don't need unless you tell them clearly and precisely. They want to help, and that's wonderful. You are going to need their help and will appreciate it deeply in the days to come. However, you need to direct the help so that it is what you need. The best way to sort out your thoughts on this issue is to spend some quiet time alone thinking about what you really want.

Pressures of all kinds, intense emotions, and conflicting information will be directed at you when you first learn of your child's handicap. Your only hope of sorting through this turmoil, which includes the storm inside you, is to take some quality time for yourself. This means being alone and in a place where you can think things through clearly.

Our society doesn't seem to value simply sitting and thinking. If someone is sitting still and apparently just staring out into space, we usually feel something is wrong. Yet the complexities of many modern-day problems require deep thought. Certainly your situation does. Quiet time alone thinking the situation through is important and valuable. It will help you make better decisions, feel both calmer and more in control, and all of this will help your child immensely.

If you feel too fragmented or upset to think even when there is time and space to do so, then talking with a counselor or a close friend might be wise. After expressing the first rush of feelings and emotions, you will be able to decide what you need and want. From there, the next big step is communicating that clearly to your family and friends.

Communicating About Help

Open, honest communication is difficult for many of us, since in many families more stress is placed on being polite than on being open and direct. However, your situation demands honest communication with others. Without it, simple misunderstandings can quickly develop into sticky interpersonal problems. For example, you may feel too tired, depressed, or overwhelmed to talk, and someone who cares deeply for you may misunderstand your silence.

Misunderstandings with other people can sometimes be resolved just by opening up and saying what you feel. This could be hard for you, and you may just need to blurt it out, saying, "Look, I'm hurting badly and just can't talk to you right now. Please give me some time."

It is both understandable and acceptable to say just exactly what is going on: "We need to be by ourselves tonight. Could you come over some other time?" Or "I can't talk about it right now. Maybe in a while." Or "I feel too overwhelmed to be with anyone right now." Or "I'm too miserable to talk now." Trust people enough to tell them how you feel, even if this means you have to say no for now.

The other side of learning to say no during these first turbulent weeks is learning to say yes. We tend to think it a virtue to keep our troubles to ourselves and somehow make do without any help. This is the worst kind of false pride. This attitude cuts us off from human warmth, something we all need deeply, even when things are going well.

Now is not time to put on a front of self-sufficiency. When people offer to help, say yes. But don't stop there. Direct their energies and goodwill so it does your family the most good. You probably know what needs to be done better than anyone else, and if you are too scattered to think about it clearly, tell your friends and relatives the truth, but don't shut the door: "I know I could use help, but I can't think clearly right now. Can I call you in a few days?"

Let your family and friends take on some of the daily activities that keep a house afloat, like food shopping, housework, or child care. If friends want to know how to help, ask them to cook double one night and bring over the extra portion so you don't have to cook. Or you can ask for some frozen dinners, homemade or from a store. If relatives or friends make offers to help in any way they can, you might suggest that they have your other children over for a meal, a night, or a weekend so you can get some rest. Relatives who want to help and can afford it can give you money for a babysitter or housekeeper or they can hire a local teenager to help you out around the house.

People who care about you and your child will want to help in the ways that count. When you let them know what you really need, you are being generous in offering them opportunities to show their concern and share their warmth. People close to you will feel good knowing that they are helping you pull through in a very real way, and that they belong to your circle of support.

Talk from Your Heart

If you are a person who is used to communicating well and saying what you mean to say, this can be a particularly difficult time for you. You are likely to be confused, numb, vague, and distracted. This will change in time, and you will begin to think and speak clearly again. Right now, try to be easy on yourself. Don't expect too much and be forgiving if you forget things— phone calls, important information. You are going through a time of grieving that naturally affects your thought processes.

If you find that you are not making sense in your conversations with others, admit that you aren't thinking clearly. Tell others that you just can't keep things straight right now. This is a very normal response to your situation, so don't feel frightened. It is also one that will change. You may feel mixed up, with your thoughts and feelings in a terrible jumble. This, too, is natural. If you can't express to others what you feel or think, just look them in the eye, smile a bit, and press their hand. Anyone with a shred of sensitivity will know you care and that talking is just too much for you right now. Give yourself time to heal, and be gentle with yourself during this first, hard period of adjustment. If you can do this for yourself now, you will find that the necessary changes and healing will come more easily. This will help you, your family and friends, and most of all your handicapped child.

Chapter 3

How Parents Can Help Themselves and Each Other

Love, concern and human connection offer hope.
Without this hope it is quite difficult sometimes
to face life, to grow from its challenges and to
refuse to be destroyed by them.

—SARA KAY COHEN

Parenting is hard work even under the best of circumstances. With a child who is handicapped, the work of parenting intensifies and so do the strains, stresses, pressures—and of course the stress responses. A parent is likely to feel constantly tired, irritable, short-tempered, weepy, ill, discouraged, depressed, or angry and brittle. Rage may come too quickly and easily, and good times or simple relaxation can seem a fond memory from some distant past.

This is not a healthy state of affairs for anyone in the family, including your handicapped child. It is important that you find a way to relieve the stress, at least occasionally, and get a break from your responsibilities to refresh yourself. If you are a single parent, you have to do this in ways that do not include a mate. I have some suggestions for single parents later in the chapter. If you have a partner, you can help each other weather the hard times by working together.

With two parents, one is often stronger than the other at enduring pressure, working under strain, or just carrying a heavy load of responsibility. Add the considerable needs of a handicapped child, and the stronger of the two partners may start feeling angry and put-upon at having to bear most of the burden. The other partner may also feel angry to cover up the deeper fear of finding him or herself so dependent. This is tinder for an emotional fire that can hurt both of you.

When one of you carries the emotional burden most or all of the time, your relationship may quickly become strained to the breaking point. One or both of you can build up reserves of anger that can lead to fights, separation, and divorce. According to Martin (1972), 46 percent of parents with handicapped children are single at one time or another.

When the strong role is not so rigidly fixed on one partner, so that you can share and exchange the burden, then each of you can spell the other. This means you each have times when you can let go, relax, and know that your family will support and sustain you. A marriage is not made in heaven, but starts here on earth with two people committed to creating a working relationship that lets them handle difficulties and life's practical problems together.

The added work, responsibility, and pressures of having a handicapped child could be the starting point to begin forging a working, balanced partnership. As with any deep friendship or partnership, however, this union of energies will not happen quickly. It takes time, communication, commitment, and determination to be successful, but the benefits far outweigh the work.

One of the things I hear most commonly from parents is that they did not so much as share a cup of coffee or a single meal together for months after the birth or diagnosis of their handicapped child. How can any relationship continue to exist—let alone grow and develop—when two people spend no time together? This would be like expecting magic, and magic is not the answer. Instead, common sense and caring are what it takes.

Any relationship needs attention to flourish, but especially a marriage or partnership. You have to plan it and work on it just as you would to create and sustain a beautiful garden. If no energy or time goes into a garden, the weeds quickly choke out the flowers and any tender shoots of new growth. The same thing can happen to a marriage or partnership.

The greatest gift you can give any child is a loving, pleasant home with mature, content parents. Your marriage or partnership is most definitely a garden worth tending. Also, the good that comes from a strong working partnership extends beyond the immediate family to touch many lives. Two important prescriptions to help you work toward this loving home and partnership are trade-offs and weekly dates.

Trade-offs for Time and Space

Trade-offs mean time off for one of you while the other shoulders the parenting load for a while. For trade-offs to work, you will need to sit down together and talk about specifics. Make a list, if it helps, of just what you can do for your spouse or partner and what you would like done for you. We often want to do great things for the person we love, but feel limited by circumstances. A single, simple, small act can be the most helpful of all. Many mothers, for example, would be grateful for an hour or even fifteen minutes alone to take a hot bubble bath or read—with *no interruptions*. It can feel luxurious indeed to a woman who has not had any time to herself for days or months. Something simple might be just as welcome to a man, who might want to work by himself in the garage for an hour.

If you sit down to discuss details, you will discover small ways to help each other out that you didn't even think about before. Communicating in this way may be new to you, but it can give you a fresh view of one another. To make partnership arrangements work, you have to open up and say what is important to you. (You also may need to give this some thought before you sit down together.)

One couple arranged to trade off weekend days, so the father took care of the children on Saturday and the mother on Sunday. That way both parents got one day a week to do just what they wanted. This might not work for you, or you could try half-days instead. Each of you would then have at least half a day to spend as you wish every week. You will find yourself renewed and able, once more, to take on the responsibilities of parenting.

You can also work out trades with your partner for the everyday household jobs and special jobs that involve getting up at night with your child or taking your handicapped child for treatments or appointments. One family who traditionally cleaned their whole house together every Saturday decided to do a thorough cleaning every other week and instead pick up better every day to keep things orderly. The extra Saturday they gained by this strategy gave them time to do something they all enjoyed. In another household, the partners divided up the jobs by choosing what each wanted to do. Then the leftovers—which no one liked—were done by taking turns each week.

If often helps make the work of running a household easier if the two of you sit down and discuss what really needs to be done. Many people care for a house the way their mothers did. And yet now jobs can be simplified and streamlined. By working together you can figure out ways to do everything without exhausting yourselves.

Both of you need to realize that the weeks and months to come are going to be unusually demanding. So you need to work out practical ways of giving each other a break. This mutual support can get you through the bad times better than anything else.

A Weekly Date

Right from the beginning, when you first learn your child is handicapped, make plans with your spouse or partner for a weekly date. This may sound like a frivolous concern at such a time, but it is terribly important. It may be one of the *most important things* you can do to ensure a loving, caring home environment for your handicapped child. A weekly date is essential.

To do this you will need to find someone as soon as possible to care for your child when you and your partner are gone. It must be someone you trust to handle any kind of problem. Perhaps you can find a grandparent, a parent whose handicapped child is grown, or just an experienced or competent young woman or man.

You will also need to budget money for this right from the

beginning. It may seem an unnecessary expense when there are so many other bills that are urgent. Again, I'd like to say that this weekly date is an absolute necessity. Leaving your handicapped child in the care of someone else very early on is immensely healthy for your child and you. You will see the advantages of doing this many years after you have forgotten how hard it was to get started.

Partners won't feel like helping each other out if they don't feel like partners to begin with. Time together need not be complicated or expensive. The main idea is just to have some fun or enjoy good conversation with each other without little voices asking for your attention. All parents need some time away from the responsibilities of parenting, but you need even more. And your time should be in regular doses, at least once a week.

Going on a date suggests an expensive dinner out or tickets to the theater—wonderful once in a while, but probably too extravagant on a regular basis. There are alternatives. Time spent browsing together in a bookstore or having coffee and dessert in a café with some uninterrupted conversation can feel like a three-day holiday. A walk in a new neighborhood, along the beach, up in the mountains, or along the rim of a lake can freshen your world view and your view of each other. A peaceful breakfast in a nearby restaurant after the children are in school can seem more lavish than a costly dinner at a fancy restaurant. During your weekly time together, make it a rule not to bring up money, the children, or any practical matters. (You'll be surprised to find how hard this is.)

Simple activities can break your routine and refresh you: Go for a bicycle ride, plan a picnic, or just go get an ice cream cone together. Choosing the flavor could be the most lighthearted decision you've made in months. The point is to discover things you both enjoy that relax and revitalize you, creating a fresh supply of energy for your everyday responsibilities. It doesn't matter, really, what you do, only that you do something together and enjoy these times.

Be creative with ideas for your times together. You may have to let go of convention and just open yourself to ideas. To help yourself along in this process of exploring areas you might not know, many city recreation departments offer a range of programs that you can investigate. Also, community pools often set aside time for adult-only swims. Or later on you could share a special interest like collecting, birdwatching, hiking, auto racing, flea-market hunts, outdoor sketching, folk or square dancing, skiing, or working out together at a gym or health club. Try going back to doing some of the things you used to enjoy together when you first met. Or perhaps you would like to try something entirely new together: learning a new language, a new sport, taking a class together, studying computers. You could certainly use your weekly date to explore ideas or activities you have each been interested in but too busy to develop.

This special time together gets both of you out of your everyday world and into a neutral space. That is what makes it so important and valuable. For at least a little time, no one makes parenting demands on you, and you have a chance to feel like an adult and see each other as adults, not just parents. If nothing else, you will feel recharged.

It takes some real work to feel like an attractive and interesting adult when all your energy goes into being a mother or father. To do this, you need to reserve some time and energy for yourselves. And you need to make the time special by putting energy into planning for it. Even if it is only for an hour or two a week, time spent enjoying each other's company pays large dividends in the years to come. Remember, a weekly date is doctor's orders.

For Single Parents

If you are the single parent of a handicapped child, your job is indeed a very hard one, and you will need all the courage and determination you can muster. I think you will find that you will develop more of both these qualities than you thought possible, and you will grow beyond all expectations.

To begin with, you must quickly develop a good support system of family, friends, and medical personnel to make it through the first rough period. During this same period you are going to need time alone to breathe and just get away from your problems for a while. You have to create ways to take this time frequently, or your body will just refuse to handle any more stress. Physical or emotional problems are bound to follow. So please take the time you need. Listen to your body, and don't push yourself beyond your limits. You have to think farther ahead than just the next few days and weeks.

First you need to explore ways to have adult time to yourself or time to share with other adults. If you are lucky enough to have relatives nearby, perhaps they can offer you quality child care. It is essential that you find someone you trust so that you can start leaving your handicapped child right from the beginning and have some time to yourself. Without relatives, you are left the task of creating an instant family. One mother did this by cooking dinner for an unmarried male friend once a week in exchange for a weekly night out. She taught her friend to be an excellent caretaker, and he was happy because he enjoyed helping and being an important part of a family some of the time. You might also try exchanges with the parent or parents of other handicapped children. You could watch someone else's child for a few hours a week along with your own and then get a few hours of child care in exchange. As your child becomes more sociable, this can benefit the children, too.

Finding a friend or partner with whom to share adult time can be hard and may require a little resourcefulness on your part. Groups for single adults—such as church groups, Parents Without Partners, the Sierra Club Singles—all are possibilities. You will have to investigate the places in your own area where you can meet single adults. It is important for your mental health that you find some friends outside of any handicapped parents groups you might join. Contact beyond the world of your handicapped child is important, so your view does not become narrow and restricted to just the world of handicapped children.

Being a single parent has a positive side to it. Often a closeness and a sharing develops between mother and child or father and child that may not be possible with two parents. When a household has two parents, they can be so busy living their own lives and involved with each other that there may be little real communication with the child who is handicapped.

Another benefit of being a single parent can be the absence of tension that can easily arise when two people try to raise a child. Individuals often have strong ideas about how a child should be raised; occasionally these agree with their partner's ideas, but often they clash. People have different styles of disciplining, and this can cause conflict. Children in a home with a single parent avoid the pain of living with two parents who fight a lot. With a single parent, children do not have to divide their allegiances and they have their parent's undivided attention.

Of necessity, the children of single parents often achieve more emotional maturity earlier in life. In fact, this can come about too soon for children who have to take responsibility when a mother or father is trying to do everything alone. A particular problem can arise when a mother tries to do too much, trying to be all things to her child. Love like this can turn into "smother love," which is not healthy for a child. I have seen relationships, too, where the child and the mother were almost extensions of one another.

Carole Klein wrote something in her book *The Single Parent Experience* that I like: "To raise a child who has strong enough feelings of identity that he can move towards an unknown future with confidence is difficult but not impossible." The consensus among professionals is that with enough ego strength of her or his own, a single parent can do just as good a job as married parents can, and sometimes even better.

There is another positive value to being a single parent—or in this case a single mother—and that is sensitivity and awareness. So often a male child raised in a household with a father is not allowed or encouraged to develop sensitivity because his father was taught to hide his own feelings when he was growing up. With just a single parent, the boy often has more chance to know that it is okay to express feelings and not feel ashamed of them. A child who grows up in an accepting atmosphere like this will be a more aware and feeling adult; he will know that if he wants to show emotion, he can.

A final value of the relationships in single-parent families is that the children perceive their parents as being much more real. Most single parents don't have the energy to cover up feelings or pretend when they are frightened or hurting. For many reasons, they allow their children to see them as they are and do not work so hard at projecting a false image. Because of this, there is a real openness between the parent and child or children that is wonderful for everyone in the family.

Role Models in Single-Parent Families

A possible problem in families with a single parent is that of role modeling. This particularly occurs where a mother is raising a boy or a father raising a girl. Mothers have to be very careful about being seductive with their sons, expecting them to replace an adult male figure in the household and become the mother's male companion. The reverse is true of fathers and daughters. I am not talking about physical seduction, but rather emotional seduction, which can be very harmful to a child. A child who is made to fill an adult role may suffer long-term consequences and become either an overly responsible adult or one who will not assume responsibility.

Finding a support system of caring people is very important for a single parent. Such a network should include adults of the opposite sex, so that the child has some good role models to choose from. One woman did this by hiring adult males who belonged to her church to care for her ten-year-old after school. Some were college students, and one had a job that left him free in the afternoons. The boy, who had been having problems in school, responded very well to spending time with men, and even went with them on short excursions. His school problems became fewer as he became happier.

Another value of having an extended substitute family with a single parent is that the child needs to learn to get along with all different kinds of adults. While it is good to give the child options when it comes to spending time with adults, it is particularly important in the case of a handicapped child to be careful in choosing a parent substitute. Handicapped children are often less likely to be able to care for themselves and protect themselves, and any child can, unfortunately, be intimidated by an adult. (See page 58 for pointers on how to find good child care.)

Discipline

Discipline can be a problem in any family; it is especially difficult in a family with a handicapped child, and this is compounded in a family with a handicapped child and a single parent. Parents often feel guilty about their child's handicap or guilty about the fact that the child doesn't have two parents. Reasons for feeling guilty seem to be plentiful, but all this achieves is to interfere with good parenting.

Good parenting requires discipline, and discipline is really just another word for love. It is the parents' job to show their children how to survive and if possible to flourish in the world. This means training in social and academic skills and simple survival techniques, such as handling money, crossing streets, calling for emergency help, or saying no to a stranger. In setting limits, establishing guidelines for appropriate and inappropriate behavior, and voicing expectations, a parent is saying, "You are a very important person who deserves a lot of attention, guidance, and love, which I'm going to give to you."

Children may voice complaints about restrictions or expectations and test limits to see if they will hold, but in fact they want and need limits. A child without limits feels very anxious and insecure. Although children sometimes talk and act as if they would like to run the world and everyone in it, they simply do not have the judgment and maturity to do this, and they know it.

A single parent needs to have or develop a fair amount of ego strength to set limits and establish firm but fair guidelines. But the rewards are great if you can do this, and you will have much happier children. You don't do children any favors by raising them to be demanding, whiny, and manipulative. To get help in learning how to be a strong parent, look for parent-support groups, classes on parenting and child rearing, library books on raising children, and people who seem to have done a good job of parenting. If you can find some good parents to use as role models, ask them questions and seek their advice. Most people will be happy to tell you about what they have found that works or doesn't. You might also consider forming a group of single parents who meet to share ideas on childrearing. One group of parents I know did this: They would periodically choose a book on parenting to read and discuss at their meetings. Even though they often disagreed with the authors or each other, they shared a lot of information and inspired each other's efforts to be better parents.

Another advantage of being a single parent is that a child cannot play one parent against the other to wheedle a special privilege. Difficulties may arise, however, if the child's other parent lives close by. Then there may not be just one clear set of rules to follow, and this can become a problem for the child. Frequently each household has different ways of doing things. One woman told me she was very careful about what her child ate, what she watched on TV, and where and with whom she played. Then, when the little girl went to her dad's, she was allowed to stay up late, watch anything she wanted on TV, eat anything, and run fairly wild. Somehow, though, the child survived. She quickly had to learn that one set of rules applied in one house and another in the other.

In a two-household arrangement, the rules must be clearly defined. Then, even if one parent is more permissive than the other, the children will know what they can and cannot do. With more and more children alternating weeks between their parents, experience has shown that they can adapt readily if they just know the rules, and these rules are consistently and firmly enforced.

You can tell by now that I think being a single parent has both its advantages and disadvantages. I speak from several years of my own experience in handling this demanding job. Perhaps the greatest disadvantage is having to be all things to your children and having so many demands placed upon you. If this is then compounded by having a handicapped child who requires a great deal of time and attention, it can seem that your life demands more strength and energy than you have to give.

You can survive better if you work some quiet times and some moments of fun into your daily life. Even just a few minutes here and there can make a lot of difference in how you feel about life. Fun is very good medicine. Also, be sure you don't become isolated and cut off from others. Warm, friendly human contact is important to have every day, especially at first. Living just one day at a time is probably the very best advice that I can give you as the single parent of a handicapped child.

Chapter 4

Time Out
for Mothers

When we cling to pain, we end up punishing ourselves.

—Leo Buscaglia

Women are the usual caretakers, the constant emotional givers in our society. This may not be fair, but it is fact. As a mother, you may be so committed to the care of your children, particularly your handicapped child, that your own needs get submerged. To survive the constant demands of a handicapped child in addition to those from the rest of your family, *you must set aside some time for yourself each day.*

As impossible as this may seem, it isn't. It only seems impossible to you right now, which is different from being impossible. Such time is essential, because if you don't take care of yourself, you will not be able to take care of others.

You may only be able to set aside fifteen or twenty minutes a day, but even this short time can change the picture you have of life. You might try making time when the rest of the family is asleep in the evening or when the children are napping or at school. Some women wake early in the morning to have a quiet cup of coffee by themselves before the day's activities begin. A daily walk, jogging, exercises, dancing to music, singing, writing in a journal or letters to friends and family, reading a good book, gardening, or just sitting and unwinding can help you survive one more demanding day.

Time away from any child is part of doing a competent job of parenting. It is too easy to start seeing your child as just a lot of work, someone who needs feeding, clothing, and bathing, instead of a person with a growing personality and uniqueness. This is particularly possible when the day-to-day care is not only physically but also emotionally exhausting because you have a handicapped child. Unless you take some time for yourself away from your handicapped child and family, you will become consumed with fatigue and anger.

To make time for yourself means setting aside or finding money for babysitters or nurses for some takeover care. This has to become a part of your regular monthly budget. Money for child care is not a luxury, and money spent in this way is not wasted. Getting time away is as important to your survival as continuing to breathe and to eat.

Many mothers tell me that they feel guilty spending money to hire someone to watch their child so that they can take time off. Yet often they spend enough money on unnecessary baby products or fast foods to pay for the extra child-care help. One day I added up what a young mother on welfare told me she spent monthly on disposable diapers, prepared formulas, prepared foods, and different kinds of powders and lotions. It was hard for me to believe that no one had suggested a better way for her to use her money, as it came to quite a sum.

Well-washed cloth diapers are usually better for a baby's skin than disposable ones, and making your own formulas by mixing them with water (or nursing your child and using little formula) saves a great deal of money. Cornstarch is a good, inexpensive baby powder and great for diaper rashes unless the rash is caused by a fungus. Most health-food or baby-product stores now sell a hand grinder that quickly makes your regular meals into good baby foods without the extra expense. A blender can do the same trick, if you have one.

Mothers often argue that disposable diapers save time. It is true the cloth ones need washing, but you can use this time to think about other things, as you load the washing machine, grind the baby's food, or mix formulas. And remember that shopping frequently for disposable diapers takes time, too.

Television and magazine advertising have done a disservice, I think, to young mothers who have little money. They show many products as necessities, when you are really better off with just a few essentials and a lot less fuss. We live in a society that places much emphasis on things, and it is often hard to realize that time is really more valuable than products. Time spent renewing your own energy is worth more than many highly advertised products.

Buying less and choosing more wisely is also a good idea when it comes to children's toys. Children do best with just a few well-chosen toys instead of a roomful of breakable ones or ones with many parts that are easily lost or that may cost a great deal of money. A good set of blocks may cost a bit more at first, but they will last for years and will help your child develop a creative imagination and wonderful sense of play.

You can also exchange toys with other mothers so that your child can have a range of play experiences without costing you lots of money. Some towns even have lending "toybraries."

Children's clothing can also be expensive. Often children do not wear out all their clothes, so someone else can use the same wardrobe. This way you can buy just a few really special things and still have plenty of nice clothes. In many towns there are children's consignment shops that buy used children's clothes that are in good condition and then resell them at a reasonable price.

Certain families qualify for financial assistance to pay for help with child care. This is called respite care and most often is arranged through state or local agencies. For example, in California, both the California Children's Services (CCS) and the Regional Center can help provide respite care in specific cases. Unfortunately, it often takes time and cutting through considerable red tape to get this help, but it is available. Check with your state agencies that care for handicapped children about possible respite care for your child. You might also contact a social worker at your local hospital or at an agency with which you are familiar to find out what's available in your area.

By using all these strategies—and more that you come up with—you'll be able to put money aside every month for some time off for yourself while someone else cares for your child. It is an absolute necessity for you, your handicapped child, and the other members of your family.

In addition to stressing how important your *daily* time alone is, I feel the same is true of *weekly* time off. Once a week it is important to take an entire afternoon or evening off from your handicapped child. This weekly "time-out" should be in addition to the weekly date you take with your husband or male partner. This means you should have a block of several hours for yourself each week to go to a movie, visit the library by yourself, or talk with a friend.

Daily and weekly time to yourself not only makes life more satisfying overall, it makes day-to-day living with a handicapped child much easier. I am sure there are times that you feel completely worn out. Then you pick up a good book or some handwork, do some vigorous exercise, relax with a close friend, or do something enjoyable for a few minutes. The change that comes after such a break feels like a magical transformation. After just fifteen or twenty minutes of doing something I enjoy deeply, I can feel recharged and ready to go again.

Think of your daily times off as mini-vacations that help you manage each day better. These breaks boost your energy enough so you can work to make that day the best one possible for yourself and the people around you.

If you find that you feel uncomfortable with the idea of taking time off, you should investigate your feelings. You may feel so guilty that you don't deserve any rest. If this is the case, you may need counseling to help change your attitude. To do your best as the parent of a handicapped child, you have to learn that parents need time for themselves. This is a basic right of being a parent.

Becoming a parent doesn't mean you are no longer a person. As a parent you still have rights to your own personal growth, which will be particularly important to you as the parent of a handicapped child. More than rights, time for yourself and your own growth are needs as basic as shelter and human warmth. You need a place in this world that is just for you. You cannot make your own unique journey in life without taking time to do some of those things you truly want and must do.

Getting caught up in the details of life can move us blindly through duties without having any fun. At the end of such an existence—one can hardly call it a life—so much we may have dreamed of remains unexplored and undone. Bitterness can grow from living like this; I have seen it happen too often, and this is a tragic waste.

A good way to help you stay on track and to see how you spend your days is to keep a daily journal or record. Just jotting down thoughts as they come to you in an inexpensive notebook is a good way to get in touch with what you really feel and think. Doing this will help you to center and to think about just the moment at hand plus help you to find some new strength and direction in life.

There are several good books about journal writing, and some communities even give classes in journal writing through the recreation department or community college. One particularly helpful book, available in paperback, is called *The New Diary,* by Tristine Rainer. Keeping a journal is a private way to be aware of the activities that make up your own life. You can say anything you want to, and no one will see it. A journal can also aid you in maintaining your emotional balance from day to day.

In her book *Whoever Said Life Is Fair?* Sara Kay Cohen said that she decided to keep a journal to handle the stress and frustration she felt in life. She would put in her journal the steps she was taking in her journey toward a new life. Writing when lonely or afraid, she found she could ease her anger and fear and find some answers to her immediate problems by working out her thoughts on paper.

We pass through life only once, so each moment is precious. Time spent doing what you want is essential for you, especially since you carry the extra burden of having a handicapped child as part of your daily life. You need time for thought and reflection. You may even need some counseling to help you find a good balance for your life and to determine what is essential for you.

A Network of Friends

Friends are good medicine. We have all had friends who make a gray day brighter and a bright one more fun. Unfortunately, once women have families, they often feel that there is not enough time for both their families and their friendships with other women. Women need the friendship of others. Without friends, women stay at home with their own children and have little adult company. They can easily come to feel cut off and lonely. This is definitely unhealthy, especially for you as the mother of a handicapped child. You can easily be tempted to hold back from your friends and try to deal with your grief and problems alone, when what you really need is to reach out to others for their help and support.

Now more than ever you need a network of good friends who will be able to help you in many ways. Friends can often see practical solutions to your everyday problems that you can't see. They can come up with fresh ideas you haven't thought of. More important, their warmth and concern can make massive problems seem manageable.

For your own well-being and that of your family, cultivate your friendships and develop a network of close friends. Making contact with other women who have handicapped children at home may be especially helpful so that you can share information about practical matters as well as give each other much-needed emotional support. Your doctor, a social service agency in your town, the hospital social worker, or a parent-support group can often put you in touch with other mothers in circumstances similar to yours. Women who have faced or are facing problems like yours can better appreciate what you are going through than others who haven't been in your position. We all need a strong guide— or even many guiding hands—on a long, hard journey. Other mothers who have handicapped children are likely to have valuable tips about practical matters or advice on a way of looking at a problem that can give you a lift. Talking with women who carry the same burden you do scales your own problems to a level that seems workable.

Probably the hardest period in your friendships with others will come with your desire to hide your feelings of inadequacy. Wanting to hide these feelings from others is natural enough; no one likes to have others see them as weak and vulnerable. But you should not let this fear of exposure keep you from reaching

out to people in friendship. I think you will find that real openness brings surprising warmth your way.

Friends can energize and sustain each other. One group of
mothers I know gets together one morning a week with all their
children in tow. They take turns meeting at each woman's house,
where they share ideas and ways of raising children, coping with
problems. They even bring special books to share that have been
helpful. The women often agree ahead of time on a topic or book
for these lively discussions. Neither the children nor the mothers
agree with each other all the time, but they have been meeting
this way for over a year now, and all seem to be flourishing from
their contact and mutual support.

Another function of this group is to trade child care. Two or
three of the women (the group has about six members) have
worked out a cooperative plan whereby each mother takes two
extra babies for one morning a week. Each woman thus has two
mornings a week to herself. The children are well cared for by
these loving friends and their mothers, who are like well-known
aunts to the children.

This miniature community of women would have been natural in a tribe or small village, but we don't live in small groups
anymore. Since people move around so easily from town to town
and state to state, we are often far away from close relatives and
friends who could help us out. The next best option is to create
networks with our friends that function as extended families.

Good friends are one of life's great joys, but we need to guard
our friendships carefully and care for our friends to the best of
our ability. This care will be returned many times over, and often
when we need it the most.

Chapter 5

The Siblings of Handicapped Children

All that we put into the lives of others comes back into our own.

—Edwin Markham

A handicapped child requires, by the very nature of his or her problems, a great deal of attention. As a parent, though, you have only so much energy. What this often means in practical terms is that the brothers and sisters of your handicapped child may be pretty well forgotten, or at least it can feel that way to them.

During the same period that parents are spending time with either their handicapped newborn in the intensive-care nursery or an older child, trying to find out what's wrong, the siblings of the handicapped child are likely to be having a hard time themselves. These children frequently harbor many guilty feelings because they are "normal" while their brother or sister isn't. Worse, they can believe that something they felt or thought, said or did, caused the handicap.

No one has the time or takes the time to sit and talk to these children about why their brother or sister is handicapped, and so they whirl around in their own emotions and pain. They often feel very alone, isolated, and, unconsciously or consciously, very angry.

Characteristically, the brothers and sisters of a handicapped child react in one of two ways. Some choose being very good as a strategy of survival. Making no demands on their already over-worked parents, they try to be helpful and are rarely mischievous or troublesome. As these "good" children grow up, however, they often discover they harbor anger and emotional turmoil deep inside because they missed out on badly needed parenting.

The other common reaction of the neglected siblings is to try attention-getting mechanisms. Children doing this are either consciously or unconsciously trying to regain some of their parents' time and energy. If their behavior is ignored, these children can eventually move on to more powerful acting out, such as setting fires, destroying property, running away from home, or becoming addicted to drugs and/or alcohol.

These children need attention just as any child does. Without getting any positive attention from their parents, who are too preoccupied caring for their handicapped child, the other children can settle for negative attention. Getting their parents' atten-tion—even if it is only anger—through misbehavior and acting out is better than nothing at all.

While the acting-out children become obvious and immediate problems for their parents, the goody-goodies who hide their distress often wind up with lifelong problems. Those brought up with a handicapped child know how hard it is to achieve any place in the spotlight without going to extremes. Either they acted out or were so good that they grew up too soon without the opportunity to be a child.

If, while really talking with your nonhandicapped child, you come to feel that he or she is deeply disturbed about your hand-icapped youngster or has feelings that are depressing or fright-ening, I strongly suggest that you seek counseling. If your talk together doesn't seem to lift the child's worries or fears, he or she may need more than you can give. Early counseling, or even ongoing counseling, offered as needed, can make a real difference in a child's life later on as an adult. Such early intervention can free a child from carrying a handicapped sibling like a heavy stone around the neck.

In many cities discussion groups for siblings of handicapped children are led by professionals trained to handle the problems of these young people. If there are none where you live, look for a counselor to start such a group. Or you might also seek out someone to do individual counseling with your child or with all the children in your family. Many social-service agencies have trained counselors available at a cost based on your monthly income. Also try your local city, county, or state mental health office.

I have led several sibling groups and have always been amazed at the weights some of these children carry. Most live with strong feelings of responsibility for their handicapped sibling, either self-imposed or put there by their parents. Often they have a distorted view of their sibling's actual handicap. Many feel that their parents are focusing all their energy on the handicapped brother or sister. All this guilt, anger, and suffering build up inside these children, making life very tough for them. I think we did a lot of "abscess lancing" in those sessions, which was tremendously helpful. Your children will benefit from a chance to talk to other children who are in a similar situation. This experience can let them know, in a way you can't, that their guilt, worries, and hunger for attention are all normal. They need your reassurance.

A pediatrician told me about some of the feelings and problems she felt while being raised in a family with a handicapped child. Her family knew that something was very wrong with her little brother, but they couldn't discover what it was despite visits to many doctors. Finally, when the boy was about fifteen, they discovered the cause of the problem. My doctor friend thought of her parents as practically carrying her brother around on "a satin pillow." They didn't expect him to do any chores or have any outside jobs, which they expected of the other children. And the parents always found time and money for their handicapped son's many needs. For the other children, the parents had little time, and money was only available if they earned it themselves.

Although the parents would not tolerate any open expression of anger from the healthy children, they put up with the handicapped child's frequent temper tantrums and angry outbursts. Obviously the handicapped child knew he was the favored child, and he took advantage of it every chance he could. He manipulated both the parents and his brother and sister so that essentially he was seen as the good boy and the other children were the naughty ones.

By the time the boy's medical problems were identified and a tumor was removed, the family's financial resources were depleted almost to the point of bankruptcy. The father, a proud bookkeeper, would not accept any help from the state agency for handicapped children and tried to meet the high medical costs with his own small salary. Neither of the nonhandicapped children ever vocalized their feelings that they were being treated unfairly. They simply accepted the treatment they received as their due until they became older.

The woman who told me this story said that once, while seeing a therapist for marital problems, her counselor said to her, "You've been carrying your brother on your back all of your life, which is probably one of the reasons you went into pediatrics. You have been trying to understand what happened with your brother and why you always felt him around your neck like a millstone. You have a highly overdeveloped sense of responsibility toward other children and have tried to mother the world. This has caused emotional problems, marital problems, and has left you feeling drained, angry, and incomplete. Essentially you have had to be your own parent, and after your parents died, you felt a tremendous responsibility for your brother. By transferring his dependence from your parents to you, you created a very difficult problem for yourself. You may well know that people often grow to dislike, or even hate, close individuals on whom they feel dependent. This surely was your brother's case. First he hated your parents, and now he hates you."

This was a painful and powerful legacy that the parents left to their children. The problems with her brother took the physician a long time and a great deal of counseling to resolve. Even when they no longer were in touch, the brother frequently appeared in the woman's dreams as an evil figure. This highly respected professional woman went through years of emotional turmoil and conflict over a situation that was completely out of her control.

If only someone in the family had realized the importance of communicating with the other children. The parents could have explained their frustrations with medical practitioners who couldn't pinpoint the brother's problems. Then the family could have established a forum to discuss financial problems, chores, and other difficulties. In essence what happened in this family, though, is that the parents pitted themselves and their handicapped child against their other two children instead of working together as a unit. The nonhandicapped brother and sister became close and helped each other survive, but they talked about what their real problems had been only many years later.

Good early counseling could probably have prevented the lifelong emotional scars these two still carry. Both became high achievers in order to fill their deep needs for respect and recognition. And both, now divorced, have had to seek counseling in order to learn how to express anger and how to trust in intimate relationships. Guilt, a pervasive sadness, and a feeling of responsibility for their brother rode hard on their consciences for many, many years.

Becoming a member of the helping professions—as in the case of my friend, the pediatrician—is common among the brothers and sisters of handicapped children. Perhaps the nonhandicapped siblings want to explore what it means to be handicapped, or else they want to understand what has happened in their own lives. Many also want to rid themselves, through their work and dedication to others, of the guilt they feel or felt at being normal.

As the parent of a handicapped child and one or more who are not handicapped, you probably feel that you don't need or can't handle any more bad news at this point, especially about your children who seem fine. I raise this unpleasant subject only because, forewarned, you are better prepared to avoid some of the problems with your children that came up in my friend's family.

One-to-One Time with Each Child

The idea of spending time alone with each child might seem impossible to do with all your other responsibilities. It is probably difficult enough to find the time you need just to care for your handicapped child, and you certainly aren't likely to have any extra time to spend with the others on a one-to-one basis.

I know this is true, and I also know how intensely important it is that you do spend some time alone with each of your children. It does not have to be a lot of time. Quality time and the one-to-one nature of your contact is what is important. It can be for only five or ten minutes here or there in a busy day.

The time alone with a nonhandicapped child when no one else is around or can interrupt lets you both open up and talk intimately about special things. It also gives this child a much-needed and concentrated dose of your love and affection. If you don't make special times to do this, you might be just too distracted to express your caring openly and directly. Parents are often amazed to hear their grown children complain that they were never told their parents loved them. Parents can know they love and care for a child but become too busy to tell the child.

When you first talk alone with each child, you might gently bring up the subject of the handicapped sibling if the setting and occasion warrant it. This lets the child you are talking to know that it is okay to discuss the sibling's handicap, to ask questions about it or ask why it's there. Use "creative listening" to inspire trust and communication between the two of you. This builds a strong foundation so that you can encourage ongoing openness for sharing questions and feelings. (See *Parent Effectiveness Training,* Gordon, 1975.)

Once you have opened the way for communication with each child by talking about your handicapped youngster, you can let the child you talk with lead you to what he or she wants to share. You will find yourself listening not only to fears and worries, but also to triumphs and dreams. Achieving openness with your children can take lots more than one listening session, but it is a goal well worth achieving. The point is to start somewhere by giving each child a chance at a few moments of your undivided attention as frequently as possible.

It will take lots of ingenuity on your part to find times for private talks if you have a house full of children or even just one or two, which can sometimes seem like a houseful. Good chances for talks are going for a walk together to a park, to buy a treat, or to a child's school or friend's house; just taking a little time off from your busy schedules is special for the two of you. Sometimes just sitting across the table from each other in a pleasant space new to both of you—a little ice cream store or bakery shop—is a good way to start talking.

With certain children you may have to set the stage a little bit more to get things started. Try communicating when the others are out playing, visiting friends, or away at a birthday party, or when your handicapped child is at a physical-therapy session. The two of you can stay home, sit down, have some cookies and milk and a talk. One of the best times I found to talk with my children was just before each one went to sleep. Because they had separate bedtimes, I had a good chance to spend a few quiet moments with each one. I always enjoyed these times of sitting and talking quietly at the end of a full day, and they enjoyed it, too.

It very much helps if you do something mutually relaxing during your one-to-one contact with your child. One mother I know took one youngster each day out for short "flower walks," as she called them. Because she loved flowers, she took great pleasure in teaching her children their names as they walked. But they talked also about what was happening in the child's school and what was on the child's mind. Later, as the children grew older, she would have one or the other out with her in the yard, where they worked and talked together.

A father I knew found it relaxing to do puzzles with his children. He insisted on working with only one child at a time, and they respected this rule. He started with simple ones and went on to complex jigsaw puzzles, big enough so that each child got to help put the whole thing together—and spend time alone with their dad in the bargain. Another father had his children, even as toddlers, help when he worked in the garage, fixing things. Working side by side, with the little one handing her dad a hammer or a rule, gave them a chance to talk about things. Find some way to share the thing you enjoy in life with each of your children on a one-to-one basis.

Another trick to finding this time alone with each child is to use the time when you are driving your child to get a haircut or to a doctor's appointment. Being together in a car gives you the space to talk privately. Going to the dentist works especially well for this because a child who is nervous about going to the dentist—and most are, a little—welcomes the chance to open up and talk about anything bothering him.

One more possibility is to go out shopping together. After you have worked together to finish the grocery shopping, you can take a few minutes to do something just for this child. Nothing extravagant is needed. Getting a pair of brightly colored shoelaces or some pretty stickers can delight a child. So can a short walk and some window shopping while talking.

Working together on the everyday chores that need doing around the house can be a good way to share time. Children are often quite willing to do work if it means helping you and working alongside you. Jobs that they would scorn if they were told to do them or had to do them alone become suddenly more attractive when you tackle them together. Perhaps the best example is a thorough cleaning and organizing of a child's room or that child's section of a shared room. This naturally requires that just the two of you work alone together. But you can also work side by side at sorting laundry, washing dishes, gardening, organizing a closet, running errands, making beds, cooking a meal, polishing furniture, or just straightening up.

Besides spending time alone with one child, working on something together has other benefits. The child feels important because skills are learned that make a valuable contribution to the family's daily life. The final advantage is that you get things done that need doing.

The only disadvantage to working with your children is that it is also important to spend time with them when you and the child have no other commitments on your time. With a lot of responsibilities, it is only too easy to work all the time and never stop to relax, play, or just be still, or to enjoy seeing and hearing. Some of the very best intimate contacts with a child can arise quite naturally when you are relaxed together and the child feels free to ask a question that is important. Moments like this can't be planned or programmed, but they can be followed up when they do happen.

Fathers, too, need to spend as much one-to-one time with each child as possible. Each of you offers your children different qualities because you are individuals, and each meets different needs in your children. When a family is always together as a unit, there is no time or space for a more intimate, personal meeting of individual family members.

Remember not to be hard on yourself about this issue. No one who is human is perfect. You will inevitably go for days without even noticing your other children, but when you recall that they may be feeling left out, drop some of the less necessary chores and spend some one-to-one time with them. I can't tell you what a valuable investment this is in their future. You will all be better off for a family atmosphere that is a healthy balance instead of one that lists toward one member exclusively.

You may find it helpful or necessary to make a mental checklist once every few days to a week of the time spent alone with each child over the past few days. On top of everything else, this may seem like too much, but the time spent is a very wise investment in your children's futures. Life will be easier if you spend just a short time now with each child. Otherwise, you might have to put in too much time later on in trying to undo the damage. Moments of quality time with you sprinkled through each child's day can change a child's emotional forecast from stormy to sunny.

Chapter 6

How to Find Your Handicapped Child's Greatest Potential

Who in the world am I?
Ah, that's the greatest puzzle!

—LEWIS CARROLL

All parents have expectations for their children—they want them to grow up to be educated, or caring, or clever. It is both normal and natural to have these expectations, and there is no need to give them up with a handicapped child. In fact, expectations will be very important for both you and your child. For you, they will serve as guidelines to help you in making decisions and choices about schooling, recreation, friends, and special programs for your child. Expectations will give him something to work toward and the sure knowledge that he can do something that you believe is valuable and important. Expectations or goals can give all of you a bigger picture that will inspire you when the details of daily life threaten to bog you down. Such goals can offer a long-range perspective. This can be uplifting at the times when all you can see in front of you are too many obstacles and chores that need doing.

Although you will want to set goals for your handicapped child, the process is not the same as it would be for the parent of a nonhandicapped child. Several important considerations will influence your decisions and choices.

Setting Goals

The most important point to keep in mind in setting goals for your child, handicapped or not, is that they should be realistic. Children can develop tremendous anxieties when faced with un- realistically high goals that have been forced on them. While it is good and healthy to want your child to excel—and we have all heard wonderful stories about individuals who have achieved far more than expected—the goals you set have to be obtainable. If they are clearly impossible, such as expecting a child afflicted with severe cerebral palsy to achieve normal speech, then anxiety, re- sentment, and rage can erupt in both you and your child.

Goals that are set too high can be frustrating and finally im- mobilizing, so that children begin to feel that they can't do any- thing at all and give up trying. Push a child too hard and life becomes nothing but a burden, each day bringing more and more discomfort. Your child feels punished, and you feel like an an- gry, demanding parent. On the other hand, having no goals at all or goals that are not challenging can lead children to become bored and unable to test or develop their full potential.

You may need the help of professionals to establish realistic goals for your child. They can give you an idea of what to ex- pect. Setting realistic, obtainable goals for each handicapped child, however, requires a great deal of insight and experience, and you will want to help guide this process.

To get a good start, you must first examine your own expec- tations. Many parents simply cannot accept the very real limits of their child's handicapping condition. After you have talked with professionals about your child's condition and its limita- tions, take some time to explore your own emotional response to what you have heard. You may need some time for grieving again, here, about the fact that your child will not be able to do some of the things that matter greatly to you. It is important to pay heed to what your own hopes have been. You can acknowl- edge them, and perhaps lay them to rest if they are unrealistic or inappropriate. Only after this will you be able to focus on your child as an individual and not as an extension of your own desires and needs. This is not an easy task for any parent, whether the child is handicapped or not. Helping a child discover the answer to Lewis Carroll's question, "Who in the world am I?" is important work for each parent.

Once you have examined your own expectations and started bringing them into line with reality, you will next have to explore the expectations of the experts you are consulting. Many physicians and other medical personnel have problems accepting anything less than a perfect solution to any problem. Accepting nothing less than perfection can lead professionals to establish unrealistic goals for your handicapped child.

Keep in mind that certification by a board of medical examiners as a physician or other medical practitioner is not necessarily a guarantee of common sense. If you see medical professionals setting goals for your child that you know are impossible, you must voice your doubts openly. You as a parent are your child's advocate, and you know your child better than anyone else does. Professionals can be highly qualified in their field, but you are the expert where your own child is concerned.

One of the first problems in setting realistic goals is that it is difficult even for experts to assess accurately any handicapped child's potential. Another complication is that your child's condition or situation can change with time, requiring new goals and expectations. Changes can be brought about by natural alterations in the handicap as the child grows, new methods of testing the child's potential, or newly discovered, more effective treatment methods. Any change can then alter what at first seemed either impossible or possible. Because of this, you should plan from time to time to reassess the goals you set for your child. It is a good idea to do this annually, so that the goals can be reviewed to see if they are in line with actual experience.

A good example of the need to reassess goals is the case of a child with a progressive muscle disease. Because this leads to a steady loss of strength, what a child can do readily at the age of eight may not be possible by ten no matter how hard he tries. Sensitive adjustments to goals have to be made for children in this situation.

Another example of the need to reassess goals periodically can be seen in emotionally disturbed children. As they improve with education or therapy, their goals will need to be changed. Children who are injured in an accident or diagnosed as having a handicapping condition after several seemingly normal years may become depressed and have to learn to express and channel their frustration and anger. Once this occurs, they can start developing the skills and abilities that are there. For these children, goals have to be altered as they learn to work with their own potentials. What was difficult for an angry, upset child can become easy for one who has released his blocked energy.

Let Your Child Help Set Goals

Whenever possible, let your child take part in the goal-setting process with you. With infants and toddlers, this is unrealistic, but as soon as children begin to understand, they can begin to share in the process. Setting goals with their parents gives them a chance to express their hopes. Hope is an often overlooked but essential ingredient that works to make life better for everyone. Working as yeast does in warm dough, hope both lifts us up and lightens our burdens.

There is another often overlooked but practical aspect to having your child participate. Children will put more effort into reaching goals they have had a part in setting. They will not feel that they are having to achieve a level established by someone else.

A second ingredient in working successfully toward goals is the love and support that you give your child. Goals can be high and still be realistically based on what is possible. Many children, handicapped or nonhandicapped, far exceed expectations because they received so much love and support along the way. They felt they could afford to take risks because they knew that their parents would still be there for them even if they failed.

When you begin thinking about goals for your child, you won't know what is too high or too low. All you can do is to make your best guess, based on the information you have gathered and what your own intuition tells you. Watch how your child responds to these challenges as you work together to meet them.

Be alert for signs of overwhelming frustration and anger, but remember that some frustration is the price of learning anything new. Let your child meet challenges, because children who are protected from all problems, frustrations, or failures don't grow into mature, capable adults.

With time and experience, you will develop a feel for setting goals that are both fair and realistic. Those that are too easy don't offer any challenge or excitement. But those that are unrealistically high don't allow children to develop a sense of competency. Real successes are needed to develop self-confidence in any child.

Consulting with medical professionals and other parents who have a child with a similar handicap may help you. Expect to make mistakes in the process, but realize that at the same time you will be gaining on-the-job knowhow that cannot be matched by any number of educational credentials. Your experience will help develop insight, so you will become better and better at setting realistic, workable goals.

Society's ideas and attitudes toward handicaps and handicapped individuals is slowly becoming more open and forward-looking. You can help this process by working with your child to find out what is possible and show others how realistic goals can be accomplished.

One mother who had a child with Down's syndrome wanted to enroll her in a Montessori preschool when she was two. Other parents and the teachers were sure that the little girl wouldn't fit in and would probably disrupt the class. Finally, they agreed to give the mother and child a chance. The little girl started going once a week with an aide.

The aide and the girl's mother worked at adapting the educational materials and tasks to the girl's abilities, and the child had worked up to going four times a week by the time she was three. She also needed her special aide only two days a week. The other two days she functioned as a "normal" student in the class, getting along very well with her classmates—a triumph for mainstreaming. The once-skeptical parents and teachers became converts, and soon other handicapped children were allowed and encouraged into the classroom. One woman's vision and courage made this a reality for many, but if she had listened to what others had said instead of to her own feelings, her daughter would not have had the chance to make the progress and educational growth that she did.

Recreation

You and your handicapped child can become so caught up in keeping appointments with doctors, physical therapists, social workers, occupational therapists, counselors, and so on that your child has no time to relax and just have fun. A child who is kept so busy has no chance to play, and without time for imaginary play and other creative activities, children can't develop a rich inner life. It is this capacity for a rich inner life that can sustain a handicapped person who may be unable to do many things.

Play relaxes and revitalizes people of any age, but play is more than just fun. Children learn many skills easily and naturally with creative play. Early-childhood educators feel that free creative play is one of the best preparations for accomplishment later on in school. An introduction to music, art, and nature study are all important to children as well, and they all add a great deal to a child's perception of the world. (See Spock and Lenigo, 1965.) Wonderful books have been written specifically about creative activities for handicapped children (Silver, 1982; Cheryl, 1979; and Atack, 1982).

Dance Therapy

Dance therapy is a well-recognized way of helping people with both emotional and physical handicaps. It is fun and good exercise, and ease of movement is important to all of us. Also, showing through movement or dance what it feels like to be angry, fearful, or sad is a good way to explore, acknowledge, and release these emotions.

Movement therapy combines dance, physical therapy, and gymnastics. Amy Cluck, a registered physical therapist in San Francisco, is currently one of the few individuals in the United States to develop this type of program for handicapped children. She makes the point that children without handicaps often have music lessons, dance classes, or gymnastics, so why shouldn't handicapped children have similar opportunities to enjoy themselves and express their feelings?

One seven-year-old patient of mine lost her ability to walk because of a gunshot accident. Slowly, with good rehabilitation, she began to improve. She joined Amy Cluck's group after several months, and the movement-therapy program seemed to be an important stepping-stone back to fairly normal strength and function for her. She now talks and thinks like a normal child. Without this therapy, she might have come to see herself as being permanently handicapped.

Dance or movement therapy should not take the place of physical therapy if your child still needs such treatments. Instead, movement therapy should be a stepping-stone for your child toward more normal activities and movement. It is essential for their well-being that children see themselves as normally as possible. Anyone who sees himself as handicapped often acts in that way, and then is treated as handicapped by others. This creates a self-fulfilling cycle by which the person accepts limitations that are often unnecessary, because of his self-image.

Movement therapy should be fun. It should not only help a child's self-image, but also develop the child's balance, coordination, body awareness, flexibility, and endurance. Each handicapped child should have a program tailored to meet his own needs. For example, children with physical handicaps often have problems with movement, and working on their coordination and strength helps them feel much more whole and normal. Just watching a child who finally masters a new move glow with pride and delight is testimony to what a benefit this can be.

Think of what it would mean to a child with cerebral palsy to know he could go to a dance class just like his nonhandicapped friends. The mother who introduced her Down's syndrome toddler into the local Montessori school also took her child to kindergym classes for nonhandicapped children. At first the other parents were standoffish, but soon they were welcoming. The experience was very heartening for her daughter, Leah, who learned to develop not only her coordination but also her ability to relate to nonhandicapped children as well. The social interaction possible at a dance class or dance therapy group is another important contribution to your child's well-being. So often handicapped children are isolated, or just with their families, only making frequent trips to doctors, clinics, and laboratories.

It might be difficult for you to find a physical therapist with Amy Cluck's background in dance and gymnastics, but it is worth looking. Doubtless this field will grow as soon as its potential for helping and healing becomes recognized.

Play with Nonhandicapped Children

Playtime with other, nonhandicapped children is an area of a handicapped child's life that can be forgotten or overlooked. A child with a handicap can easily withdraw and become lonely. A handicapped child may not know how to reach out and make contact with other children, or a child might not be able physically to leave home to find playmates in the neighborhood.

Lack of socializing isn't healthy. As a parent you will need to help your child find ways to get out and make contact with other children, even though your child's handicap may make it hard to go out in public. But your attitude and actions will set the tone. If you feel that you can go anywhere and be open and friendly, your child will imitate you and learn important social skills.

At first finding people to be with—playmates for your child—will take some effort, but the energy you put into exploring what your community has to offer will be repaid abundantly. I can guarantee this because I have seen it happen so many times.

Begin checking out resources by calling the social worker at the nearest hospital. Another source of information about social programs and activities for handicapped children is health and social-service agencies. You can find them in the Yellow Pages of the phone book. Many programs have been developed to meet the specific needs of handicapped people; all you have to do is locate them. Once you find a resource, phone for a newsletter or list of monthly activities. Many centers mail these out free as a public service.

Contact agencies like the Red Cross or Catholic Social Services. In larger cities, a hotline is often set up to answer questions about what is locally available. Big Brother and Big Sister programs can also be a real boost to single-parent families, and churches offer good social programs or can tell you what is available locally.

You might also try investigating the possibility of "importing" playmates from the neighborhood or school for your child. Contact other mothers and work out arrangements to trade child care. If your child requires more care and attention because of the handicapping condition, you could trade extra time for every one hour another parent cared for your child. Also look into programs at community recreation centers, scout troups, YMCAs, YWCAs, nursery schools, and the Boys' and Girls' Club.

Whenever you are out in public, encourage your child to talk to others. If you keep your child from public contact, you encourage withdrawal, and this just reinforces the sense of isolation and of being different.

If parents can find ways to help their children relate to all people, they will give a gift of immense value.

Handicapped Playmates

Some parents find it hard to have their handicapped child spend time with other children who are handicapped. They feel this way because they can't accept the fact that their child is not "normal." If you find yourself feeling this way, please consider talking with a counselor. You may need help to resolve the issue before you can move on to fulfill your child's real needs. Every child needs contact with other children, and if you find it hard to accept other handicapped children, your child may come to feel the same way about himself or herself.

Depending on the severity of the problems, a handicapped child should spend time with both handicapped and nonhandicapped children. Nonhandicapped children can bring a wealth of new ideas and fun into the life of a handicapped child, but handicapped playmates who have different limitations are also important. It is good, too, for handicapped children to have other friends with their same problem.

One patient of mine had an unusual condition called Turner's syndrome. I arranged for her to meet another girl her age with the same disorder, and this delighted her. Even though the two lived far apart, they became friends and pen pals. My patient loved having someone with whom she could share her feelings, and who could understand exactly how she felt.

You may want your child to be with nonhandicapped children most of the time so that normal behavior can be learned and there can be as much contact as possible with the real world. It can, though, be very hard on a child to be the only handicapped one among all the children at a school or to be with children who have much greater ability.

Also, school personnel may have had little or no training about your child's particular handicap and the associated problems. The school counselors are likely to be overburdened or may be inexperienced in working with a handicapped child. They can react by simply denying that such a child or any problems exist. Often, with only one handicapped child in a school, the other children tease the handicapped one. It takes an unusual teacher to be able to teach the needed compassion to her students, so that a single handicapped child is made to feel welcome.

You will probably have to do some soul-searching before you work out a good social balance for your child. Ask yourself some straightforward questions about your identity as the parent of a handicapped child. You may discover that you have your own personal doubts, hesitations, and anxieties to work on first before you can make any clear decisions. The main point to keep in mind is how essential warm social contacts are for you and your child.

Self-esteem

Nurturing any child's sense of dignity and self-worth is critical, and that is especially true for a handicapped child. Reaching even limited goals fosters your child's confidence and feelings of self-esteem. This then helps to build the kind of emotional strength your child will need to face the major challenges of life.

There are many ways you can help your children develop self-esteem, letting them know you love them, respect them, and are sensitive to their needs. Your time, interest, and energy cannot be replaced by any number of objects you buy and give them. The most important thing you have to give your child is your caring attention. This says to children that they are valuable and valued.

Encourage an open expression of ideas and opinions, even if you don't always agree, and guide your child to express emotions and negative feelings. Also, criticize the child's actions, not the child. One of the most important things you can do to help children grow in self-confidence and self-esteem is to avoid doing anything for them that they can do for themselves. This may sound harsh when a child is handicapped, but I want to caution you against doing too much for your child. You may feel pity or guilt because of the handicap, and then get into the habit of doing too much. You do things that your child could do alone or learn to do in the mistaken belief that you're helping your child.

A handicapped child needs all possible chances to try doing things alone. Even a small achievement can be very important. By watching your child—or other handicapped children—work to gain competency, you can begin to see how valuable it is to give as many opportunities as you can to obtain a sense of personal achievement. Each small task your child masters is like a step up the mountain. It is a triumph that helps a child to know, as words cannot, that he or she is a valuable human being.

When your child is young, the challenges encountered can be as simple as holding a spoon or cup. Expect your child just to perform tasks that are realistic for the age and handicap. The balance you seek is a delicate one between doing too much and expecting too much.

As your child grows older, you should decide upon daily chores and responsibilities around the house that are appropriate for the age and handicap. These should be done consistently at the same time each day. Many parents tell me that their children do chores or take care of their own needs on weekends. Just doing chores on weekends or at special times doesn't develop any sense of responsibility or family participation. Simple chores or responsibilities need to be worked into the daily schedule. Having regular duties helps a child feel like an important member of the family, and this goes a long way toward building self-esteem. Children quickly realize that being effective in the world means knowing how to do things. And all children want to play some real part and make a meaningful contribution.

You may need to make special physical arrangements so that your child can do a specific job correctly. This may take extra planning, but you'll soon find that the outcome is worth your initial effort. The same approach applies to teaching children how to do things for themselves. It often seems easier just to dress or undress a child or to clean his room rather than to teach him these skills, particularly if he is handicapped. I know parents who handle major management problems with ease at their business, yet they won't take the time to plan how their child could do chores at home. Parents like this often wind up with a "problem child" instead of a "child with a problem." We must let our children learn what they can do and to teach them to do what they can learn. If we keep them from meeting and mastering challenges on their own, we rob them of precious chances to discover their own capacities.

Discipline

Loving discipline is essential to raising any child well. Discipline is especially necessary in order to do a good job of raising your handicapped child. Many parents of handicapped children feel so sorry for their child that they forget discipline, the need for setting limits and establishing guidelines for acceptable behavior.

Parents often feel that raising a child with discipline is not being loving. They believe that discipline means punishment rather than limit-setting.

In his excellent book *Dare to Discipline,* Dr. James Dobson points out that good discipline is in itself a form of love. (See also Silberman, 1980.) Dobson says that children who are not disciplined feel that they are not loved.

The primary aims of discipline are to help children grow into mature, emotionally secure adults and to have a good balance of mutual respect in families. Without this mutual respect, family life can be much like a war zone, and there may be many casualties.

Children need limits, and they want to know the rules. The child who knows the limits feels a true sense of security in knowing that the parents are in control. Children intuitively realize that they are too little to be in control of a family, even though they may act as if they want to be.

The family rules have to be fair, and they have to be consistent with the age of the child. They also have to be clearly understood. In an atmosphere like this, with caring parents, a child feels safe to grow into an adult. Discipline really is love, and when you take the time and energy to discipline your children, you are teaching them respect for others and love for themselves.

The usual result of a home without discipline is whiny, unpleasant children. We have all known at least one or two youngsters like this, and no one wants to be around them for very long. A child who is unmannered and unpleasant drives others away. Children who grow up without discipline become unlovable and learn disrespect for rules and for other people. With handicapped children, being undisciplined or "spoiled" can add a burden of emotional pain to their handicaps when they are shunned by others. A child like this can grow up more isolated and lonelier than ever. Parents who raise their children without discipline surely do them no favors.

One mother told me a story about her son Rick, who was confined to a wheelchair. He and his brothers were laughing and joking one day, when Rick made a rude remark. His mother spoke sharply to him and immediately had a horrified feeling that she shouldn't speak that way to a child in a wheelchair. Looking at him, though, she saw him begin to smile, and she realized that she had treated him for once just as she would his brothers, and he was delighted.

It is a difficult job to be a parent and particularly hard to be a mother. It has always amazed me that we need licenses for everything except the most demanding job of all, parenting. For that we don't require even one single qualification, and yet it is probably the most important job in the world.

You may not feel comfortable with the kind of discipline you received in your parents' home, or perhaps you feel shaky about disciplining at all. Some guidelines I would offer for disciplining children would be:

1. Establish fair limits, according to the child's age, that both parents agree on (if there are two parents in the home).

2. Reward good behavior by positive remarks.

3. Strive for a good balance of mutual respect.

4. Discuss with your child what is expected so that he or she will know the limits.

5. When the time comes that one of the rules needs to be changed, or if you feel you have made a mistake with one of your rules, be open about this, too. A family conference is a good forum for discussing such changes.

These few rules may look easy enough on paper, but disciplining in this way requires (1) adults who feel good about themselves and are able to set limits firmly; (2) adults who are not afraid to have a child dislike them temporarily but remember that the long-term goals are more important than immediate approval; (3) adults who can confront and, if needed, erase patterns from their past, such as the idea of spanking children at the drop of a hat.

I have never favored spanking except in situations that were potentially dangerous. Good examples of this would be where a child runs out into the street or starts a fire while playing with matches. Once, out of curiosity, I asked my grown children which form of discipline I used had worked the best. They both answered, almost immediately, "Your voice." They knew if I said something, I meant it and stuck by it. They expected me to set limits, and if for some reason I didn't, they always made me aware of it. They knew that behind the discipline was a great deal of love.

Spanking can get out of hand, particularly if a parent is angry. A good rule is not to spank when you are angry.

Anger must be acknowledged, and expressed in ways that won't hurt a child. Some suggestions about what to do when you feel angry at your child are listed below, but also explore ideas of your own about how to release and handle your anger harmlessly. Let yourself feel your anger, but it is important not to release anger on children who are smaller and weaker than you. Also, handicapped children are usually even more at risk, as they can't run away or defend themselves as well.

If you are angry, try:

1. Taking several deep breaths.
2. Leaving the room for a few minutes.
3. Counting to a hundred.
4. Imagining yourself in your child's place for a few seconds before you respond.
5. Taking a cold shower!
6. Telling your child that you are very angry and you need to be alone for a while.
7. Calling for a time-out and then not discussing whatever it was that made you angry until you can approach it calmly.
8. Telephoning a parent-crisis line and telling the person who answers how you feel or that you're afraid you will hurt your children.
9. Calling up a friend to say you don't think you can take another minute of what is going on.

We all know that the daily demands of raising children can feel overwhelming. These demands can be particularly difficult when there is a handicapped child or if the family has other problems, such as financial or marital problems; if there is a single parent, or both parents are working full-time, or the father is raising the children alone. All of these can be a cause for anger, which may flare if a child is acting out. In situations like these, firm discipline is even more important and even more difficult.

Handling Manipulative Behavior

All children try to manipulate others to get what they want. This starts in infancy as a way to obtain basic food and warmth.

Later, children learn that certain actions bring desirable responses. Handicapped children, in particular, learn to manipulate others early in life. Because they are often limited in their physical movements, they quickly devise many ways to bring everyone running to do their bidding.

Children who become adept at manipulations often turn into spoiled, immature, unhappy adults. It is up to parents to set limits and establish clear signals about appropriate behavior.

The mother of Kelly, a child with spinal atrophy, shared an amusing anecdote. When Kelly was four, she tried to wheedle her grandmother and mother into doing something she could handle herself. Her mother was firm, and so was her grandmother. Foiled, the child said with complete candor, "This isn't turning out at all the way I planned it!"

Though she didn't know it then, Kelly was very fortunate to have a mother with enough self-esteem to say no when she knew it was best for her little girl. Saying no to a handicapped child is hard to do, yet it helps a child grow into a mature, confident adult.

Learning to Discipline

There are many resources to help parents learn about discipline. Many cities offer inexpensive Parent Effectiveness Training classes (Gordon, 1975) or groups run by professionals that focus on parenting. Many churches also sponsor parenting groups that meet to discuss problems and solutions, listen to guest speakers, or organize panel discussions about specific issues. Your family doctor or pediatrician could probably suggest additional resources. Other possibilities are the Red Cross, YMCA or YWCA, social service agencies, or parenting institutes. Some colleges sponsor classes on parenting or have special seminars about particular problems. There is always the local library, which will usually have books on parenting or can order a particular one you have heard about. Also, try to locate a parent-support group for handicapped children and ask them if they discuss the issue of discipline. Check as well with local agencies concerned with handicapped children for referrals.

Perhaps your best resource is other parents. Talk to the mothers and fathers of children you like—neighborhood children or those you've seen at church, school, clinics, or physical-therapy offices. Ask these parents about their approach to discipline. Even if their children are not handicapped, you might be able to pick up some basic guidelines. Your best resource of all might be the parents of any well-adjusted handicapped adults or young adults you know. Such people could be a storehouse of helpful information if you can locate them. An alternative is simply to interview well-adjusted handicapped young adults or adults about how their parents raised them. You might learn a lot that would help your efforts to raise children who are comfortable with limits and discipline.

When I am teaching medical students about children, I like to give them a paragraph written by Dr. Willis J. Potts, a pediatric surgeon who seems to have a real feeling for children.

> The mystical heart of a child is a precious and beautiful thing. It is marred only by the wounds of a thoughtless and not-too-intelligent world. In a physical sense, the heart is a tough organ; a marvelous mechanism that mostly without repairs, will give valiant pumping service up to 100 years. In an emotional sense, it is susceptible to wounds of indifference, thoughtlessness, and neglect, and during episodes of illness is especially vulnerable. The heart of a child is mysteriously molded by parents, teachers, playmates, and all those with whom it comes in contact. Physicians wish during those short but violent episodes of illness to avoid wounds that will leave irreparable scars. I am convinced that the heart of a child, sunned by love, security, and understanding, will be able to withstand storms of illness and pain.

To his wise words "sunned by love, security, and understanding," I would add the word discipline, because that is needed to help your child feel cared for and secure in this turbulent world.

Hugs, Fun, and Laughter

Many parents get so lost in the everyday details of the physical care for their handicapped child that they forget how important it is to take time for hugs, fun, and laughter. It's okay to skip a bath occasionally or to miss a therapy session in order to have some fun or some quality one-to-one time with your child. We all need daily doses of affection, especially when we're children. It's especially important that a handicapped child feel love.

The quality of a handicapped child's life is a constant juggle between pleasure and pain. Many handicapped children must endure intense physical pain from repeated surgeries, therapy sessions, medications, or radiation, and this pain has to be balanced with some enjoyment and fun. As a parent, you are the one who can tip the balance so that the pain of daily living doesn't outweigh the pleasure there can be in life for your child. It is up to you to discover the formula for fun in your house if you haven't already.

One mother I know learned the secret for her family by happy accident. Being a hardworking woman who prided herself on being a "good" mother, she drove her children to appointments, taught them important skills, bought and cooked good food, and so on. With her high standards and expectations, she had an exhausting schedule, and, not surprisingly, her children's lives were much like her own—hectic and somewhat driven.

One winter afternoon, with too much on her list for even her to do, she gave up and just plopped down on the living-room rug. Her two children, delighted with her unusual presence at their level, quickly draped themselves all over her. Soon, just lying there like a lump of clay, she found herself playing happily in a puppy pile with her children, tickling and laughing, being tickled and rolling around.

She told me later she hadn't had such fun in years. Her children loved their mother's discovery. Their lives hadn't been much fun for them either. The bonus was for her, that she felt relaxed and energized when she got up after a half hour of this, to make dinner.

Maybe this kind of fun isn't something you would enjoy, but you need to search for your own kind of fun. One mother decided to start singing more. As a child she had sung with her sisters when they did chores, so she sang old songs to her children. They loved them, and later they began to make up new ones together.

Fun activities can be simple. In fact, the best relaxations may be the simplest, and everyone needs the relaxation that having a good time gives. Hugs, fun, and laughter make life worth living, so give yourself and your child large regular doses of good times, and you will soon notice a difference in how you both feel about life.

Chapter 7

How to Find the Best Professional Help

Who shall decide when doctors disagree?

—ALEXANDER POPE

As soon as you are told your child's diagnosis, you should seek more information and help. At first you will want to know more about the diagnosis. You may also wonder if there is a drug or special treatment being researched that can improve or cure your child's handicap. Because you have a child who is handicapped, you will have to see physicians and other medical professionals frequently, and you will want to obtain the best medical advice possible. To begin with, you want to be confident that the diagnosis is correct.

The Right Diagnosis

When they learn that their child has a handicap, many parents immediately start searching for a better diagnosis from another doctor. This search may continue for years, from one doctor or medical center to the next. You may already have sought one or more opinions, or you may be thinking about looking for another—better—diagnosis.

91

Looking for another opinion brings up many difficult issues. On the one hand, once you have received a catastrophic diagnosis of any kind, it is a good idea to consult one or two other experts if you have any doubts in your mind. Often there are several approaches to treating the same medical problem. And occasionally a diagnosis can be mistaken. On the other hand, parents can get caught up in going from doctor to doctor, subjecting their child to endless tests. This puts tremendous stress on both the parent and the child, and the final diagnosis can still be unclear, though the process is certain to have been costly. In some cases the parents of a handicapped child make a full-time career out of seeking a better diagnosis, and they never confront the child's handicap or day-to-day needs. Some parents not only see many physicians, but also go to nutritionists, faith healers, and acupuncturists. A great deal of time, money, and energy can be wasted this way, and a child's days can be spent in trying different procedures, medications, and therapies.

I had one small teenage patient in a wheelchair who had a marked eating problem in addition to her chronic disability. In asking questions about her eating habits, I found that a nutritionist had put the girl on twenty-six different vitamin pills plus other food supplements. The youngster simply had no room for any good food. After I convinced the family to stop all the pills and supplements completely, the girl started eating once again.

Your best resource for finding the right diagnosis and good care for your child is your family physician. This could be the doctor who delivered your child, or one who has been caring for your family over the last few years. It might also be the pediatrician or family practitioner who cares for your other children. The important point is to start with one doctor whom you trust, someone you already rely on and can talk to honestly. This is essential, because the best person to check on the medical qualifications of one doctor is another doctor. My best advice if you are planning to consult a new specialist is to start with a doctor you know.

When looking for a physician to consult or someone to direct the care of your handicapped child, it helps to have some criteria in mind before you start looking. With the important qualities defined before you start, you will be better prepared to find a good physician. First, you want someone who is competent and knowledgeable. You also want someone who is warm and caring, a doctor who will talk openly with you about your child. Finally, you will want a physician who is gentle with your child rather than cold and sterile, and someone who will talk with and to both of you rather than at you.

Begin your search by getting the names of doctors who are experts in your child's handicap. First ask your own doctor and then get other names of doctors by talking to parents of children with similar handicaps. You might also try calling the agency for handicapped children in your state, such as the Crippled Children's Services (see Appendix E) and asking for referrals to physicians specializing in your child's handicap. (Remember, though, that you may just be talking to clerks in these offices. If you are concerned about the information they give you, ask to talk to the medical consultant for that program.)

Once you have a list, your primary doctor can help you check the doctors' qualifications and personal qualities. After you and your doctor have narrowed your list down to one or two, make appointments with them. Remember that even if a doctor has had excellent training or has a wonderful reputation, you still have to feel comfortable with that doctor as a person. You also have to like the way that physician relates to your child. Without these two essential ingredients, the two of you might not be able to work together well enough to help your child. If the first two you chose do not feel right to you, try one or two more. It is worthwhile to put genuine attention and energy into finding the right doctor now, for several reasons that I'll discuss.

Large Clinics and Medical Centers

Many parents believe they can obtain the best diagnosis and treatment by going to a large clinic or a university medical center where there are many specialists. The problem with such large medical centers is frequently the same, however, as when parents go from one doctor to another. Often many tests are done and many physicians are seen, and yet there are still no definite answers, but just a pile of medical bills.

Working through one doctor you trust is the best strategy for obtaining a reliable diagnosis and good follow-up care for your handicapped child. This is not to say that large clinics are worthless. They can, though, be confusing places to start. Once you have chosen your primary physician, or the one who will be in charge of your child's care, large clinics or medical centers can be an excellent resource for consultations and specialized tests.

A large clinic may have a team of specialists and other medical personnel, all of whom will usually see your child during a single clinic visit. With one knowledgeable doctor coordinating the care, these various specialists can help plan the most effective therapeutic program for your child. Without such coordination, tests or X rays may be duplicated or done unnecessarily, and your child will receive fragmented care.

Because the individual doctors working in medical centers or large clinics are often highly specialized, routine pediatric procedures may be overlooked. The routine but important pediatric procedures that may be missed are standard immunizations (see Table 1 at the end of this chapter), hearing and vision tests, blood counts, and urinalysis.

A three-year-old girl was referred to me a few years ago by a pediatrician in private practice. The child from birth had had bronchopulmonary dysplasia (a rather severe lung disease), and had lived in a children's hospital for the first two and a half years of life. She was then in a foster home, and the doctor asked me to review her enormous medical records to help him plan for her posthospital care.

The girl had been seen by neonatologists, or doctors specializing in newborns, plus specialists in infectious diseases and in diseases of the heart, lungs, and bones. During the two and a half years in the hospital, immunizations had not been given, nor had she had any kidney X rays despite a suspected kidney infection. Some other things were also missing that were required for good general medical care. Luckily, though, the child now had a good pediatrician who was not afraid to ask for help. We worked out a program to bring her medical care up to date and protect her in the future as well.

A case like this—which is not unusual—is just one example of why it is valuable to have a single qualified physician in charge of any child's care. This is particularly true of a child with a handicap or with multiple handicaps. The doctor in charge functions like the hub of a wheel, pulling all the information into one place so that it all passes through one central person and cannot become lost or misinterpreted. With a system that functions this way, you, the parent, also should have relatively easy access to the central doctor because you know who is handling your child's case. She or he can then communicate to you what all the specialists have found. Your doctor-in-charge can also help you understand and assess the recommendations of the specialists, outlining and commenting on the advantages and disadvantages of various suggested courses of treatment.

Preventing Fragmentation of Care

Having a single doctor in charge is the first big step in preventing the kind of fragmentation of care that can happen too often in the treatment of handicapped children. Fragmentation happens more today than in the past because there are many more specialized areas of medicine, and even these are fast becoming subdivided into narrower and narrower specialties. One doctor needs to coordinate, interpret, and help analyze the information from all the specialists, so your child can receive the most accurate diagnosis and best care possible.

As a parent, you can play an important part in preventing fragmentation of care. First, buy a notebook that is small enough to carry with you at all times. Keep it just for this one purpose. In one section, perhaps in the first few pages, put the names, addresses, and phone numbers of all your child's doctors and other medical specialists. In another section keep a list, in chronological order, of all the doctors' visits your child has as well as any surgical procedures, medications, and treatments your child re-

96 Charlotte E. Thompson, M.D.

ceives. Put down the specific date opposite each entry so that anyone can tell what took place on each date.

Medical records can become temporarily misfiled, so if you carry your own list of medical treatments and physicians with you in compact form as you take your child to various appointments, you will be helping greatly. A notebook like this can be very valuable to a doctor seeing your child for the first time, as the doctor can quickly review your child's history and treatment without having to wait weeks for medical records to be forwarded.

This notebook can be a personal benefit to you as well in helping you to use medical consultants wisely and fully. Before any medical appointment, write down any questions or areas of concern you have. Questions that come easily to mind while you are washing the dishes or straightening up your desk can slip your mind during an office visit. Write down what you want to know when you think of it. Also, take a few minutes before any visit to collect your thoughts and focus on what you want to ask and to accomplish during that visit. One question may bring up others if you allow yourself enough time to reflect, and one of those questions could lead to some important but overlooked information. So organize and record your questions before the actual visit.

Most physicians will welcome a chance to answer your questions or explain a specific procedure or treatment plan to you. If one does not, then he or she is probably not the one you want to have for your child. Be suspicious of doctors who discourage questions or make you feel uncomfortable about keeping a list. This shows little understanding of how hard it is to handle all that you have to and how difficult it can be to remember the important questions right when you need to. You don't want someone with so little sympathy and understanding treating your child.

Keeping Good Medical Care

After you have found a good doctor, there are some things that you can do to ensure that she or he will want to continue caring for your child. I have found that parents who have children with chronic illnesses often get lax about doing their part to ensure good care. Probably they become so overburdened with the care of their child that they simply don't realize their responsibility in helping obtain the best possible medical care.

For example, I have received messages that a parent has called and, on trying to return the call, find the telephone busy for a long time. Tying up the phone when you are expecting a doctor to return your call shows a lack of consideration, unless there is an emergency situation. I think a feeling of mutual respect between parents and physicians is essential to a good working relationship. To do your part, I recommend the following to help your relationship with your physician:

1. Regular appointments are important. They are times to go over ongoing problems and to anticipate future needs for the best preventive approach to your child's care.

2. If you must cancel a regular appointment, do so at least twenty-four hours ahead of time. (The exceptions, of course, are sudden illness or an accident.)

3. Be on time whenever possible. This usually means leaving earlier than usual to allow for bad traffic conditions, time to find a parking place, or unforeseen incidents that can slow you down.

4. Supply current billing information or the relevant insurance forms at each visit.

5. Be sure to pay your bills on time.

To help maintain your child's records accurately, it is important that you have all X rays copied and that you carry these with you when they will be needed. Most medical centers and radiology offices keep their films on file for just seven years. The X-ray report alone is usually not adequate, as the X rays themselves often have to be reviewed.

Most people assume that hospital X-ray departments or radiology offices always have their films on file—many doctors make this assumption as well—but I have found that this is not the case.

The same warning applies to muscle biopsy slides. If your child has had a muscle biopsy, try to have a set of the slides on hand when you go to the first appointment with a new doctor who is to review the case. Such slides are often either misplaced or destroyed after a relatively short period of time. It is a shame to have your child suffer any extra pain or inconvenience to have a procedure redone or to undergo a treatment for something that could have been prevented with just a little better organization of the medical care.

Hearing

One of the areas of medical care that deserves more and better attention than it usually gets is hearing. Approximately fifty thousand school-age children are deaf, and many of these hearing losses were detected far too late to really help the child adapt and adjust well. Unfortunately, many children who are physically handicapped are afflicted with multiple handicaps that often include visual and hearing losses. These are often not detected early because the hearing testing done in pediatricians' offices and in the schools may be cursory and inadequate.

If you have any suspicion—even just a feeling—that your child is not hearing, make sure he or she is tested in a diagnostic center where they routinely test children. Testing children for hearing problems requires a great deal of patience and experience to do a good job. If your child is not making sounds by 3 months, he or she must have a hearing test done by a qualified expert. The sooner a hearing loss is detected in a child, the more chance there is to help that child develop normal speech and learning habits.

Betty Johnson, the mother of a deaf ten-year-old, is now a licensed hearing-aid dispenser. She does both hearing testing and fitting of hearing aids. Mrs. Johnson makes some important points about the amount of delay there was in picking up her son's deafness. To begin with, she felt that the doctors wanted so badly for her child to be normal that they thought for a long time that *she* was the problem, a nervous first-time mother.

She went on to say how often people commented on what a good baby her son was because he slept through any kind of noise. She knew that something was definitely wrong the day she saw him "talk" on his play telephone the way any small child does, but he just moved his lips and no sound came out. He had seen her do the same thing—but he could not hear her voice.

Betty Johnson is fluent in sign language and has convinced all her son's close relatives and their families to learn it as well. She feels that parents should start both signing and oral communication when the child is young. Her final important point is that if you, as a parent, feel that something is wrong with your child but the experts contradict you or do not take you seriously, "Go from your heart and not from your brain," and keep looking for answers.

This is excellent advice, and it applies not only to suspected hearing problems but to other handicapping conditions as well. It is up to you to follow your intuitions about your own child, because you are the expert.

Throughout the process of seeking and using good professional help, keep in mind that the final choices are yours to make. You will certainly ask others for recommendations or suggestions, but ultimately you make the decisions because you are the one who lives with the results of those decisions. The doctor or doctors you choose for your child must feel right to you. You need to feel that your doctor respects your intelligence, and you must firmly believe that the doctor you have chosen will be honest with you. You will want to find someone you can trust as a healing, helping physician. Your intuition, your research, and your common sense working together can make these choices clear for you.

Table 1   IMMUNIZATION CHART

AGE	IMMUNIZATION
2 months	DPT #1, Sabin #1
4 months	DPT #2, Sabin #2
6 months	DPT #3
9 months	Tuberculin test
15 months	Measles, mumps, rubella
18 months	DPT #4, Sabin #3
2½ years	Tuberculin test
4½ to 5 years	Dip-Tet booster, Sabin #4

Tuberculin test every one to two years; Dip-Tet booster every ten years unless required by camp or school. (Guidelines established by the American Academy of Pediatrics)

Table 2   ROUTINE PHYSICAL EXAMINATIONS

To six months of age	monthly
To one year of age	bimonthly
To four years of age	every six months
Yearly thereafter	

Chapter 8

How to Cope with the Costs of Raising a Handicapped Child

A man who both spends and saves money is the
happiest man, because he has both enjoyments.

—SAMUEL JOHNSON

The day-to-day expenses of raising any child have become enormous. The basics of food, clothing, and shelter—without anything extra—can be very costly to supply. Add to this the additional burden of high-priced medical care when a child is handicapped, and a family's financial situation can seem overwhelming and unmanageable. Without an adequate insurance plan—sometimes even with insurance—a family's financial reserves can be destroyed by the medical expenses of a seriously handicapped child. For this reason, most states have passed legislation to help the families of handicapped children with their finances.

To do the best for yourself financially, you have to do two things as soon as you find out that your child is handicapped. First, you must start a program of good money management. This not only means management of everyday money, but it also

101

means keeping very careful track of your medical bills and payments. Sylvia Porter's book *Your Own Money* is a good guide to help you get started in good money-handling habits, and there are many other guides as well. Check your local library for one you think will help. When things settle down a little, check out adult-education classes about how best to work out budgets, finances, and money management.

The second thing you must do immediately after receiving your child's diagnosis is to seek out information about any and all financial-assistance programs. Unfortunately, such information appears to be a well-kept secret, and it can be hard to get the facts on what programs are available or how to apply for them.

You need this information, though, and it is especially urgent in the case of a handicapped newborn. If the state agency caring for handicapped children is contacted *immediately,* it may *be able to assume financial responsibility for your child's care right from the start.* Too often so much attention goes into the medical problems that the doctors, social workers, or other personnel in the hospital forget to mention available sources of financial aid. Yet if the child is not referred to the state agency immediately, parents may lose any chance for state aid right from the beginning, which means they are responsible for paying enormous expenses that could have been covered. It may be left to you as a parent to ask about this help and then pursue the information.

You will probably have to be well focused and persistent to get the answers you need, which is a lot to ask of yourself right now. Just do the best you can. To start with, try the hospital social workers. Some are quite knowledgeable about money matters, though not all can help. You should be able to get some referrals or places to start.

If you can't get the help you need at the hospital, call the public health department in your area. Public-health nurses are a good resource for information about what's available to you locally. At the very least, they should be able to give you several suggestions about places to call.

Be prepared to make lots of calls just to get the names of other people to call for possible information. You will need paper and writing materials, but your best tool will be your own energy and expectations. If you know ahead of time that you will be making many calls, some leading to dead ends, you will be realistically prepared to follow through on those that can get you what you need. (This will be difficult to do if your children are underfoot, and it is better done during a quiet time when they are either out of the house or napping.)

Try calling voluntary agencies. Many can help in the care of children with specific handicaps, such as the Spina Bifida Association, the Arthritis Foundation, the Cystic Fibrosis Association, or the United Cerebral Palsy Association. Look in the phone book for these names and numbers. (See the listing of special agencies in Appendix C.) The limitations of specialized agencies is that they know only about their own area of concern and usually don't have information about ongoing general resources, such as crippled children's programs, financial services, or respite care.

Another place to check is the list of state government agencies under "State Government" in the phone book. Most states have specific bureaus and departments to oversee programs for handicapped children. The people in these offices should be able to supply you with a list of resources for handicapped children and financial aid.

You can also contact the National Information Center for Handicapped Children and Youth in Washington, DC, at P.O. Box 1492, Washington, DC, 20013. People at this center can help you with specific questions, and they have a wealth of information that they will mail you. (See Appendix D for programs listed by state.)

All in all, confronting the financial demands and finding help in meeting them is not easy. Your family may be one that "falls in between the cracks," which means you have too much income to qualify for state and federal aid but too little to finance an adequate medical program on your own. The key is to keep trying—to get more information, to follow up leads, and to continue applying for various types of financial assistance. This may seem like an endless paperwork maze to you, but with luck some of the paper at the end will be the green kind that can help pay your child's medical bills. Keep at it.

Chapter 9

How to Find the Best Educational Program for Your Child

The mystery the child is searching for is itself.

—Leo Buscaglia

Helping handicapped children reach their highest potential means putting a great deal of time and energy into finding the best educational program for them. Education doesn't start with a preschool or kindergarten; it starts at birth for all of us.

From day one, infants use their senses to learn about their surroundings. If there are problems with vision or hearing, early sensory loss can make a real difference in their development. If early information can't be obtained, potential can be limited. Thus, it is very important to be sure all the senses are functioning as well as possible. There are now some special tests that can be done even on infants to be sure their vision and hearing are working well. These are called brainstem audiometry and visual evoked responses. Most large medical centers with intensive-care nurseries can arrange to have them done. Babies who have been in intensive-care units as a result of a serious illness, birth defect, or premature birth are particularly at risk and should be watched carefully as they are more likely to develop visual, hearing, and other sensory deficits.

104

Because handicapped infants often have to spend long periods of time in hospital nurseries, many hospitals and outside agencies have developed or are developing programs for infants. These programs are designed to stimulate physical, emotional, and mental development of babies. Infant-stimulation programs, as they're called, were started after researchers found that just taking care of the physical and medical needs of newborns was not enough, particularly when they were in the hospital for long periods of time. Well-fed and medically stable infants were still often listless and uninterested and lacked the lively quality that healthy babies have from birth on. They responded to being held, talked and sung to, shown colors and toys—all the things parents naturally do with newborns at home. A positive change was noted in the infants who received this added kind of nurturing, so infant-stimulation programs were designed to provide a healthier and more natural environment for each infant's best growth.

All to the good, but—and this is an important but—an infant has to be healthy enough first before it can begin to benefit from such a program. Newborns with multiple birth defects or spina bifida must first get through their initial rocky days and become medically stable. Premature infants may have an even longer period of ups and downs. Once stability is achieved, then the infant may be able to handle and profit from an infant-stimulation program.

Your baby may seem too sick to handle such a program and yet may be receiving it. If so, I urge you to talk over your concerns with the doctors in the nursery unit. An infant-stimulation program doesn't do any good until your baby is stable and healthy, and it can be potentially harmful.

Once your infant is ready, such a program can be started, if it is offered by your hospital. Many people who work in these infant-stimulation programs do an outstanding job, and you may pick up some ideas from the person working with your baby.

Not all of these programs are good, though. Some seem to be filling time for themselves, as well as for the babies they are treating. After hospital discharge, infant-stimulation programs are also available, and the Easter Seal Society sponsors some good ones.

The Important Preschool Years

Birth to three is a critical time in the education of your child. However, federal law guarantees education for handicapped children starting only at age three. Between the ages of eighteen months and three years, education for handicapped children is considered optional in different parts of the country. As parents you need to call the special-education office of your local public school system to find out what special programs are available for your young child and at what ages they are available. Remember, even though your child is entitled to early educational programs (especially after age three), you may have to search them out.

Language, growth, and pre-academic concepts are particularly important to handicapped children between the ages of three and five years old. These are the foundations upon which a child builds school skills, and your handicapped child may need extra help in order to stimulate learning through his senses (hearing, touch, and vision).

In general, children under age three or four need to be with their mothers part of each day or with a mother substitute. Long hours in a day-care or other special program may not be best for them. Handicapped children do need time to have special training and to play with other youngsters, however, and mothers of young children need breaks from constant child care in order to do a good job. If you are a mother or father who has to earn a living and you have no choice but to use some type of day-care in addition to a special program, you will need to review carefully what is offered.

Ideally, small children, particularly handicapped children, need to be in small groups. If the program is designed as an educational one, no more than four small handicapped children can really be taught well together. There should also be some one-to-one time with the teacher. The teacher thus will have an opportunity to see that all the senses are working or to help those with problems to use their remaining senses to the greatest degree possible.

A half day is preferable, but if it is necessary for a small child to stay all day, then a rest period and free-play period are important. Free play may have to be taught to physically handicapped children or children who are blind and deaf.

The quality of the preschool program is more important early on than concerns about integration with nonhandicapped children. Beware of overstimulation, particularly with children who were premature or children with multiple anomalies.

Visit any school that interests you and spend some time watching the daily program. Observe how the teachers and the children interact. Do they seem generally to like and respect one another? Are the children enjoying themselves? Watch the children to see if they appear relaxed and interested in what is going on. Is there special equipment and how is it used?

After you observe for a while, spend time talking with one of the teachers after school and ask about the program. Some nursery schools offer a wide range of specialized activities—art, music, and specialized play, well-chosen toys and equipment— that are just right for specific problems. Any good program for this age group also includes enough adults and open time for the warm contact these little ones need.

Other nursery schools are nothing more than babysitting services with no planned activities or sense of what handicapped children need. You should thus check each one carefully.

For example, try to discover how any nursery-school staff handles hygiene, toilet habits, and food preparation. Also, is there time for naps?

I have visited both regular and handicapped nursery-school programs that were so poorly organized or in such a bad setting that I wanted to run out the door as fast as I could.

One important question to ask is what the policy is with sick children, especially with respiratory infections, like colds or sore throats. Many parents send their children to school with a low-grade fever or even when they are coming down with the flu, simply because the parents have to work. This makes the nursery school an incubator for germs, encouraging illnesses to spread rapidly if sick children are allowed to attend.

If your handicapped child already has serious medical problems, this added contact with infections can make matters worse. Exposures to respiratory infections can be particularly harmful if your child has a hearing problem. Some children are allowed to stay in school although they have repeated ear infections. I recently visited a nursery school for deaf children where one child, only partially deaf, was continuing to lose his hearing, and it was felt to be due to repeated ear infections.* A child's hearing is particularly precious in the early years, because with poor hearing, his language and social development may be delayed. Frequent ear infections can cause hearing problems, with a thickening of eardrums due to infection and fluid staying in the middle ear after the infection. I was concerned that the school was not doing something more to correct the child's situation, but as nonmedical people, they may have been doing what they could.

Adding the burden of a hearing loss to any child, and particularly to one who already has multiple handicaps, is just unacceptable to me.

Alternatives

Special programs may not be available to your child or you may need a nursery school or day-care program in addition to some special training. If you cannot find a nursery school you like, there are workable alternatives. One possibility is to form a play group with two or three other mothers who have small children. These might be women you've met through a parent-support group, in which case children would have handicaps similar to your child's. Another possibility would be the mothers of young children in your neighborhood, children who will probably not be handicapped.

Other women may welcome a chance to cooperate on child care, so that each of you gets some time to yourself. Of course you will need to spend time beforehand setting up a routine and

---

*Unfortunately, loss of hearing (though not all due to ear infections) is a real health problem in the United States today. Other causes of loss of hearing are meningitis, genetic (25 percent of all cases), trauma, prenatal viruses, and toxic drugs to name a few.

agreeing on health and care standards. You may want to try an unstructured play group three mornings a week, or you may want to provide a structure, even though the children go to different homes, by opening and closing with the same song each time the group meets or setting up a regular plan for the group's morning activities.

Mothers working on shared child care will have no shortage of topics to talk over: discipline, snacks, toilet training, play activities, outdoor times, naps, health care, toys, and equipment. If you decide to try this, don't expect to work everything out in just one meeting. Each of you will come up with new ideas as you go along, so you may decide to meet regularly as a group. While the children are playing nearby, you can talk over what you've all learned about toys, games, or how to handle difficult situations. Talking together like this can help break down the isolation many mothers of young children feel.

The advantage of a cooperative child-care arrangement is that you know the situation your child will be in. You also know that your child will be getting good care from other mothers. The disadvantage is that it takes some of your energy, initiative, and creativity, but it may be something you would enjoy doing.

You might not want to go so far as to organize a play group, but you can still work out an informal exchange with one or two other women. With two exchange partners, you gain two periods a week free of children and two times when you have an extra child. Sometimes this can make your own child care easier, as the children can entertain each other while you supervise them.

A third possibility is to hire a neighborhood youngster to entertain your child with games and toys while you do housework or catch up on other chores. Your child will benefit from the contact and stimulation, and you will have some spare time.* Because you'll be nearby, the child you hire can be quite young, just so he or she enjoys being with other children. Also, you need not pay much. One mother did this several afternoons a week with a neighborhood eight-year-old girl who came after

*Remind the neighborhood youngster to talk to your child, even though there might not be much response, if there are communication problems.

school. She paid the girl fifty cents an hour, though the young lady probably would have been happy to do it for nothing.

Schoolchildren Age Five and Up

The main decision with schoolchildren from kindergarten on up is whether to put them in a regular classroom or a special-education setting. Before making this decision, you may need to have your child tested by a qualified psychologist and communication expert to see if any learning problems often associated with physical problems such as spina bifida, cerebral palsy, or Duchenne muscular dystrophy are present. There may be visual-motor or fine-motor problems, auditory-processing, visual, or language-processing difficulties.

Schools should provide for testing with special-education children. Testing will let you and the school know your child's potentials and limits, and with this knowledge a better decision can be made about school placement and the need for specialized services.

It is essential that a qualified psychologist do this testing. Many with excellent training who do marvelous work with "normal" children have little or no experience testing handicapped children. It takes someone with a wealth of experience and a great deal of patience to test handicapped children, especially those who are both deaf and blind. Many handicapped children can't be tested using methods or tests that work well for nonhandicapped children. Also, if there is a language problem, this, too, can create added difficulties.

Be sure that the person who tests your child explains why particular testing methods were used. For example, you probably don't need an IQ test for your child, but you need what is called, in medical or psychological terms, a "psychometric profile." This shows where your child's strengths and weaknesses lie. It also will show learning disabilities or special "holes" that need educational attention—the kinds of things you will want to know about before you choose an educational program.

If the school does not have psychologists trained to test handicapped children, inquire around to find someone qualified for this job. Start with the doctor caring for your child and ask for a recommendation, but remember, a family doctor or pediatrician may not see enough handicapped children to make a recommendation. State clearly that you want someone with lots of experience testing children with your child's particular handicap. If your doctor doesn't know anyone, ask him or her to make some calls for you. You may find it necessary to travel to a large city in your area, but finding a psychologist qualified in this field is worth considerable effort to save yourself and your child a lot of false starts once the child is in school.

Remember that the testing should be set for a day when you think your child will not be extra tired from lots of weekend visitors or after a strenuous vacation. Also, choose the time of day that your child seems to be most alert. If he has a respiratory infection or other illness, the testing should be canceled, because you want him to be in the best possible physical condition when tested.

Another factor in testing is that a child should be reassessed every year or two. The general requirement for the schools is that a major retesting be done every three years. Repeated testing will show changes in your child's ability, so you and the teachers can make appropriate adjustments in the educational program.

Regular Classrooms and Special-Education Options

The use of the word *mainstream* is one you will hear commonly. It is a concept that became popular when Congress passed Public Law 94-142 in 1975. To the maximum extent possible, handicapped children are to be educated with children who have no handicaps. The specific language of the law states that handicapped children should be placed in the "least restrictive environment" for their schooling. This means that a handicapped child may be in a regular classroom or at least be able to interact with nondisabled children part of the day or an entire school day. One alternative is to have a child in a special-education class that exists within a regular school setting, so that he can attend some regular classes and also have some special-education help. There are, of course, schools that are just for handicapped children and schools for children with specific handicaps, such as deafness. Some students need highly specialized and concentrated instruction in order to be able to participate more fully in the mainstream life as adults. Many children now are spending part of their day in a regular classroom with an aide to help with physical problems or someone to sign or interpret if they are deaf. The ideal setup is probably to have a range of alternatives from which parents and professionals can select the services best suited to each child. The supplementary services sometimes cannot be achieved in regular classrooms.

Both mainstream and special-education programs in schools have their advantages and disadvantages. Rural areas have more problems providing a range of services because they have so few students with handicaps. Sometimes, in order to get services, parents may need to move or to have a child away from home for a period of time in a special program.

There is no one simple answer to whether your child should be in a regular classroom or placed in a setting specifically for handicapped children. The thing to remember is that each child's situation is unique and may also change from year to year. It may help you start making a choice by getting advice from people you respect. Consult with your child's physician or other parents you know, even if their children are not handicapped. Your own ideas will often grow clearer as you describe the various options to someone who is not personally involved. As you sort through the issue enough to explain it clearly to someone else, you may discover that you have already reached a conclusion, but it was buried in the facts.

First, consider the general pros and cons of different options. The concept behind mainstreaming and its primary advantage is that it offers a handicapped child contact with nonhandicapped children in a regular school setting. This gives the child a chance to see and learn from role models who have a normal range of skills and interests. Handicapped children can be positively motivated by this contact and are likely not to feel so isolated or shut away from society. The potential disadvantage is that the solitary handicapped child in a regular classroom can be the focus of cruelty by other children. Children also won't have the special education their specific handicaps warrant if there are not enough special-education resource people to go to all the normal classrooms.

I spoke to a speech therapist one day about a child that needed a great deal of help. She felt that she was giving him adequate time, and when I asked how much this was, she said that she saw the child thirty minutes once a month! She did consult with his regular teacher, but the regular teacher was teaching thirty other children.

Other disadvantages of mainstreaming are that many schools are not properly staffed to work out good supplementary programs for handicapped children. Be sure each teacher has the appropriate credentials to serve your child. Problems may arise because of the shortage of trained teachers and other personnel. The shortage is said to be due to a lack of money, and many say that the legislators who passed the law didn't provide the money to make it really workable. Given proper funding, mainstreaming might be a useful approach.

This puts the burden on you to find out how handicapped children are placed and taught in your school district. Ask to observe in classrooms and look at all the possible options available for your child. Talk with the teachers and, if you can, the parents of other handicapped children who attend the school programs. Ask the school personnel directly about the range of problems or handicaps they are trained in and prepared to handle.

I have had as patients several children with aphasia who were incorrectly placed in classes for severely mentally retarded children. Aphasia is basically an inability to use or understand spoken words due to some malformation, disease, or injury in the brain. If these children had been started out in a special speech program, their progress would have been much better. However, no such classes were available in that particular district, so they were put in a class for mentally retarded children, which was the only available option. Aphasic classes should be one of the options available in each district, but unfortunately they are not. Children with specific handicaps like aphasia need teachers who are trained to work with such problems. They need to be put in a class in a private school if nothing is available in the public schools, and by law the public schools are required to pay for this. It may necessitate hiring a lawyer and spending time in court to accomplish this, though.

Although in many school districts across the country the goal is to place handicapped children with nonhandicapped children, there still are numerous self-contained classes with unique services for handicapped children, for example, language-impaired or orthopedically handicapped children. The advantage of a special-education placement for a child is that the teachers are specially trained in how to teach children with handicaps. Teachers often specialize within special education to teach children with specific handicaps, such as those trained to teach deaf or blind children. Another advantage is that the environment and equipment in special-education settings are geared to the particular learning needs of children with handicaps. This is not to say that special equipment cannot be used in regular classes with appropriate special-education support services.

On a social level, it may be comforting for children with handicaps to know that there are others in the world like themselves. They may feel more accepting of their own limitations or problems if they see or know others who have similar difficulties, and they may be inspired by handicapped children around them who can understand the frustrations they feel. A handicapped child may also have an easier time making friends in a special-education classroom or school.

The disadvantage of a special-education placement is that the child with handicaps may come to feel shut away from normal society. This can increase the feeling of being different or "weird" and can also lead to the child's not learning how to function in what we think of as normal society.

You may find it possible to arrange a balanced combination of both kinds of programs—mainstreaming and special education. For example, your child might be mainstreamed in a regular classroom and then have a tutor or tutors to help in areas of special needs. This would give the child a full range of normal social contacts, as well as extra help in particular problem areas.

A reverse combination might be to place your child in an appropriate special-education setting and then provide outside social contacts. For example, you could arrange for your child to join some regular school activities or a scouting troop of nonhandicapped children, a local Boys' or Girls' Club. These would offer the advantages of a special-education setting in which to learn needed skills and a regular education program as a source of social contacts with similar-aged nonhandicapped children.

To pursue an educational program for your child, you will want to be familiar with both the national and state laws that pertain to the education of handicapped children. Parent support groups are most likely to have this information. School personnel can help review the information with you to be sure that it is up to date and complete. Some areas have legal advocates who can help you understand your rights and the rights of your child. You can often request a pamphlet about special education that explains the rights and responsibilities of both pupils and parents.

An important feature of special education are IEPs. These are the individual educational plans mandated by law for handicapped children. The IEP, or Individual Education Plan, is rewritten at least yearly at a school meeting attended by parents, an administrator, teachers, and any other needed special personnel, such as a speech therapist or occupational or physical therapist.

Recommendations are made and recorded and signed by all present. If, however, you as a parent are not satisfied with what has taken place or find that the recommendations have not been carried out, then a new IEP can be requested. (Parents can request a new IEP at any time.) If the school personnel refuse, they must explain why in writing.

Much has been written about the IEP process, and one particularly good pamphlet is available from the National Information Center for Handicapped Children and Youth in Washington, DC Only handicapped children who require a special education are eligible for IEPs. Things that you should know about IEPs:

1. Tape-recording the IEP is legal and might be a good idea.
2. Both parents or partners should go if possible. Also, a legal advocate or support person can go with you.

3. Make notes and ask questions. Don't be shy, but do try
    to keep from becoming angry if you feel your child is not
    getting what is needed.

4. Try some role-playing with a friend or partner at home
    before the meeting if you are shy about going and speak-
    ing up.

5. Write down your goals and questions and be sure to take
    this list with you.★

If the school refuses your request for a new IEP, a legal process has been established, with specific steps that you need to
follow. This may ultimately involve a hearing. It is somewhat
complicated and extremely time-consuming, and you may need
a legal advocate to help you get what you want.

Ask about your child's curriculum. Some places do not have
well-established curriculum guides for teachers. Too often special-education teachers have to rely on their own resources and
make up their own curriculum as they go along.

Regular education, on the other hand, has specific state and
local board-adopted curricula and guidelines for different ages and
levels of ability. These have yet to be established for those special-education students who need a modified curriculum. This is
unfortunate. However, it is very important even for children with
markedly limited intellectual abilities to learn as much as they can
at school so that they can understand the world around them
better and have their own lives enriched. As a parent, you can
become active in a parents' group or advisory group and work
toward getting your district to develop curriculum guides for
teachers in special-education programs.

Court cases against the schools are becoming more and more
common, when parents feel schools are not able to provide the
kind of program a child needs. These are expensive, time-consuming procedures that take a great toll in emotional energy.
They identify parents as "thorny" or difficult, so if you as a par-

★Adapted from *Take Charge!* by Diane Nousanen and Lee W. Robinson (National Association for Parents of the Visually Impaired, Inc., Austin, Texas,
1980).

ent can work within the existing framework, it is probably best. If not, find an altruistic attorney or volunteer child advocate who will help you and not bankrupt you. A legal battle is a long, drawn-out process, so be very sure that you know what you're getting into before you begin. Then, if you need to do it and are well prepared—financially, emotionally, and physically—go ahead.

Nonspeaking Children

Dr. June Bigge has often discussed with me the communication problems of handicapped children. This is a specialized area with too few skilled professionals. However, with instructions in alternative communication methods and the surge of knowledge in the computer industry, computers and electronic communication devices are now being tailor-made for individual students who have limited speech and cannot use their hands because of a severe movement handicap. Such children are able to use electronic devices to speak and write for them.

There are many aphasic children and children with cerebral palsy who have the mental ability to speak but who simply do not have the motor control or nervous system connections that allow them to communicate. It behooves the rest of us, as professionals and parents, to find ways for them to do this. Assessment by professionals highly trained to work with these children is, again, a high priority.

Instead of trying to communicate, it is only too easy for individuals to slip unconsciously into the habit of treating noncommunicative children as though they were retarded and younger than they actually are. People are uncomfortable because they don't know how to communicate with these children. Often these handicapped children are not spoken to, but at. Be sure every nonspeaking child has some way to let others know how best to communicate with him or her. The method may become quickly obvious, as when a nonspeaking deaf child signs or pulls out a pencil and paper to write a message. Some methods do not become obvious, and a note attached to a child's wheelchair or placed near the child is often helpful. The note can give clues such as "I look up to say yes; I look down to say no." It takes a great deal of time and waiting for a nonspeaking child or teenager to use a communication board or communication device. (See Bigge, Chapter 4.) Some aids are simple to make, and others are very complex. Some are electronic and others are not. Even though family members do not need to rely on these communication aids, they do need to understand how they operate so that their child can be helped to practice developing speed and accuracy using the aid.

It is not always clear which communication methods should be used for individual students. Many issues arise. For example, signing is a form of communication currently taught in classes for aphasic children. There are pro and con arguments about whether teaching a child diagnosed as aphasic to sign keeps the child from learning to speak. This is a problem shared with deaf children. I think the answer for parents and professionals is to find an expert in the field, have the child seen by that expert, and then rely on his or her judgment. We cannot be specialists in everything.

School Programs

Many schools do not have classes for children with language disorders or aphasia, and children may be placed in orthopedic or handicapped classrooms. In addition, children with such disorders frequently are not identified or identified early enough so that proper schooling or training is obtained for them. As parents, you *must* be your child's advocate, unless you can afford an attorney skilled in such matters. (Some postaccident children will often need a special language-disorder class for a period of time.) A special battery of tests by a psychologist skilled in working with these children is needed to identify problems in children with communication disorders. Prior to the testing, a hearing test *must* be done. This should not be done in a doctor's office unless the doctor is an ear, nose, and throat specialist and has his or her own skilled audiologist. A quick school examination is not adequate, but a comprehensive examination in a hearing center must be done to determine that a child has adequate hearing.

Any child who does not make sounds or vocalize by three

months should be suspected of having a hearing problem. If hearing is adequate, further testing for aphasia or some other problem is needed. To be put in language-disorder classes, children who are handicapped must have normal intelligence. If aphasia is identified as a problem, a small aphasic class or other intensive instructional program is a must. If such services are not already available, the school district is required by law to provide such services either in another district or in a private school. Once again, if the school district will not arrange for this, be prepared to go through a long, drawn-out legal proceeding.

Remember, however, that schools often find themselves in a bind. The most appropriate class for a child may be full, and a less appropriate class may have room. Look very critically at all instructional placement options for handicapped children and be sure you understand the reasons and appropriateness for your child's placement in a particular classroom. It may be that if enough children are not available to have a special class, for example, in a rural area, intensive tutoring services could be provided. Inquire about long-range planning for your child. Many exciting avenues in the working world are opening now for even some of the most handicapped youths. School programs should have provisions for preparing students to work and participate as citizens in their community once they become teenagers and adults. The support of other parents or a parent-support group is extremely important to help you stay on course, as is taking care of yourself and finding time for your own needs.

Chapter 10

How to Help Your Child Find Some Fun In Life

The world is so full of a number of things,
I'm sure we should all be as happy as kings.

—ROBERT LOUIS STEVENSON

Childhood should be a time of magic—a time to learn, to grow, and to play. Think how hard it would be to chase butterflies if you could not run, to hear the birds sing if you were deaf, or to see the animals in the zoo if you were blind. Put yourself inside each of these children and your own handicapped child, and imagine how difficult it is to have a quality of life that allows for more pleasure than pain.

I came across a sentence in a medical journal one day that parents and doctors of a handicapped child need to remember: "Life is worth living only when the pleasure outweighs the pain." (Dudale, 1968.) Handicapped children often have so much pain in their lives that it is important for you as a parent to pay a great deal of attention to fun and good times for your handicapped child. It is the quality of life, not the quantity, that counts, and each day should have some fun in it.

The early years are particularly important, as these are formative years, and play is an essential part of learning how to live in the real world, to handle problems, and to have as rich an imagination as possible. Life can be narrow and restrictive for a child with a handicap. Having a special interest or hobby can change

120

children's lives so they become more outgoing, find new friends, and see their whole world become bigger and richer. To find some ideas for your child, start by wandering through your local toy or hobby store. With a child who is severely handicapped, you may have to be very creative, but you will be able to find some hobbies. People usually think of hobbies such as collecting stamps, buttons, thimbles, or doing crafts, but these are just a beginning. A child can listen to music or books on tape, enjoy art, watch movies, or learn about special subjects. There are also pen pals, in this and other countries, who share different hobbies. This can be an added benefit for a child who needs new friends.

One of my patients learned as a teenager how to do reweaving. He was in a wheelchair, but his hands and arms were strong enough to do this. He later turned this into a small reweaving business in his home. It gave him a real sense of independence and a feeling of accomplishment, as well as making him a little extra money.

Another patient loved opera and became an expert on old opera stars and opera history. He was frequently asked for information by music students and teachers, and he even dictated occasional articles.

A teenager with cerebral palsy loved classical music and became quite an expert. He went to concerts in his wheelchair and then dictated reviews for a local newspaper.

The possibilities are endless. Your child could start with a postcard collection, a comic-book collection, an old poster, plate, or spoon collection. There are individuals who love garage sales, fairs, swap meets, and flea markets. These are all ways to make friends and have as normal a life as possible, in addition to a much richer life. If your handicapped child doesn't have a hobby, seriously think about helping him or her find one to enjoy.

Hobbies have other benefits as well as the ones I've mentioned. Some of the things children do can also be therapeutic. For example, finger painting or artwork can train and strengthen hands that might be tight or injured. Blowing bubbles or blowing up balloons can be made into a game; this is excellent therapy for children with respiratory problems, as it helps develop and increase their lung capacity. A similar game for such children is to have them blow a small, lightweight boat across a tub of water and try to race someone else's boat.

Throwing beanbags, tennis balls, or Ping-Pong balls into boxes or baskets is a way to help children with limited upper-extremity strength or dexterity. Such activities can increase their range of motion and strength.

Horseback riding is wonderful for many handicapped children. In Denmark, riding horseback is routinely ordered for children with muscular dystrophy. It stretches the muscles at the back of the legs (or the heel cords), and is very good exercise. There are horseback-riding programs designed for handicapped children in different parts of this country, and many are available at either little charge or no charge.

A good recreational therapist, occupational therapist, or special-education teacher will have other suggestions. Also, ask your doctor for referrals or call the local branch of the agency that handles your child's disability.

Pets are a wonderful way for a child to have more pleasure in life and develop a sense of responsibility as well. Children can help with the care and feeding of a pet, and pets do not have to be expensive. Fish or small turtles can be purchased in pet stores and are easy to care for. Guinea pigs are easy pets, too. You can obtain dogs and cats through the Society for Prevention of Cruelty to Animals if you have enough space in your home and if time is not too much of a premium.

The hearing dogs that are being trained in some areas by the SPCA can offer deaf children not only a pet but also a hearing friend to help alert them about cars coming, falling objects, and calls to come home.

If you can't locate a helpful professional in your area, there are some good books to help you. Look in the children's section at a bookstore or a public library to find a treasure chest of ideas. The activities suggested can be adapted to the needs of your handicapped child. There are books that talk about planting seeds and watching them grow, a fun experience for anyone, as well as a way to learn about nature. Books are available about butterflies, birds, fossils, and many other subjects. Take some time on a day when you need a change and visit your public library or

local bookstore. If you do this alone, you will have a better chance
to see what is there and get some ideas about fun things your
child can do. When my children were growing up, I used to keep
a list of ideas for snowy or rainy days.

On one of my recent trips to a bookstore, I discovered an
excellent paperback book called *What to Do When There Is Nothing to Do*. It was put together by a group at the Boston Children's Medical Center and lists activities by ages. This helpful
book even suggests things you can make for babies. Many of
these ideas can be constructed just from everyday things found
in most households. The book also cautions you about harmful
objects or things that could cause accidents.

Another idea is a dress-up box. I used to keep one for my
children and they had lots of creative fun with it. You could
easily put together a dress-up box for your handicapped child.
Most children can have clothes draped around them to do a little
playacting, and what a wonderful way for a handicapped child to
be part of a group and have fun. Also, dressing up can take them
away from their own difficulties for a little while. Visit a Goodwill or Salvation Army store, church rummage sales, or local
garage sales to find an abundance of inexpensive clothing, material, hats, scarves, gloves, boots, and accessories for costume play.
Also, look in grandparents' attics for wonderful treasures.

The other thing I did was to have a bag of little surprises
whenever we took a long trip by airplane, bus, or train. A quick
visit to the dime store, drugstore, or even toy store for such an
occasion was always a must, and it made trips much easier. Very
little money is necessary here; just some thought and planning.

Toys received as birthday or Christmas presents do not all
have to be played with at once. You can put some away for a
rainy or sick day and bring them out as needed. Some parents
rotate their children's toys, leaving out a limited number at a
time. This way old toys brought out from the top of the closet
can seem new and exciting again. I think too many toys at once
just confuse children.

For painting and drawing, I found that a roll of white shelf
paper or the end of a newspaper roll kept on hand was an inexpensive way to have poster-drawing paper available. Call your

local newspaper, as these newsprint ends can be reasonable; you can buy white shelf paper in any grocery store. My children were always very creative about making long scrolls, posters, and banners. Old wallpaper samples or wallpaper books are great, too, and many stores will save these for you to take home when their new ones come in if you will just ask. Don't be timid about doing this, because it can help you survive many days of rain or illness. Brown paper bags are also wonderful for making a multitude of things—puppets, masks, hats, bags, piñatas.

If you don't live in the western part of the United States, you may not know about piñatas. These are a part of the Christmas celebration in Mexico. A piñata is generally made of papier-mâché or clay and filled with candy and toys. It is hung high on a cord strung from a tree limb or a hook, and people stand around in a circle while an individual who is blindfolded has to hit at it with a bat or stick. When it is broken, everyone scrambles for the candy. There are, of course, many variations of this, and even children in wheelchairs can participate. We used to make our own piñatas, at Christmas or other times of the year, out of large brown paper bags, and then decorate and fill them with wrapped candy, little toys, or pennies.

Television has replaced so many creative activities that children today can grow up without a chance to be creative and often have very narrow lives. I heard Dr. Benjamin Spock say recently that not only does the average child watch television a great deal, but during the growing years, a child sees some eighteen thousand murders. This is an incredible statistic. Surely some artwork or a hobby is far better than watching eighteen thousand murders, as well as countless acts of other violence. Hours of television aren't good for any child, but when children are in a wheelchair and not out playing, television can become the only perception of life they have. Many handicapped children already have difficulty with anger and hostility because of their problems. They don't have normal opportunities to act out their anger or get rid of it by running and playing, so murderous thoughts can be a problem for them anyway. Adding eighteen thousand murders seen on television is surely not a prescription for good mental health.

One child I care for watches as much as eight to ten hours of television a day. This may seem easier for her mother, but the child is essentially a nonparticipant in today's exciting world, and I feel that is sad. I have suggested changes, but I am afraid that her mother is too tired and has essentially given up. The child's wheelchair has become her prison.

These children need some creative activities that can help them express their feelings and give them some fun. Puppets are fun and creative, and they can be made from crepe paper, paper plates, cartons, sticks, newspaper, tissue paper, socks, mittens, food, spoons, or clothes—the list is endless. Puppets also give children a chance to act out a range of feelings in a harmless and creative way. A simple stage can be made from a cardboard box. Spending a lot of money is not necessary, because many play materials can be obtained at little or no cost. Buttons can be sewed on for eyes, nose, and mouth with a big needle and thread. Pieces of scrap yarn or rope are good for hair or mustaches. If your child works with you, good eye-hand coordination can be fostered.

Just a little research and searching on your part can save you and your child from some bad times as well as helping the child to improve eye-hand coordination, develop a much richer inner fantasy life and some creativity; it can yield many other benefits as well. Limiting television watching to just some special programs pays off abundantly.

There are lots of packaged crafts that have everything already organized so you needn't do a lot of searching for different materials. Finger paints can help your child develop a good tactile sense, and clay can help develop the use of hand muscles and a three-dimensional sense. Buy nontoxic clay that doesn't dry out.

Collages are also fun, and you can use any small pieces of material, wood, beans, pasta, or paper that you have around. Save old wrapping paper or magazines for backgrounds. Paste glue is hard for some children to use, but liquid glue can be watered down for collages.

Remember that if you buy art supplies they should be water soluble and nontoxic. Large brushes, sizes 10 to 16, are best for young artists, I am told. Tempera, which can be washed out of clothes, is available ready-mixed or in powder for you to mix, and it is fairly inexpensive and has good clear colors. You can tape pieces of paper on an easel or on the garage wall for young artists. Save cottage-cheese cartons or plastic containers for paint-brushes.

Drawing or painting can be therapeutic for your child. The artwork can also offer you some insights into what a child is thinking. Having children draw pictures of themselves or their families is a good way to begin understanding some of their feelings.

If your child needs some ideas, offer some general suggestions. Themes such as holidays are good to draw about; doing theme pictures keeps a child from being self-conscious about the drawing. (Be sure to hang drawings up and exhibit them even for a little while after a child has completed them.) When you comment on a drawing, try the approach of "tell me about" rather than trying to say what it is. You could easily hurt your child's feelings if you can't see quite what the child thought was being drawn. Also, just comment on the positive things, such as "It's a pretty color" or "What clear lines!"

Noodles are fun to string, to paint with tempera, or to make into collages or jewelry. Avoid marking pens because they tend to get on everything. Cleaning up after an art project helps teach your child a sense of responsibility and thus has an added benefit for children. As your child works—or rather plays—he learns how to organize materials, to work on a project, to finish some-thing, and to return the materials to their places. Play can ac-tually teach a child many skills as well as strengthen the child's muscles, coordination, creativity, and self-esteem.

Traveling

Traveling is a wonderful way for children to see and be intro-duced to many different life-styles and cultures. For handicapped children in particular, who often have many limits placed upon them, traveling can both enrich their lives and give them a greater understanding of people. Traveling requires thought and prepa-ration for any of us. When you add a child who may be in a wheelchair, uses a walker, or has limited ability to get around, the problems increase manifold. They are not insurmountable, though, and that's important to keep in mind.

Much more attention has been paid in recent years to making places accessible for the handicapped, including national, state, and even regional parks, museums, art galleries, and public monuments. There are also good guides and pamphlets available now about special facilities, toilets, ramps, and so on for handicapped individuals. Also, there are travel agents who specialize in making arrangements for handicapped travelers.

Sometime before you start on a trip, I suggest you buy a small notebook and start thinking about and jotting down special things you are going to need to take along as well as any necessary plans for the following: (1) lodging; (2) availability of medical care; (3) medicines and prescriptions; (4) eyeglasses replacement prescription; and (5) letters from your doctors detailing any special care your child requires. By anticipating possible problems, you can resolve them with little stress. No experienced traveler expects to have a trouble-free trip, and seasoned travelers learn how to handle problems, both big and small. It is always a good idea to check with your child's physician before starting and ask about calling if you need to.

Recently one of my families went to a family reunion several hundred miles away. Everything went well until the return trip, when their son, who is in a wheelchair with a muscle disease, became quite ill. They stopped at one of the new twenty-four-hour walk-in clinics that are springing up everywhere and were seen by a physician. For some reason, he checked the blood sugar and found it to be a little high. Without any further testing or consultation with the boy's regular physician, he started the young man on an oral diabetic drug. Fortunately, the mother did not give it to him, but instead the family started home. They arrived with a gravely ill young man who required an emergency midnight hospital admission for pneumonia. All of the next few weeks of illness probably could have been prevented by the doctor at the walk-in clinic being alerted to the need to take a chest X ray and probably start the patient on some antibiotics. One long-distance telephone call is surely less expensive than weeks of hospitalization. It causes a lot less discomfort and anxiety, too.

Some large hotel and motel chains are now offering special services for handicapped travelers. They are installing such things as electronic devices to activate lights as a way of signaling people who are deaf. These and other devices will become more prevalent in the future.

The Society for the Advancement of Travel for the Handicapped has a free brochure giving details about travel in the United States. Material is also available on a free cassette tape and in Braille. Their address is 5014 Forty-second Street, N.W., Washington, DC 20016. Telephone (202) 966-3900. The National Easter Seal Society for Crippled Children and Adults in Chicago, Illinois, has pamphlets with information on handicapped travel also.

Amtrak has a special booklet for handicapped travelers that you can obtain by calling (800) 872-7245; the TTY number is (800) 523-6590, or 6591. In Pennsylvania, it is (800) 562-6960. They also have special discount fares that you should ask about.

There is an International Directory of Access Guides that you can get from the Rehabilitation International U.S.A., Inc., 20 West Fortieth Street, New York, NY 10018. This lists access guides all over the world. There is also the Travel Information Center at Moss Rehabilitation Hospital, Twelfth Street and Tabor Road, Philadelphia, PA 19141, telephone (215) 329-5715, which gives information about hotels and transportation for the handicapped.

As time goes on, more and more information about access, transportation, facilities, and services will become available for the handicapped. Networking with other parents or your local agency will keep you in touch with new developments in this area. And it always pays to ask. Inquiring about special services and rates for handicapped travelers can at least plant the idea if no services are currently available.

Family Fun

One of the best ways to make sure your handicapped child has fun is to have some yourself and make some time for family fun. As the parent of a child with special needs, you can become overly involved in responsibilities and forget the tremendous power a good laugh has to relax us and heal us as well.

Fun need not be expensive or take much time. Having fun is mostly a matter of attitude and being open to playfulness and spontaneity. It may seem silly or frivolous to waste time having fun, but believe me—having a good time, laughing, and playing are valuable, worthwhile activities. Everyone needs a little playfulness in each day, and a child who is handicapped needs a strong dose of good times daily to make life feel worthwhile.

Learn to have fun if you don't already know how, and create occasions when your whole family can relax and play together. Be sure fun and play are close to the top of your priority list.

Chapter 11

How to Survive Your Child's Adolescence

Rashness attends youth, as prudence does old age.

—CICERO

When my own children were teenagers, there were days I can remember going into my bedroom, firmly closing the door, and wishing I didn't have to come out until they had left for college. Yet my children were normal, healthy, caring teenagers with no disabilities or handicaps. Being a teenager is itself handicap enough these days without the extra problems of also having spina bifida, cerebral palsy, or some other major disability. Coping with physical, emotional, and intellectual changes leaves many adolescents feeling moody, confused, and unsure of themselves. The additional complications of a serious handicap can make a teenager even more difficult to live with.

Teenagers are generally very self-conscious about their appearance, and it is extremely important to them to look like their peers in school or the community. Handicapped teenagers with visible problems suffer even more self-consciousness than non-handicapped teenagers do. Adolescents with handicaps often have to be helped with counseling to accept their disabilities and focus on their positive qualities. It is particularly hard for teenagers to accept any differences in themselves, but this can lead to strength in meeting other challenges.

In some ways invisible handicaps can be harder on teenagers, as they try to hide them so they are not recognized. Teenagers who are deaf or who have learning disabilities may have real problems because everyone expects them to perform like their peers if the problem is not known; they certainly don't want to bring attention to themselves by letting others in on their disability.

I saw a new patient one day, a handsome boy with little vision in his left eye and no ear canal or hearing on his left side. He was doing poorly in school, so I called the school to see if I could find out what kind of problems he was having. It turned out that he had been sitting in the back of the room where he could not adequately see the blackboard or hear the teacher. It was a new school for him, and the teachers did not know about his problems. Naturally, he was not about to tell them.

After discussing the situation with the teenager, I asked that he be moved to the front of the class where he could see and hear well. His schoolwork improved dramatically with this simple solution, and he was not upset by the change.

Independence

Adolescence is the time when youngsters should begin to change from children into independent adults; that is what most parents are working for. This transition should be gradual, with parents giving their child more and more responsibility and freedom as new situations and demands are handled well. By the time a child is a teenager, the process should be well enough along so that a teenager will have some measure of independence. Parents of handicapped youngsters have to find other ways to foster independence when their children are obviously physically dependent on others. How does a parent encourage independence for a child who is in a wheelchair, blind, deaf, or has a progressive condition?

Of all the challenges facing the parents of a handicapped child, this is the one that may be the trickiest. It is both essential and difficult. Some parents so smother their handicapped child—through guilt or remorse—that the child becomes terribly dependent. This pattern is hard to break once it has been established. Many parents, and mothers in particular, find their reason for living in the care of their handicapped child. They make themselves feel valuable, needed, and worthwhile by catering completely to the child's needs and whims. The child becomes totally dependent on them, and this makes the parents seem important and indispensable. Parents of nonhandicapped children often live through their children, too, but the opportunities to do so are much greater with a child who is handicapped. In many cases like this, the father often gradually relinquishes any authority in the home and retreats to work while the mother takes over everything but breathing for the child.

One patient I had was severely disabled emotionally. Her mother was always with her and gave up all her outside activities to take care of the girl. All of the mother's energies were totally focused on her daughter. I tried repeatedly to get the mother to accept family counseling, to no avail. As time went on, the girl became increasingly dependent on her mother and was finally homebound.

Several years later, the mother died of cancer, at a fairly young age, and her daughter gradually reentered the real world. She grew more and more independent, started driving a car, and began helping with children at a playground. Her father simply would not—or could not—give her the same level of attention that his wife had. It is sad that the girl had to lose her mother in order to regain some independence and emotional health.

There is an important message in this story for parents of handicapped children. Not only did the one daughter have parenting problems added to her handicapped condition, but a brother became so alienated from his mother that he did not even come home for her funeral. The parents' marriage also suffered, as alcohol became the father's companion to replace his wife.

It is essential to encourage, support, and help motivate your child's independence. As parents, your goal should be to make your role much less important as the years pass. If your handicapped child is the center of your world, try to pull back and reevaluate what you are doing. Seek out some professional help if you feel you cannot change the pattern of your life. Parents who have raised their handicapped children to be well-adjusted, capable adults are the ones who have met this challenge head-on and have found ways to let their children grow and then go.

Teenagers who are physically handicapped may need special equipment so that they can navigate on their own. Electric wheelchairs and vans with hydraulic lifts and hand controls are indispensable for true independence in wheelchair-bound teenagers. Parents can sometimes get these through state departments of rehabilitation. If you decide to try this route, be ready to spend many hours filling out forms, "reminding" counselors, and waiting a long time. You probably need to start before your child reaches the legal driving age.

If you meet other parents who have obtained a van, ask them what they did and whom they contacted. Parents who have lost a child are often happy to have their son's or daughter's van used by another handicapped teenager.

Education

With the new emphasis on mainstreaming handicapped children into regular classrooms, a handicapped teenager could be the only such student in a classroom. This does not have to be an insurmountable problem.

One of my patients who was wheelchair-bound told me about his first day of school in a regular junior-high class. No one had talked to the class or prepared them for his arrival. Even the teacher was uncomfortable with his presence, and the boy took a great deal of ridicule and torment for the first few months. The other boys called him names like "fag," "crip," and "retard" because he was not sports-oriented and could not be outgoing. They put objects in his wheelchair spokes to keep him from moving and even tried to tip him over.

I asked the boy what his message would be to parents and school personnel for other handicapped students starting in a new regular classroom. He suggested that they prepare the class and themselves for the handicapped student. He felt it would be helpful to have a special discussion in class about the specific handicap and involve the teenager in both the planning and the discussion.

If you have a teenager who is about to enter a new classroom or a new school, talk to the teacher or teachers ahead of time. Most junior high and high schools have counselors who can help you set up meetings with school personnel and aid you in working out good strategies for talking with teachers and students. You might ask your child's doctor, physical therapist, or other medical support person to make a presentation at the school. I have taken slides and muscle biopsies for microscope viewing to classes with handicapped teenagers. I have also shown pictures and discussed particular handicaps with students and teachers. This kind of presentation can help give a handicapped teenager or child a special place in the classroom instead of making him or her different and an outcast. It can also teach nonhandicapped youngsters compassion and proper behavior around someone who is handicapped. Many teenagers simply have not had contact with such an individual and are uncomfortable. Once they can understand and find some common ground with a handicapped classmate, they can begin to look at life from another's point of view. In this way, having a handicapped student in a regular classroom can be a real benefit for the entire class.

Special circumstances apply to children who become handicapped after an accident. On returning to their school, they can find themselves either objects of ridicule, or else they are just ignored because they can't take part in the normal activities. They may become very isolated and lonely.

One patient of mine was hurt severely in an automobile accident. When he returned to school, the school personnel were so afraid of his creating a liability by falling on the school grounds that they forced him to sit in the office during recesses and free periods. They made no provision for any physical education or social contact with the other students during his free time. This changed only after we visited the school and talked to the teacher and principal.

Self-esteem

Teenagers with major physical problems such as disfiguring facial or orthopedic problems often have a negative and very distorted self-image. Studies of teenagers with curvature of the spine (scoliosis) or multiple handicaps have shown (by having them draw pictures of themselves) that they see themselves as much more distorted than they really are. Counseling is often necessary to help these young people change their self-image. If it is not changed, teenagers' entire lives can be affected, because they see themselves as badly damaged persons.

A favorite teenage patient once told me that the hard part of being in a wheelchair was that people thought she was retarded just because she couldn't walk. In fact she was both capable and intelligent. Other people, particularly her classmates in a new school, saw only the wheelchair and did not think of her as an individual. She once refused to go to school because the bus for the orthopedically handicapped students broke down and the bus for the retarded students was sent to pick her up instead. She said that would be all she needed, to appear at her new school on the retarded students' bus.

Many teenagers who are handicapped do not want to associate with other handicapped teenagers or handicapped people in general. This can create real problems. It can also be a sign that the individual has not accepted his or her own disability.

One handicapped teenage girl I knew wouldn't do anything with other handicapped people. Gradually she also withdrew into herself as nonhandicapped friends and boyfriends drifted away. She became more and more isolated and lonely. Although she finally received some badly needed counseling, her family would not become involved in the counseling. It was both too late and too little to help her, and she eventually took her own life.

Sexuality

Sex education is an important subject for any teenager, even if the adolescent is handicapped. It is important for teenagers to receive accurate information about sexuality so that sexual feelings can be accepted and handled appropriately. Sexuality can be a difficult problem for a teenager handicapped with cerebral palsy, paraplegia, or many other disabilities.

One young woman patient with cerebral palsy was literally trapped in her deformed, writhing body as her feelings and fantasies about sex became an obsession with her. She would rub against anything or anyone she could, frequently stuffed bulky objects into her underpants. A gentle and understanding psychiatrist helped the girl recognize her feelings, and she learned to handle them appropriately.

Another patient loved to see buildings explode in movies or on television. He constantly drew exploding volcanoes, which mystified his family. A psychiatrist who worked with him talked to him about his pictures. He felt that they were the boy's way of releasing sexual feelings, and anger as well. This seemed a safe way for the youngster to express feelings for which he had no other outlet.

Fortunately, there are now programs that train counselors in how to discuss sexual feelings and problems with disabled teenagers and adults. The United Cerebral Palsy Association has sponsored some of these programs. Contact them or other programs you hear about if your teenager seems to need some help in this area. Parents often do not feel capable of handling these issues on their own. Other resources are hospital social workers or the social workers or counselors in a local agency you know. Ask them about programs or suggest that they consider starting a program locally.

Sexuality encompasses not only actual intercourse but also love given and received in many ways. For young adults who are physically handicapped, there are other ways to express feelings of love, and these need to be taught. Male paraplegics who have lost sensation or cannot have an erection can still enjoy sexual happiness by learning other ways to meet their need for holding, touching, love and warmth. Women paraplegics can fill many of their sexual needs by learning appropriate methods from trained counselors. What is important is to find ways to touch, and be touched, and express warmth and love.

More and more we are becoming a society where touching is taboo. As we become more isolated from each other, we forget how to reach out and contact other people with warmth, humor, and caring closeness. The popularity of Leo Buscaglia's series of books on love point to this real lack in our society. Social isolation and lack of touching and warmth may be an even greater problem for a handicapped teenager or adult who is already isolated because of a handicapping condition.

Try to make sure your teenager is learning how to relate warmly to others and share affection. You are the role model for your teenager's warm and caring behavior with others. Some of your own ways and behavior may need modifying or changing to be the best role model for your child.

Risks

The very nature of life for all of us is change, new challenges, and growth—unless we're stuck in a rut. To encounter life fully involves taking risks—risks in trying something new, learning a new way of thinking, feeling, or relating, and exploring new relationships with others. If handicapped teenagers are not allowed and encouraged to try new things and to handle the inevitable mistakes, their quality of life can be shallow and dreary.

One teenage patient showed up at a recent appointment in my office with her parents. The girl was in a wheelchair and in the past had never shown any interest in being independent. Now she wanted to visit a cousin in another part of the state, and I was delighted to hear of her plans. It created some furor in the family as I encouraged her to make the trip on her own. She had carefully thought out potential bathroom, transportation, and eating problems, and she seemed well prepared. Finally her family allowed her to go, and she had a wonderful time. When she returned, she was a much happier and healthier young woman, ready to try more new adventures.

Gradually her parents began to accept her newfound independence. They discovered the pleasure of spending time by themselves again after years devoted to their handicapped child. Without their being aware of it, their relationship had suffered, and some repairs were badly needed. Fortunately, their daughter's new independence gave them time to do this before it was too late.

Not all teenagers will want to travel alone, but each person needs to find something exciting and challenging. Often you will have to guide and aid your child to take risks and accept challenges. If you start this process at a young age, your teenager will already know how to risk and to achieve new independence. Giving your child the needed support and yet knowing when to push her out into the world takes a great deal of wisdom and love.

Chores at Home

I am always surprised to find how many teenagers have no chores at home or make no contribution to the family life. These adolescents could be helpful in many ways around the house, but nothing is demanded of them. Even simple tasks in the kitchen are not done, and they would literally starve to death or have to live on cold cereal if no one were around to feed them.

This is sad, because teenagers who don't contribute to the family's well-being miss out in several ways. First, they do not learn day-to-day survival skills that will make them able to care for themselves as adults. Second, they miss out on the satisfaction that comes with knowing they are an important and contributing part of the family group. Finally, a handicapped child, or any other child, can feel worthless or a burden at seeing others do all the work when they receive a "free ride."

It is important for everyone in the family that the handicapped member do what is possible. Parents and siblings can grow to feel resentful if no contribution is made by the child. These feelings are often buried and may surface elsewhere in the family relationships. Siblings who are constantly forced to give and care for a handicapped brother or sister can themselves become emotionally handicapped and shun close relationships later in life due to anger or fear of the sacrifices involved.

It does take more time and effort for handicapped teenagers to learn how to do things around the house, but that's not a good reason for not assigning them regular chores. I feel strongly that household chores done regularly and well are important steps to adulthood and independence. Teaching your children how to do practical, basic tasks is an essential part of being a good parent for a handicapped child—or any child for that matter.

You can involve your child in decisions about his chores, and this will encourage him to do a good job. All of us are more motivated to do something we choose rather than something we are simply told to do. You might begin by making a list of the chores your child can handle at present or can learn to handle. Then let him choose the ones he would like to do. Write up a schedule of how often and when the chores must be done. Make sure they are real jobs that need doing, like setting the table, taking out the trash, putting laundry away, cleaning the bathroom sink, and so on.

When you first teach your child how the job is to be done, set aside plenty of time so you won't feel pressured. Big jobs can be broken down into smaller steps, and these can be practiced in the right sequence. Be sure to point out that jobs have a beginning, a middle, and an end, the end being when everything is picked up and put away. You don't want to have to clean up after your children have done their chores.

In the first stages, you will have to praise often for small accomplishments, but after a while your child should be able to master the whole job if it is appropriate for her age and ability. It is important to express appreciation for a job well done or to point out things that need changing. Too often we take the services of other family members too much for granted and don't express our appreciation.

As time goes on, you may want to change or add to the complexity of the jobs. The goal is not to load your child with work but to teach skills that help her become a capable, independent, and contributing family member. You may find it necessary occasionally to remind yourself and your children of this, because all they may see is that demands are being made. Only later in life will they be able to appreciate fully what you taught them and the opportunities you gave them for independence.

One young handicapped woman told me that her mother taught her about cooking when she was little. Her mother worked full-time, so the family planned meals together. The mother bought the food and the children cooked, according to their mother's instructions.

This woman had often felt that she was given too much responsibility during her teen years, but when she talked to friends she grew to appreciate the many valuable lessons she had learned from her mother. By twenty she could run a household well and care for herself and others. Teaching a child to work and to be capable is a valuable gift. The ability to do things—and to do them well—is a wonderful survival skill for parents to pass on.

Planning Ahead

Handicapped teenagers need to learn to plan ahead. A physically handicapped teenager who wants to be able to function as normally as possible needs to know how to ask the right questions about elevators, bathrooms, doors, and public transportation. Careful advance planning can make things go much more smoothly for someone in a wheelchair or on crutches.

When your child is young, you as a parent will do most of the planning. Then, as soon as possible, you will want to involve your child in the process. You can start out quite simply by asking, "Can you think of anything we've forgotten?" As your children grow, allow them to plan for outings or trips to town, and then review the possible circumstances and what else might be needed before you set out.

You can also teach your child to use the telephone and other resources to check out facilities ahead of time. This can avoid embarrassment and unnecessary work.

I was in a leg cast using crutches not too long ago, when a friend took me out to a new restaurant we wanted to try. When we got there, we laughed because it was up a steep stairway and the elevator was a long way away. My friend had called ahead to find out how accessible the restaurant was but didn't find out specifically how far the elevator was from the entrance. I made it, but it wasn't easy, and we both learned a valuable lesson—to ask for very detailed information.

Role Models

A teenage boy who is disabled may be raised in a single-parent family by his mother. Fathers frequently drift out of their sons' lives due to guilt or anger because of their "defect." It is very hard for most fathers to accept a handicapped child, particularly a handicapped son. A great deal of our heritage and culture looks to sons to carry on traditions in jobs or professions. When a male offspring has severe cerebral palsy, blindness, or other serious handicaps, the dream of a son to carry on family tradition is shattered or distorted. It takes an unusual father to handle this shattered dream and find a creative new reality.

Because of this, teenage boys are frequently cared for at home by their mothers and at school by women attendants, women teachers, and sometimes even women bus drivers. Their nurses, physical therapists, and aides may all be female, which leaves a boy with few, if any, male role models.

When a boy spends so much time with women, his ideas of maleness and his sexual identification may be vague and formless. A single-parent mother can help her teenage son by encouraging his association with male teachers, scout leaders, counselors, or physical therapists. Male attendants should be hired whenever possible, and male relatives should be encouraged to form close relationships with the boy.

Single mothers may form unhealthy relationships with their sons, in which they become dependent on them for their emotional needs. The sons in turn may rely too much on their mothers, particularly if they are handicapped. A warm closeness is one thing and can be good for both, but when it starts getting too "sticky," it is not in the best interest of either the mother or her teenage son. Teenagers need to be out in the world relating to their peers, making friends, talking to other adults, and becoming as independent as possible.

Communicating and Relating

When children become teenagers, talking to them or with them becomes a lost art in many families. In part this is because adolescents want to be with their peers or by themselves. This is a healthy move toward independence, but it shouldn't mean a complete breakdown in communication with their parents.

Teenagers and parents differ—in their views, their energy levels, their interests, and most other things. Yet it is vital to keep communication channels open, even if all you do is to agree to disagree. Often it is up to the parents to initiate and nurture communication at this stage. One mother of a boy with a muscle disease suggested that some questions might start communications if there seemed to be a barrier. She found that asking one or more of the following questions at the appropriate time and place helped her teenagers open up with their parents:

1. Are you feeling angry?
2. Are you feeling upset?
3. Are you feeling sad?
4. How would you like things to be different?
5. If you had three wishes, what would they be?

Bringing up your own feelings can sometimes help start talk flowing. You might mention that it makes you sad to see your child unhappy, and you'd like to help if you could. Once your youngster starts talking, you must follow up by using a combination of common sense and your best parenting instincts. If there is mutual respect and love, it will help you listen in a way that will help feelings to be expressed. Often a teenager just feels better having someone listen, without the listener doing anything to change the situation. It is important to acknowledge the feelings your child is expressing and to let her know you understand how she feels.

Your teenager will often respond to your interest and attention by talking to you more often. This does not mean that you must solve anything; mostly it means that your youngster trusts you to listen carefully and to respond with sensitivity. Knowing this, your teenager will feel more confident about tackling the problems discussed with you and may even want your advice.

It will probably be necessary for you to make periodic reassessments of your relationship with your teenager and your teenager's relationship to life in general. Disabled teenagers can become so involved in medically related activities or have so many hospitalizations that they have little time left over for fun with their friends, parents, brothers, or sisters. When you take stock of his relationships, look for ways for your teenager's life to have more fun and quality time. They need fun time with their family and friends, as well as quality one-to-one time with each parent—and time alone as well. This is hard to create and sustain, but a life that consists of just doctors' visits, schoolwork, and therapy is dreary and discouraging at a time when life should be fun.

A parent's task of creating quality time can be especially hard with a child who has a progressive disease or one who is nearing death. The demands here are quite different, and often desperation makes parents and child wonder, Why try if death is inevitable? I try to instill feelings of hope in all patients who have progressive diseases, and in their parents, too. Given the tremendous advances in research, genetic engineering, and medical discoveries, there is good reason to have hope. For example, diabetes was a fatal disease until a young medical student working in his professor's laboratory discovered insulin. Other cures will be found for today's progressive diseases, perhaps in the not-too-distant future.

When I was a medical student and pediatric resident in the 1950s, leukemia in children was a fatal disease. Now, thirty years later, many children with leukemia have been cured. Technological innovations have wrought many other changes since then, too.

If your child has a progressive disease, support her hopes, but give her plenty of good times to relish and enjoy. Laugh whenever you can, and measure each day by whether it has had some joy and special times in it. Appreciate each moment you have together, and live fully in that moment. Live just one day at a time, and let both the past and the future take care of themselves.

Chapter 12

Advice from Parents and Patients

Many receive advice; only the wise profit by it.

—PUBLILIUS SYRUS

Someone who is handicapped or who is the parent of a handicapped child has insights that even professionals who have spent years working with handicapped patients can never have. Because of this I interviewed several parents of handicapped children for this chapter, asking them about what they thought was most important in raising a child with a handicap. I also asked patients with handicaps similar questions. They were willing to share the problems as well as the joys in raising a handicapped child, and insights into what being handicapped means.

Marsha Longdon, the mother of a child with multiple handicaps had three pieces of advice:

"Even if you are smart or semi-smart, you get overwhelmed.

"Hang in there until you find the right doctor.

"Never quit!"

Cathy Dressler, a parent I met recently, talks about her five-year-old son, Philip.

On what having a child with birth defects means:

"Although I have nothing to compare it with, I think for the most part being told in the delivery room your child has birth defects does not significantly affect the way you feel about your child. The love, the bonding, caring affections, are still very strong, and the defects in no way distance you from your child.

"The one area that may be different is in expectations. We have no ambitions for our son other than to allow him to live to the fullest of his capabilities.

"The hardest thing is getting information: information on which to base medical decisions; for example, Who does this surgery? What is the success rate? Who *else* does this surgery? And the second kind of information is practical, such as how to toilet-train a child with an imperforate anus."

Brian Keith Walker, a young man on crutches because of polio at age two, had several things to share:

"If you don't spoil your handicapped child, life won't be so hard because there is lots of rejection to deal with. You need a feeling of self-worth to be independent, and life is more challenging if someone isn't always giving things to you.

"You can't change your disability, but you can change other things. If you're spoiled, it leaves you bitter and hostile and makes you helpless. It's important to remember that people think just because you are on crutches that you are retarded or 'bad in the head.' Your mind is not funny just because your legs don't function.

"Parents of normal children often don't want their kids to play with a handicapped child. When I was little, they thought I had something contagious.

"People assume you can't do things without even asking."

Holly Biancucci, the mother of a lovely seven-year-old with spinal atrophy says:

"To a new mother there will come a time of acceptance, but you will be a different and, yes, a better person because of the child you have. You will see the world in a different light. Problems that are great to others seem minor to you.

"There are hard times. I get tired of all the questions. I would like to have a printed sheet to pass out to everyone. And the look I occasionally see in my child's eyes when she sees others running. But it will do no good to dwell on the negative, and pity is the very worst!

"We do have a lot of support within the small area where we live. Sometimes, though, I think Lauren gives more to them than they give to her."

Nadine Fowler, the mother of a wonderful girl named Kelly, writes:

"As for my response to her disease at the beginning, I can honestly say my initial reaction was not 'Why me or why her?' but I found it much more productive to channel my energies into coping with the problem than to grieve over it. I set out to find out exactly what we were dealing with, the prognosis, and, most important, what we could do for her.

"She has never been taught to feel sorry for herself or to let others feel sorry for her.

"My mother once said that Kelly doesn't know she's handicapped, and that's the best way to describe her outlook.

"Kelly is more than willing to try to manipulate, cajole, persuade, or con other people into doing things for her. It is a continual battle for me to circumvent her attempts to find the easy way out and be lazy.

"Don't be afraid to urge, coax, push, prod, or shove if necessary."

In answer to what advice she would give the parents of a handicapped child, this mother made three points:

"Face reality and learn all you can for the sake of your child. Don't become a basket case; it won't help your child.

"Be patient. Progress can be and often is slow.

"Don't sell your child's capabilities short. Encourage every step of the way and help them to believe in themselves."

Roxanne Sowell, the mother of Kathy—a special ten-year-old with myositis—says:

"To me the bottom line is that society teaches us to be selfish and run away from problems and responsibilities. But if you handle responsibilities, such as caring for a handicapped child, you're the winner, and the rewards are fantastic. The people who walk away lose terribly.

"It's an inner accomplishment, not an outer one. The world may think you are the loser, but good guys do finish first.

"I think you have to have an inner spiritual strength that helps you to know you are doing the right thing. When you do the right thing, other things just fit together."

Janette Raybin, the mother of Garrett, a handsome fifteen-year-old with a rare muscle disease, told me about how she persisted in finding the right diagnosis. Most physicians told her, "Don't come back. We don't know what your son has," and "Don't bother us." She wrote to all the medical centers she could throughout the country and still did not get an answer until this year, when we first met.

When I asked her how she had raised such a normal, emotionally healthy young man with so little medical support, she replied:

"I didn't treat Garrett any differently from any other child. What he could do was fine. I was just happy that he could walk. I have never cared if he made a team. I was just happy that he wasn't in a wheelchair.

"The worst time was at age seven after an insensitive doctor made some depressing statements in front of my son. Garrett came home and kicked and screamed. I said, 'Look, everybody has something wrong that they have to live with even if it doesn't show. Your cousin can't read, someone else has a hearing aid, and someone else wears glasses. This is your thing.' Since then he has never complained."

Jennifer Mackey, the mother of a perky little boy with congenital muscular dystrophy, has started a book of her own, but graciously allowed me to share excerpts with you. They give insight into some of the struggles and triumphs parents of a handicapped child may experience.

Her child, Ian, recently had major surgery, and she described some of her thoughts before and during his hospitalization, when she stayed with him. As she packed for the hospital, she noted:

"I needed to keep my mind busy on most anything instead of just relaxing to confront some of the fears and anxieties I had about leaving for perhaps a full month. Leaving something familiar, your support system, your husband, your other child, and going into an environment where there are no known faces and a whole different division of educated people."

Her thoughts about relating to medical professionals:

"I think it is also important for a parent to get on an emotional level with the professionals, with the doctors, the nurses, the therapists, whoever it might be—to let them know that this is tough, it's not easy. There will be times when it will be emotionally trying, and it is important for the parent to be 100 percent high energy, to realize that their response level might be slower because they are going through a lot, so the parent has to be patient and sometimes go ahead and discuss those emotions."

About keeping a brave face:

"What is that stuff that I'm holding back? What kind of things am I not letting come through? Am I afraid that I will go out of my mind if I let down my guard? Am I just tired? Am I not accepting reality?"

About crying:

"We can cry on the surface, but to really open up our hearts and let it out, we don't. And why don't we? I'm so scared that if I start I'm never going to stop. I don't know if I'm going to go out of my mind. It's this huge vessel that is so full of so much emotion. I know psychologically it's not good to hold it in, and I should go through the pain and let it out, adjust to it."

About the eleven days in the hospital with her son: "It's been a long stretch of a different reality, a world unto itself, looking at other children, other children that suffer, parents that are in limbo, parents that have done everything they could and still feel inadequate, still feel lost, still feel confused, still feel angry, still want to know why."

About coming home:

"I came home thinking I was exactly the same person as when I left and I fought against my husband who said no, that I had changed. I seemed distant. I had gone through a soul searching for two and a half weeks and my husband was not involved in that."

About the hospital experience:

"The hospital experience, spending time with other families, other parents, sharing ideas, sharing emotions—it has changed me. When I was there I thought how great that people get to the core of their feelings right off the bat, knowing that I could share these feelings with others, and that they were right there for me. It's incredible how quickly you develop real meaningful relationships in a situation like that. You get right on to the real business.

"As I left, several people said that they would miss my energy. They said, 'You have changed the whole environment. Thank you for your strength.' Just incredible compliments, and I'm hoping that if I could have actually done that for people—who in return, of course, did the same for me—I want to try. And I'm hoping I can remember or try to remember what it was exactly that was so helpful. I mean, we can give lots of strength without really seeing the truth because it's only through real honesty with ourselves in this kind of situation, with a handicapped kid, that we gain our greatest strength and greatest understanding.

"I realized how important I am and how capable I am. And how much I really know about my child and what is best for my child in that hospital situation. And, in fact, in everyday life."

Ann Gervasi, the aunt of a teenager with cerebral palsy, sent me some important insights. She has cared for Thad, her nephew, since he was a small boy. He is one of the most severely afflicted cerebral palsy patients that I have had, and yet he has turned out to be a special and unusual young man. Ann had this advice to parents who have a special child:

"Please try not to become depressed or frustrated but enjoy him or her. And most of all treat your child like any of your other children as much as you can. Your handicapped child will demand more of your time, but thanks be to God there is now a lot of good help out there to help you cope with some of your child's needs.

"It is so important for your child to have the proper therapy, whether it be physical therapy, speech or occupational therapy, or all three. But it must be started as early as possible and be carried on religiously throughout the growing period and longer if necessary. Don't ever be passive and accept the opinion that 'therapy won't be of any value to him.' This simply is not true!

Every little amount helps, but it must be consistent. I know now that Thad would have been much better physically had I persisted in therapy with him and not listened to the 'experts.'

"Always keep in mind when you start feeling sorry for yourself that this tedious job you were called on to perform could be turned around. Any of us might be in a disabled state. How would we handle that, and how would we want to be handled? Count your blessings and be thankful."

Thad's aunt had a lot to say about school for a handicapped child. Thad first attended school at the age of nine. Before this he had never been separated from his parents. He was totally dependent on them for all his needs, and the first day of school was really a traumatic experience for this child:

"When he started school and was left alone, he became hysterical. He gradually adjusted, and I was content to have him in this protective environment. However, I wish now that he had never been in that particular environment and had been integrated into a classroom right from the beginning. It was very difficult for him to enter an integrated program.

"We have had much fun and much quality time with Thad, who is a loving person. He really cares about everyone and always remembers special days like birthdays and anniversaries. I am amazed when he remembers these dates, because I tend to forget more often than not. He always thinks of getting a gift for someone or asks me to make a call to see how someone is getting along. He has an infectious laugh and is quick to pick up the punch line of a joke.

"On the other side of the coin, he's had some pretty frustrating times. He hated his body as he became a teenager and felt that if he couldn't walk there was nothing else left for him. This started when a doctor gave him the glorious hope that with a series of therapy he would be walking using a walker. Then this was dropped with no explanation, and naturally, he became really depressed.

"Special equipment has also been a source of frustration, and 'custom-made' seems to be a preconceived design with just a few alterations. With all the research and expertise, most equipment is still primitive."

* * *

The parent of a favorite teenage patient who is a postaccident paraplegic shared some valuable thoughts:

"When my daughter was hurt, another woman said something to me that I didn't believe at the time but never forgot. She said, 'A lot of the hurt goes away, and it does get better after one year, two years, or four years.' Time does heal.

"I think parents need to remember that your life and your child's life are not less valuable because the child has been hurt and is in a wheelchair.

"Actually, I believe my daughter is in a better position to do something for others and for her community now, since the accident. You need to turn a horrible, horrible thing into something that will do good. Use it as an opportunity.

"Reading Norman Cousins's book about healing by laughing and learning to laugh even while grieving a lot helped both my daughter and me through the first few months I think. Also Elisabeth Kübler-Ross's book talking about the stages of grieving helped, and I could see us going through those stages. I guess we still are."

In answer to my question about whether she cried in front of her daughter, she said only once or twice. In general she said she tried to have her makeup on and to put on a cheerful face, particularly in the hospital.

She felt that the single most important thing that pulled her through, other than her supportive family and friends, was her spiritual strength.

Her daughter was twelve when she was injured, and I asked this young lady how she came through such a terrible ordeal so cheerfully. This youngster is a wonderful, outgoing person whose visits I always enjoy. She said:

"I never felt that I had to go through a major transition, as my parents and relatives were so supportive. My religion helped a lot, too."

She had always been taught and felt, she said, that her life was a gift, as was the use of her legs. She was allowed to use that gift for twelve years and hoped one day would again.

She shared what I found a wise insight: that a parent's attitude should stay the same after a tragic happening, as the child is still the same. She agreed with her mother's decision that parents should try to cry in private but should be open about discussing their feelings of sorrow with their child. If parents can't be positive, then she felt they should stay away, as they convey their attitudes to their child.

Many physicians try to be compassionate, she felt, yet often seemed apologetic, pessimistic, and uninformed. Hope was not a commodity that many shared freely. She valued honesty by both her parents and her physicians.

Mandi Palfreyman is a bright, attractive teenager. She has cerebral palsy, and walking is slow and difficult for her. I look forward to her visits, and during her last one I asked how she handled the questions and stares of others so well.

"Generally, when people try to be helpful, it makes it more difficult for me. Some people pity me, I think, probably 'cause they think that I'm in pain all the time. Children are confused and often ask questions about my legs, especially small children. Recently, four separate children asked me why my shoes were so ugly. I was informed by one small boy, 'You know you walk like my grandpa, except he walks faster than you.' "

She is now working at a preschool and is a senior in high school, preparing for college—a real success story. Her mother wrote:

"Shoes have been a terrible problem because they wear out so quickly. We have finally found something called Shoe Goo that you can buy in sporting-goods stores. Tennis players use it to make their shoes last longer. I put it on at night or Mandi does, and her shoes now last four times as long.

"Sundays or special occasions are difficult because Mandi can't wear high heels, boots, or sandals. Try going to the beach in braces or squeaking around the halls at school when your braces have been in the rain.

"Mandi has been the most wonderful daughter, and we are so blessed to have her. She has made us laugh and cry, but most of all she has made us proud we are her parents. We love her very much and wish everyone could be touched by her sweet spirit!"

* * *

Rebecca Cushing, a small, attractive teenager with spinal atrophy, draws people to her with her warm smile and engaging manner. We have known each other as physician and patient for several years, and her visits have always been a special interlude in my days.

During her last visit I asked her what kept her spirit up in spite of severe weakness and being confined to a wheelchair.

"I like life a whole lot. The best part is meeting new people and thinking about your future. When I was little, my mom said, 'You can't dwell on being in a wheelchair, but you just have to do what you can.'

"The things that I get upset about are just stupid things. It's the little complications that bug me more than being in a wheelchair."

Her advice to parents:

"Don't hold back from letting your child do things, but don't push your kids either. Just let things happen."

From her experiences as a handicapped young person she has learned some important things:

"I found that most doctors don't have the time or don't want to take the time.

"When I had to hire my own attendant as a fifteen-year-old, I tried not to be shy about telling them personal things and what they would have to do. I had to make sure that they realized all my physical needs."

Rebecca has just been the assistant director of her school play, and she is looking forward to majoring in theater in college.

Jill Evans, a twenty-two-year-old with spina bifida, had several things she wanted to share with parents. About teasing:

"Children between third and sixth grades can be very cruel because they don't understand differences. By helping your child understand that kids grow out of teasing and letting them talk about it at home, they can make it through this bad time."

About trying new things: She felt she was not encouraged to try new things but decided that she was going to do something new at least once. Then, if she couldn't do it, she couldn't. She started roller-skating against her parents' wishes and was taken to the doctor's office to be told it was dangerous for her. Instead everyone there was overjoyed and bragged to all around about her new ability! She felt parents need to encourage their handicapped children to try new things and to be ready to lift their spirits if they find they can't do something.

In the area of emotions, Jill feels that all of us, but particularly handicapped children, should know how to express our emotions and not keep them bottled up so that they explode all at once. She believes crying is important as it is needed, and a handicapped child certainly has a right to cry.

About parenting, she feels the hardest part is letting go.

Chapter 13

Special Needs

Let independence be our boast,
Ever mindful what it costs.

—JOSEPH HOPKINSON

Your handicapped child will probably have some special needs. Clothing may have to be altered to go over braces or body jackets, or you may have to have some clothes custom-made. Your child may also have to have special equipment ordered from medical-supply houses. It is often difficult to learn where and how to purchase such special equipment and how to use it, but many people can help—other parents, medical personnel, and home-care agencies. However, there is something more important than finding resources for special equipment and clothing.

The first thing you must do before ordering any equipment or considering special adaptations is to put a single goal at the top of your list. The goal is this: *Any special clothing or equipment you get should make your child as independent as possible.* Keep this goal in mind, as it's easy to get caught up in buying things that seem to offer either help or comfort. Unnecessary gadgets can just clutter up your life, cost extra money, and not help your child to develop as much independence as possible. Children who are independent, who can do for themselves, feel capable and proud. Such children naturally feel good about themselves.

When you plan to alter clothing or buy a new piece of special equipment, first ask yourself if this will help your child become more independent and gain self-mastery. You can use this as a general yardstick in making decisions about any special items you are considering purchasing.

A second important factor is that the special equipment also helps you. As the parent of a handicapped child, you already carry a heavy responsibility. Find ways, if you can, of lightening this burden by avoiding unnecessary work. Anything that helps your child become more independent will help you as well by saving time and energy. Your goal is to save your energy and time to spend with your child and do things for yourself and your family.

Help for you is critical in one particular area—that is, in lifting your child if necessary. You need to train yourself or be trained to lift your child—or any heavy weight such as a wheelchair—properly. To lift, bend your knees to get a grip on the object or child. *Don't* bend your back. There are specific exercises that can be done to keep your back and abdominal muscles strong. These are particularly important for mothers who may have weak stomach muscles from carrying a child during pregnancy.

As a physician, I worry that the mothers of handicapped children will end up with weak and painful backs. Your child needs a strong, healthy mother and father, and you need a strong back, not one that aches. Use special aids when you can, especially in the bathroom, where you may be forced to do more lifting. There are special pieces of equipment available, such as Hoyer or sling lifts, but unfortunately many of these are too large to fit into the usual home bathroom.

The stepfather of one wheelchair patient devised an overhead ceiling track attached to a hydraulic lift. This fit into the small bathroom in their house and worked very well. The same generous dad helped several other parents build these in their bathrooms.

Equipment

Remember that any equipment you consider should be used to help achieve the goal of making your child as independent as possible. Try to ask as many questions as you can think of when considering a purchase, and do some exploring on your own. Many times something that is standard in one area is unknown or unused in another, even with telecommunications and our advanced information devices.

Occupational therapists, physical therapists, rehabilitation doctors (physiatrists), and other medical personnel familiar with handicapped children will make suggestions about your child's specific needs. Within the new fields of rehabilitation and biomechanics, wonderful devices are being developed. In the years to come we are going to see in general use marvelous equipment to aid the handicapped, run by tiny computers. A few of these are already in the working stages. Because most such devices are still experimental, they are expensive. Sometimes, though, financial help is available for specialized equipment through a specific agency, and you can always ask.

Another encouraging trend is that many medical schools and universities are establishing bioengineering and biomechanical medical departments. A specialist in the rehabilitation department in a medical school or hospital or the orthopedic department in a large city hospital may be able to tell you about some new developments and resources. There are now, too, rehabilitation engineering departments, and some universities and private companies are working on highly specialized equipment to aid handicapped individuals.

In our area we are fortunate to have a creative orthotist named Wally Motlock at the Center for Orthotics. He makes all kinds of braces and wheelchair adaptations to meet children's special needs. I asked him for some words of advice about how to evaluate equipment that is made specifically for a child and how to choose an orthotist. His suggestions were the following:

1. View each piece of equipment (braces, wheelchairs, standing tables, and so on) as a tool to make something better. This means that you must first identify what that something is! Too many times this process is reversed or omitted, and the equipment is acquired before proper analysis. This ends up creating more problems than it solves.

2. Parents and family ultimately make the final decision. Like any wise buyers, they should consider suggestions from professionals and others and then develop *their own plan of action*. Armed with their plan of action, they can then proceed with implementation piece by piece until they reach their goal.

3. It is best if the orthotist and other suppliers are included in the overall advisory group in the beginning, but if this is not possible, parents can discuss their plan with several orthotists to see which person is best suited and experienced to help them carry out their plan.

4. Regarding equipment evaluations: With present-day fabrication techniques, there is no excuse for poorly fitting devices. Don't settle for equipment that doesn't do what it is supposed to, especially after you have identified the need for it in your plans and participated in its design and fabrication. Get it adjusted, modified, or reworked until it works properly.

I would add some general points: If any blisters or red areas develop, particularly with new braces or a back jacket, you need to notify both your physician and the equipment maker. Children with decreased sensation, as in spina bifida or paraplegia, can develop skin breakdown and ulcers, which take a long time to heal if there is too much pressure. They simply cannot feel the friction and thus will tolerate it more than an ordinary child.

Braces

When I moved from one part of the state to another to run a handicapped program, I discovered that heavy, old-fashioned braces were still being used for children with orthopedic problems. This was at a time when the lightweight plastic braces were available. These newer braces are not only easier to keep clean, but they also weigh only about a third as much. You can imagine what a difference this makes to a child whose muscles are already weak.

These lightweight braces fit into ordinary shoes, even sneakers. To be able to wear the same kind of shoes as the other kids is very important to a child who must wear braces.

If the proper material is not used, however, plastic braces can become unbearable in hot weather. Be sure to ask about this before any braces are ordered, especially if you live in an area that gets hot and humid.

Lightweight braces are particularly important for a small child or one who has extensive muscle weakness. If your doctor is not aware of these newer bracing techniques, see a specialist. Consider consulting an orthopedic surgeon, a physiatrist (a physiatrist is a medical doctor who has had special training in rehabilitation medicine), or get a consultation from a progressive orthotist (brace maker).

When you look for an orthotist, choose one who has had experience working with children. Your child's needs will differ enormously from those of an adult, and children's braces also have to be modified frequently to keep up with their growth. This can certainly be a major expense, but often you can obtain such equipment or modifications through funding from special children's programs and agencies like the Muscular Dystrophy Association. The important point to remember about seeking help in making special-equipment purchases is to *make your payment arrangements before you order the equipment, so that your child won't have to wait for the braces*.

Wheelchairs

Many physicians simply write a prescription for a wheelchair, unaware that detailed information is needed before a wheelchair is ordered. For example, wheelchairs have many features, such as detachable arms and elevating footrests. The precise height of the chair and its arms, the width and length of the seat, and other measurements should be stated exactly. Because of this, children must be specifically measured for a wheelchair, as they will spend many hours in it. If a wheelchair is not the proper size—if, for example, it is wider than necessary, it will not go through many doors—or if it is improperly fitted, it can increase contractures or tightness of the muscles. This means that the wrong wheelchair for a child could actually lead to further deformity or other difficulties.

Wheelchairs come in different sizes, and there are also electrical and manual wheelchairs. An electric wheelchair can give a wonderful sense of freedom and independence to children who cannot use their legs or who have limited ability to walk. Many parents say that when children have a new electric wheelchair, suddenly they are never at home and have to be called in for meals just like other children. Another recent innovation is a stand-up wheelchair. It resembles a regular wheelchair but has a mechanism that pushes a person to a standing position, allowing a child to do things in an upright position. (How nice to be able to see the world occasionally from a standing position rather than always from a sitting posture.)

A wheelchair is an expensive piece of equipment. As with any other major purchase, do some research before you order one.

It is possible to have modifications made to an existing piece of equipment. This is usually done by the service people at a good medical-supply house, but you should make sure first that the person you are dealing with is knowledgeable. Good resources to contact for information and advice on equipment are physical therapists, occupational therapists, and physiatrists. Ask other parents of handicapped children, too. They usually know a lot about special-equipment needs and specialists. Try to find professionals in these areas who have specific experience in working with children.

In general, a prescription has to be written by a physician for any special piece of equipment. This prescription makes special-equipment purchases tax-deductible as well as payable by insurance if you have that coverage. Insurance companies will not honor bills for equipment without a physician's prescription and a letter of medical necessity.

In orthotic centers, there are now wheelchair inserts and adaptations that can be made to make life a great deal easier for wheelchair-confined children and teenagers. The new stand-up wheelchairs are good for helping keep a child's legs straight. A child can watch television or study in a standing position—this keeps the leg bones straight and well calcified.

Standing Tables (Tilt Tables)

Standing tables allow a handicapped child or adult to be supported in an upright position. It is very important for children who sit in a wheelchair most of the day to be kept standing for at least three hours daily. This is necessary to prevent bone fractures and to keep the spine straight. If no weight is placed on the bones day after day, they become thin and can break easily (osteoporosis). The same things happen to elderly people and those who are bedridden.

Rosie was a child we saw one day in spina bifida clinic. At twelve, she was quite large for her age. She had broken her large leg bone or femur sometime before. The bone was not healing, and our orthopedist suggested increasing her calcium and watching her to see what would happen. After several visits, when the bone still showed no signs of healing, we almost gave up. Then it occurred to me that since she was in a wheelchair, her leg bones would be very thin, or what we call osteoporotic. The circulation to these bones is poor, and because they have no weight put on them, they are just not as healthy as they would be otherwise.

I suggested to Rosie's mother and the orthopedist that Rosie be put in a standing frame or on a tilt table daily for as long as she could tolerate it. Gradually X rays showed the bone beginning to heal.

Keeping your child in an upright position for a period each day in braces or on a tilt or standing table has many benefits. Many specialists believe that standing helps prevent curvature of the spine, or scoliosis. Preventing scoliosis also helps decrease a loss in lung function. When there is marked curvature in the spine, it is harder for the air to get in and out of the lungs. Such restriction can lead to more colds, pneumonias, and other respiratory infections. A downward cycle could be avoided by insisting that your child spend time upright each day.

Discuss with your child's doctor or with the group of specialists you consult the need for equipment to help your child stand upright. Beware that there is often a real difference of opinion among doctors. So, once again, find one specialist you trust to help make the final decision with you.

Bathroom Aids

Helping a handicapped child bathe or go to the toilet may necessitate a lot of lifting for the parents. Ideally a bathroom should be large enough so that you can transfer your child from a wheelchair, for example, directly to the toilet. Transfer boards are small smooth boards that allow a child to slide easily from wheelchair to toilet seat, making this a relatively easy procedure for you and your child.

Unfortunately, most bathrooms are far from ideal. Small or crowded and poorly arranged, the average bathroom is not big or roomy enough for special equipment to aid in lifting. If you can find a way to use special equipment in your bathroom, it is especially useful in encouraging independence and preventing back injury. If you cannot find a way to use aids, be sure to be careful when lifting your child.

A variety of special equipment is made for bathroom use, including special toilet chairs, bath chairs, bathtub lifts, and bathtub rails. All of these can make life easier for you and your child. When used correctly, this equipment can make a child feel both steadier and more independent. It can also make all the difference in your day-to-day energy as a parent. Remember, a healthy mother or father with a good working back is essential for your child, so protect your own backs just as you protect your child.

Also, keep in mind that a bathtub is slippery when wet. Always use a rubber mat, nonskid appliques, or even a towel in the bottom of the tub. Bath chairs or a wooden box or stool can offer stability for a child who has problems with coordination, balance, or vision.

Bladder Controls and Aids

Urinary-tract or kidney and bladder problems usually accompany paraplegic, quadraplegic, and most spina bifida children. Many children with an incomplete or mild paraplegia or spina bifida can be taught to empty their bladders approximately every two hours and so keep dry. Others have to use a catheter or tube to empty their own bladder. These are primarily used with girls, though in some centers boys are also taught to catheterize themselves. In girls, this can be done with a glass or other catheter in a nonsterile way, so that it can be done at school and elsewhere. I have had bright little five-year-old girls learn to catheterize themselves well by having a mirror held up for them to locate the opening to the bladder (called the urethra).

Boys can be fitted about age five or so with a snug bag over the penis connected by a tube to a leg bag. This can then be emptied when necessary. There are several different types, and I have recently discovered one called the Byram Pubic Pressure Urinary device, which is very good.

A condition exists called sacral agenesis, in which children may have some, but not complete, control of their bowel and bladder. I have seen these patients referred to psychiatrists and counselors because parents thought they were being naughty by soiling and wetting, when in fact it was beyond the child's physical ability to maintain complete self-control.

One six-year-old girl from another state came because her mother knew something was wrong with her, but she could not convince her doctors. They thought the child was wetting and soiling as a way of acting out. The child had very poor closure of the rectal sphincter (opening to the bowel) on rectal examination, and an X ray of her lower back showed a classical sacral agenesis, or absence of part of the "tailbone."

It is unfortunate that in many medical schools today rectal examinations are not being taught as part of a routine yearly or new physical examination. Because of this, children with this problem are often missed and not diagnosed or helped.

A high spiking fever may be the first indication that something is wrong with one of these children, as there can be associated urinary-tract infections. If a urinalysis or urine culture is not done, the cause of the fever can easily be missed, too. My teaching has always been that a child should have urine examined each year. This has paid off many times with patients. Good, simple, thorough medicine still wins in the long run, despite all the advances in genetic engineering and highly technical research we have today.

Infection in the urinary tract in both paraplegic and spina bifida children is a common and worrisome problem. Periodically, urine should be cultured to check for infection. Many of these children will have a continual low-grade infection in their bladder. If they have no other symptoms, this should not be a problem. However, a physician who knows about kidney and urinary-tract infections should be seen periodically.

Some children have to be kept on what we call maintenance antibiotics. This means they need to take a low dose of medicine most of the time to keep them from getting really sick with a kidney infection. A kidney infection is called pyelonephritis. X rays of the kidneys or intravenous pyelograms (IVPs) should also be done at least every two years to be sure the kidneys are not being damaged. One of the most important things that doctors look for on these X rays is if there is so-called reflux, which means urine going back up toward the kidneys. This is a common cause of infection.

One of the problems I see, particularly with girls who have either spina bifida or are paraplegic, is that they try to decrease the amount they drink in order to stay dry. In turn, this can cause a problem with infection or kidney stones at some time.

Children can be encouraged to drink plenty of fluids by having them carry folding cups and small plastic water bottles. It sometimes helps a child drink more if the two of you together set a daily goal of so many glasses or cups of water. Explain to your child the importance of this, and see if you can make a game out of it.

It is essential that school personnel understand bowel or bladder problems, too. Without such understanding, children can be punished for not having control or may be forced to go into a broom closet or similar place to change their diapers (I have seen this happen). To avoid putting your child in this position, ask specific questions at the beginning of the school year or whenever you change to a new school, such as:

1. Who will help my child with the bowel and bladder problems?
2. Where are the diapers or leg bags going to be changed?
3. How often will it be done?
4. What are the facilities for getting water in the school?
5. Do the other children in the classroom and the teacher accept the problem, or is the child always going to be left out of things?
6. Are there any other children in the school with similar problems, or has the school ever had a child with a similar problem?

In the past I have found it is usually necessary for parents to talk with the teacher, principal, and school nurse at the beginning of each year to get all this organized and to pinpoint answers to these questions. It is also a good idea for the physician caring for your child to do this, too. When a school knows that the physician is closely observing what is going on, school personnel tend to be more particular about what happens with a child. If your physician has neither the time nor the interest to do this, perhaps the nurse or other members of your child's medical team can take responsibility for seeing that it is done. Ongoing communication with the school is necessary not only in this area but in all areas, since a child spends so much of the day at school.

Colostomies

A colostomy is a surgically created opening from the intestine to the abdomen that allows fecal material to be collected in an external bag. Colostomy care is a highly specialized field that changes often as new and better products are developed and manufactured. The best advice I have for you if you have this special need is to find an enterostomal therapist in your area who is knowledgeable about colostomy care and can work with you.

There are also special ostomy groups you can contact for more information as well as helpful articles and special materials. See the Bibliography as well as the specialized agencies in Appendix C.

Bowel Programs

If a child has spina bifida or is a paraplegic, there may be partial or complete damage to the nerves that go to the bowel, and the child may need help for regular bowel movements. Soiling or having bowel movements in his or her clothes can quickly make any child an unwelcome classmate or playmate.

I had one spina bifida patient whose teacher required that he sit outside his classroom in the hall when he was "smelly." You can imagine the emotional problems this created.

For a child to have regular bowel movements, it is essential that the right foods are eaten and bowel movements are attempted at a regular time. The important foods for children with bowel problems are protein (fish, poultry, meat, or cheese) and lots of fiber-containing foods (nuts, vegetables, and grains). If the stools are too loose, laxative foods should be decreased. Laxative foods are all the fruits except for apples and bananas, which are constipating, or make stools hard. Lots of the refined-sugar-containing foods also have a laxative effect.

By keeping a few days' food diary, you can check what your child eats over a period of time and make the right changes to help regulate the firmness of the stools. When I work with parents, I have them mail or bring the food diaries in, so we can go over them together. Parents are often surprised at what they find out by keeping a simple food diary for a few days to a week.

One spina bifida patient had many loose stools each day, and his mother said he had never been able to have normal bowel movements. When I asked about his diet history, I found out that he love a sugared breakfast cereal and ate it all day. When this was stopped and his diet slowly improved, with a few guidelines, his bowel movements became more solid. With the use of a daily suppository to regulate his bowel movement, he was able to stop wearing diapers. You can imagine how delighted his mother was.

Another patient with spina bifida was referred to me as a teenager. The pediatric surgeon was planning to do a colostomy, but first he thought he would refer her to me to see if I could help and thus avoid surgery. It took lots of work on her part and mine, but we did eventually get her bowel movements controlled, so she didn't need surgery. Her problem, like that of many spina bifida and paraplegic patients, was that she had had long-standing constipation that had to be cleared up before we could start her on a good bowel program. She loved salami and junk foods, and it took a long while to get her to eat good protein, grains, fruits, and vegetables. She still occasionally backslides—a typical teenager, but she is a much happier one because a colostomy wasn't necessary.

Sometimes it is more than a change to a good diet or a sensible bowel program that a child needs.

Stephen had a very low-level spina bifida with minimal findings on his physical examination. From his tests and a clinical examination, I couldn't understand why he was unable to go to the bathroom normally. Then, as I got to know the family, important facts began to emerge. His parents were recently divorced, and his mother was spending a great deal of time with a new boyfriend. The boy's soiling became worse and worse despite all our combined efforts. We suggested counseling to the parents, but they were not interested. Finally the father asked if Stephen could live with him for a trial period, and the mother was delighted. Father and son began to develop a close, warm relationship, and Stephen's bowel problem slowly disappeared. He didn't need a bowel program—he just needed some loving, firm parenting.

Another handsome, bright but lonely teenage boy with spina

bifida was referred to me. As a little boy his doctor had not helped him develop a bowel program, so the child grew into adolescence still wearing diapers. Naturally this isolated him from others, and he was intensely lonely. By the time he came to me, both the emotional and physical patterns were set and hard to change. We tried for a long time, but made little headway. I often wonder what his life will be like, and feel badly that he did not receive earlier intervention when it could have made such a difference.

It is unfortunate that few doctors have any interest in helping to work out a bowel plan. It isn't a difficult thing to do; it just takes some knowledge of nutrition and a little time and effort.

I try to get all the children I treat to have a bowel movement that is firm. Then nightly after dinner they are given a Dulcolax or glycerin suppository. Once they are old enough, they can use it themselves. When this is done regularly and combined with a proper diet, there should be few problems. One other important addition is that plenty of fluid is required for normal stools (for all of us). This means about six to eight glasses a day. Bulk formers can also be used if needed. Metamucil is one that can be bought without a prescription.

Another small but important thing is to make sure that when little children are sitting on the toilet, their feet can touch the floor or some support. If they cannot push against something, it is more difficult for them to have a bowel movement. You can buy a small stool or even use a wooden box so their feet can rest on a firm surface.

Some children also need side rails on the toilet seat to make them feel secure if they have poor balance. If your child seems fearful, try to be understanding and do what you can to provide a sense of balance and security.

Psychogenic Megacolon (Encopresis)

This condition occurs in about 3 percent of the children in this country. If your child has any bowel or bladder problems, you should know about this problem.

Mark was the brother of one of my spina bifida patients who often came to the clinic with his mother and sister. One day the mother told me her worries about Mark. He was soiling, and she thought he was just being naughty, as he was still very much a baby. They had seen a psychologist and psychiatrist, but no one had really examined him clinically. The mother wondered if he, too, might have a mild form of spina bifida. The X rays of his lower back were normal, but his rectal examination was definitely not normal. He had such a large amount of constipation that he was simply soiling or leaking around it, and it took time and many enemas and laxatives to get him cleaned out.

Mark's problem started when he was a baby. His mother said he had some mild constipation because he loved milk so much. Because of the constipation he developed a painful crack or fissure around the rectum. This caused him to start holding back on his bowel movements. Thus began a whole cycle that ended up with his retaining a large amount of stool. This is common in babies. In addition, Mark had emotional problems. His parents were divorced, and his teenage sister with spina bifida had many problems that took a good deal of the mother's time and attention.

To get Mark to have a normal bowel movement required a great deal of work over a long time period. First we had to get his bowel back to a normal size, as it had become so badly stretched by the large amount of constipated material. Once we did this, we had to get him started on a good diet and a regular bowel program. We also got some counseling started for the mother and son, and over time—quite a long time—he began to grow and mature. He no longer acted like the baby in the family but demanded and received respect, and his bowel problems cleared up as he matured. It was great fun to watch him grow and change.

This story points out, once more, the value of a rectal examination to help clarify the source of problems. In Mark's case, we saw him when he was still quite young and we could really make a difference.

Clothing

Time is a precious commodity for most families with a handicapped child, so many things need to be done. If clothes are not functional and easy to put on, you can waste a great deal of time trying to dress your child. This is particularly hard early in the morning, when everyone has too little time to get to work or school and may be tired and sleepy as well.

Clothing for a handicapped child must often meet specific needs. For example, clothes might have to fit over or under back braces. With a little research and effort on your part, you can adapt regular clothing to your child's special needs. There are some publications that can help you with this process. (See Glorya Hall, *Source Book for the Disabled*, 1979.) You can also get pamphlets from specific agencies, nurses, physical and occupational therapists. Certain mail-order supply houses also carry special clothing for handicapped people's needs. Parents of other handicapped children might have some good suggestions for you as well, so check among your resource network.

One simple change that is easy and helpful is to use Velcro fasteners instead of buttons and zippers. Zippers and buttons are usually too difficult to handle for a child who has cerebral palsy or one with limited muscle strength. And in general, clothing that opens in front is easier for most physically handicapped children. One-piece clothing is difficult for some children to manage by themselves, and since independence is your goal, it is important, always, that handicapped children do as much as they can by themselves. This encourages a child's feelings of independence and self-worth. Avoiding unnecessary frustration in the first place can be a good starting place for independence and self-esteem.

Fortunately, clothing has become more comfortable and varied. Jogging suits or warm-up pants, for example, slip easily over braces or paralyzed legs. Some are costly, but many low-cost family clothing stores carry a line of inexpensive sports clothing, or "sweats" as they're called. An added attraction is that these clothing items are usually brightly colored and easy to launder.

Children and teenagers who have little or no bladder control frequently need diapers. Large diapers are sometimes hard to find in stores—you may have to order them through a medical-supply house or special catalogue. Check a large local drugstore first, though, since many now have a special-needs section near the pharmacy. If they do not have what you need, ask to talk with the owner or manager and see if the store will order these for you.

Because so much of your energy is focused on taking care of basic needs—food, clothing, and medical care—you can easily overlook the value of clothing to bring fun into a child's life. Without spending too much time or energy, see if you can find a few simple items to brighten up your child's wardrobe so that it is fun *and* functional.

Accident Prevention

Some special areas of concern arise with handicapped children that a parent might not think of because so much else demands time and attention. A most important one is accident prevention. The parents of handicapped children usually have so many things to do that they are unable to give much attention to preventing accidents. In addition, financial problems, worries, marital troubles, fatigue, and loneliness can all intensify stress levels so that more accidents are likely to occur around the home of a handicapped child.

In some ways accident prevention for handicapped children might be easier than for active children who have more physical capacities. A physically handicapped child often cannot move as quickly or easily as a nonhandicapped child. This gives you a little more control. Nonetheless, there are certain general guidelines you need to remember for accident prevention. And keep in mind that each age and stage of development has vastly different problems, as does each particular handicap. Below I have outlined some general guidelines:

1. Never leave a baby or child alone in the tub. (You can buy bath chairs or build support for children with poor balance. Even a wooden box or stool can support a child in a tub. However, the child must still not be left alone.)

2. Bath water must be tested, particularly for children with poor sensation (turn water heaters down to low).

3. Fire is a tremendous potential hazard for children who are blind or deaf or cannot move easily. You can buy smoke detectors inexpensively and install them with little effort. Children should also know what to do in case of fire, particularly if they are in a wheelchair or above the ground floor. Fire-resistant clothing and cigarette-ignition-resistant upholstered furniture both aid protection.

4. Hanging toys with strings and mobiles in a crib or playpen can catch a small toddler, particularly one with poor balance or limited dexterity.

5. Pacifiers around the neck on strings have caused strangulation and death.

6. Pacifiers that come apart can also cause choking.

7. Hungry children will eat or drink anything. This means that it is essential to avoid putting caustic substances in food bottles, containers, or unlabeled bottles. Also have all poisonous substances high up out of the way.

8. Keep polishes, dish powders, and other poisonous substances somewhere up high and not under the sink. (Dishwasher detergent can cause burns in the mouth and down into the esophagus.)

9. Children with head problems who fall frequently may need to wear a helmet.

10. Be sure all medicines are properly labeled and put out of reach. Remember that your children can learn to get to out-of-the-way places.

11. Vinyl on cribs and playpen rails that is chewed can come off and choke a child. Also, plastic coverings on disposable diapers can cause choking if swallowed.

12. Electrical outlets should be covered. (You can buy special covers for little money.)

13. Check toys for small parts that a child can swallow.

14. Check all electrical cords to make sure they are in good repair, with no frayed areas or wire showing.

15. When possible, unplug electrical cords from the appliances, not the wall—particularly coffeepots.

16. Tape or nail all rugs to the floor. (At hardware stores you can buy tape that is sticky on both sides to hold down your rugs.)

17. Have—and use—a gate at the top and bottom of all stairs.

18. Use a proper car seat with a seat belt for the appropriate age and weight of your child.

19. Seat belts also should be worn by children in wheelchairs.

20. Post emergency numbers near the phone.

Poison Center Telephone _____

Nearest Emergency Room Telephone _____

21. Have a one-ounce bottle of syrup of ipecac in the house to administer in case your child swallows the kind of poisonous substance that would not burn or destroy tissue if vomiting occurred.

22. Know CPR (cardiopulmonary resuscitation), particularly with children who have lung or seizure problems. The American Red Cross gives courses without charge to lay people, and your local hospital may do the same. Call around to see where you can learn this lifesaving skill.

23. Post the telephone numbers of doctors and an ambulance near or on the phone.

Ambulance Telephone _____

Doctor's Telephone _____

Times When Most Accidents Occur

As with many things in life, accidents run in patterns. And when you look at the list below, you'll see the logic of why this is the case. These are the danger times that accidents can happen:

1. Saturday mornings, when parents want to stay in bed and children are free to wander unsupervised
2. Dinnertime, when everyone is tired
3. Moving time, when hazardous substances can be readily available in boxes and everyone is too tired or distracted to supervise children adequately

Accidents also cluster around particular places in our homes and yards. You can probably add a few danger spots to this list.

1. Grandmother's purse or the purses of visitors who have no children
2. Grandmother's cupboards or bedside-table drawers
3. Grandparents' houses or the houses of other relatives or friends who have no young children
4. Open windows
5. Roofs
6. Open truck backs
7. Old stored refrigerators
8. Balconies
9. Stairs
10. Toy chest with a heavy lid or an airtight seal

It is a delicate balance for a parent to be careful and attentive without becoming unduly worried and overly cautious. If you remove as many of the potential household hazards as you can and keep a weather eye on your children to see what they are doing, you can usually keep them safe without constant warnings to be careful. Such continuous warnings can inhibit a child's explorations and natural curiosity, so that the child becomes fearful and regards the world as a dangerous rather than interesting and exciting place.

Hospitalizations

One of the sad but simple facts of life for a handicapped child is hospitalization for a variety of procedures. Though many handicapped children have been through the trauma of a rush to a hospital emergency room, even more worrisome for them can be the anticipation of surgery, chemotherapy, or some other treatment. A sudden emergency admission usually means that things happen so quickly, little time remains to think or worry. When the children know they will be hospitalized well in advance of the date, anticipation and anxiety can actually create additional problems.

I once stopped in on the night before surgery was scheduled to see a teenage patient who had been hospitalized for a relatively simple orthopedic procedure. His mother and I had both done our best to prepare him for the surgery so he wouldn't be anxious, but I knew that something was bothering him. When I asked what it was, he said that the nurse had told him he would probably have a hard time going to the bathroom the next day and might need a tube or catheter. I was upset that anyone would make such a statement, especially a registered nurse. I assured him that I had never had a teenager who had difficulty going to the bathroom after his particular kind of surgery.

Despite my assurances, the nurse's remark did its work. The young man could not void for two or three days after surgery because the power of suggestion was so strong. As you can imagine, that nurse never said anything like that to any of my patients again.

The anxiety of children or adolescents is difficult enough to handle, but the anxiety of parents is often even worse and can have a real effect on their child. Children can usually sense what a parent is feeling. If your child is about to be hospitalized, it is important to make yourself feel as comfortable as you can about the hospitalization. To do this, you will need as much information as you can gather. This will help you feel that you have some control and are not just sitting on the sidelines, letting others make all the decisions.

As the parent, you should be actively involved in the medical decision-making process, because you will have to bear the brunt of these decisions. Fortunately, these days parents are asking more questions and making doctors and hospitals more accountable.

Below is a list of some of the questions you may want to ask. Don't stop with these, though. Ask about whatever you need to. No individual should be beyond trying to answer the sincere questions a parent has about a child.

1. What is the nature of the procedure or surgery?
2. Who will do it?
3. What are the possible complications of such a procedure?
4. Who will be my contact person, and when is the best time to reach this person?
5. What are the hospital admission procedures?
6. Are we allowed to have a bed in the child's room, or is other inexpensive housing available in the hospital or nearby?
7. Can friends or family visit, and what are the hours?
8. How long will the hospitalization probably be?
9. If there is a surgical procedure, who will be the anesthetist and when will we meet the doctor before the procedure?
10. What are the financial arrangements that are necessary?
11. Is a second physician's opinion necessary? (Many insurance plans now require this for a surgical procedure.)
12. How long will my child be at home after the hospitalization?

13. Will physical or occupational therapy be needed at home?

14. Is schooling provided in the hospital?

15. Who will arrange schooling at home if it is needed?

16. If there are problems after my child is at home, whom do I contact and what is the number?

17. If the contact person is not available, is there a second name you can give me?

Once these questions have been answered, take some time to see how you really feel about the situation. You will always feel some anxiety, but you should have the feeling that the doctor performing the procedure is competent and caring and that the procedure is beneficial. If you have doubts, delay the procedure if it seems safe to do so, and check with another physician or other specialists.

Once your child has entered the hospital, the whole experience will be more positive if you do what you can to make sure he or she is comfortable. You might want to have your child visit the hospital and take a tour a few days before entering. If the hospital does not have a formal visiting program, ask your doctor to arrange for a visit. Many good books describe hospital stays, too. One, *Going to the Hospital* by Bettina Clark, is a pop-up book that is fun for smaller children. It might also help your child to do some role-playing with a make-believe surgical gown (a sheet halved and tied or pinned behind the neck is a close approximation), a doctor's kit, and maybe some inexpensive thin rubber gloves for the "surgeon."

Having your child talk with other children or teenagers who have had the same kind of surgery or treatment can reduce the child's fear—and yours as well. Ask your physician for the names of other families you can contact. You might also pick up some helpful hints from their parents on how to make the hospital stay feel as comfortable as possible.

It is important that a child be encouraged to take to the hospital special toys or a special blanket or pillow—anything the child loves and treasures. Hospitals should have toys and games that children can use—most do—but I remember one child who came with no toys, and the hospital staff provided none either. He was also by himself because he came from far away, and his family had to return home immediately. No one paid any attention to this child's loneliness, and I had to see that some games and books were taken to him.

Crayons, colored pencils, and make-it projects are perfect for a child in the hospital. Some hospitals have recreational therapists who plan activities for the patients, but don't count on this. You and other adult friends may be the only "recreational therapists" available to your child, so think ahead to plan ways of keeping the patient busy and happy.

You will need to tailor visits by friends and family to your child's needs. These differ from individual to individual. Too many visitors or a large group all at once can be tiring, as can a whole string of visitors coming one after the other. The best policy is to start with people the child loves best and have their visits spaced so your child can rest between.

Rest and quiet are the best medicine for maximal healing. The child needs to see you, but sometimes it isn't necessary for you to live at the hospital. Though many mothers feel they have to stay there the entire time, it may be just as important for you to get out of the hospital. If the nurses seem competent and your child seems happy with them, you may be doing everyone a favor—including your handicapped child—by going home.

I have seen mothers who literally lived in the same clothes for days with no adequate food or rest. This helps no one—the patient, the medical staff, the mother, or the family at home. Even if you feel uncomfortable returning to your home to stay before your child is released, you can certainly take time out to freshen up, visit friends or family members, or eat a good, nourishing meal out.

One thing to ask about in the hospital is the consistency of the nursing staff. Because many hospitals now use nurses from a registry rather than their own regular staff, there can be a large turnover in a single week. This means your child could have the same person for just a day or two and have no chance to be cared for by anyone who is there every day for several days at a time.

Another thing to be wary of is the tendency some children

have to suddenly become amazingly helpless when their parents are around. Little bumps become big concerns. A sore muscle becomes paralyzing, and the poor parent who is already worried becomes a slave to the child's whims. Often the clue that the child is exaggerating comes when the parent is out of the room or away from the hospital and acts in a more mature way. This usually means the nurses and other personnel can accomplish a lot more if you are not always hovering. Talk with the nurses, and see what they have to say about your child. If it sounds as if they are talking about a stranger, consider your own role in the relationship and think carefully about whether you are staying in the room for the child or for yourself.

One of the most disquieting things about being in the hospital environment is the medical terminology. It often sounds like gibberish. You will feel more comfortable and confident if you know some of the language of medical abbreviations that you are sure to see written on charts and exchanged between the medical staff. Here are some of the most common:

NPO: Nothing by mouth

STAT: Immediately

MICU: Medical intensive-care unit

PICU: Pediatric intensive-care unit

SICU: Surgical intensive-care unit

ICU: Intensive-care unit

ICN: Intensive-care nursery

NICN: Newborn intensive-care nursery

Monitor: To use instruments to measure and often visually record blood pressure, pulse, and so on

Vital signs: Blood pressure, pulse, respiratory rate

IV: Intravenous, or by vein

IM: Intramuscular, or in the muscles

IVP: Special kidney X ray taken after an injection into the vein

Upper GI: X ray of the upper intestinal tract or stomach and intestine

BE: Barium enema, or X ray of the lower bowel with a special enema preparation

Flat plate: A simple X ray of the abdomen

Infiltrate: Either an IV can infiltrate out of the vein or there can be an infiltrate in a lung

OT: Occupational therapist

PT: Physical therapist

Sepsis: Infection

IPPB: Intermittent positive pressure breathing

CAT Scan: Special detailed X ray study

EEG: Electrical test showing the brain waves

EKG: Electrical impulses recorded from the heart

EMG: Electrical impulses recorded from a muscle

SMA-6, 12, 25: Special blood-panel studies

Learning to take care of all your child's special needs—whether for clothing, equipment, unusual treatments, or hospitalizations—is going to make you a semi-specialist in many areas you once knew nothing about. If you're lucky, you will also have many opportunities to pass on what you have learned to other parents. Remember, though, that you are always the specialist where your child is concerned. You are the parent and the one who makes the decisions—along with lots of help from specialists in all the areas where you need it.

Chapter 14

Keeping Up on New Treatments, Medications, and Research

Hope springs exalting on eternal wing.

—ROBERT BURNS

Any parent of a handicapped child hopes for a breakthrough—some new information, equipment, or medication that will mean a chance for a change in the current diagnosis. Such things do happen in medicine. Research can lead to dramatic changes, so the hope is rooted in fact. Cures for deadly diseases have been discovered, and new medicines have suddenly changed lives for the better. Because of these possibilities, you should be vitally interested in any new developments that relate to your child's disability.

There are many ways to keep up to date on new medical findings. The most direct and effective is to contact an agency that specializes in your child's handicaps. Agencies now exist for almost every major handicap and condition and even for several that affect relatively few children (see Appendix C). Agencies that focus on a single problem usually publish a monthly newsletter with a section on new medical information. They also give out pamphlets with specific information on such things as clothing, special equipment, and traveling with your handicapped child. Many of these organizations, such as the Spina Bifida Association, sponsor parent groups as well, so there are many good reasons for contacting the local branch of an agency that covers your child's handicap.

A parent-support group offers another way to keep up with information. If the parent groups you contact have no system for keeping up to date, you can suggest starting one. The best way to obtain current information is to stay in touch with an expert in the field and ask him or her to keep you abreast of any new findings. It would be a waste of precious parenting time for you to try reading the vast medical literature available in medical libraries. You would be better off leaving this highly specialized reading to experts who can translate the information for you. That way, you can concentrate your energies where you are most needed and will do the most good.

If your child can grow up seeing the world as an exciting, interesting place and feeling special, needed, and wanted, you will have achieved something remarkable. Working toward this goal is not easy. In reality it means a long, hard, uphill effort. But keep trying. The view from the top of the mountain can be breathtaking.

Chapter 15

How to Handle a Progressive Disease or One That Leads to Death

---

Death, when faced with honest courage, can give birth to the most unexpected loving and open relationship.

—JOHN PETRONI

A progressive or fatal disease in a child is tragic. Yet children almost always handle this better, in fact, than their parents.

One of my parents sent me a very special letter after her child's death. I asked if I could share it with all of you, because I think it is beautiful.

She wrote, "Her death has left in us a deep aching wound that cannot soon heal. At first, it had seemed as if the entire world, in its anarchy, should be unable to function without her; the absence was unrelenting and too painful for mere pain. It was a time where all logic, frustrating in its great eclipses during the normal course of events, failed mercilessly. The equation was irreversible. Even now, nothing has rushed in to fill the vacuum, though our equilibrium has recovered, and we live on the edge of sadness. There is something unnatural about the death of children."

Many parents and doctors simply cannot accept the fact that there is no answer or solution to a particular disease. They may try every possible way to block out what is actually happening, especially when the disease is fatal. Over the many years I have cared for both normal and handicapped children, I continue to be amazed at how well children handle a fatal illness. To begin with, they seem to have an uncanny sense that their disease is fatal, even though no one has actually told them the outcome.

During the thirty years I have been treating children with progressive neuromuscular diseases, I have been asked frequently how I manage talking to a fatally ill child about death. What do I tell them about death? What do I tell a child when he or she is going to die? Or *do* I tell them about their death? My response is that I just answer questions as each child asks them, as simply, directly, and honestly as I can. But I always try to leave the door open for further questions. I get to know the children very well over a period of years so that as I work with them, I think they feel free to bring up anything they wish.

I believe that specific statements to a child or parents about the outcome of a disease are unwise. With the excellent medical technology we now have, there is realistic hope that someone will discover treatments or cures for even the most catastrophic diseases. Because of this we cannot make definite statements about a child's future. So each time I see the parents and the children, I try to encourage them to live as fully in the present as they can.

Parents often are much more caught up in the nightmare of death than their terminally ill children. I have seen this dread so consume parents that they lose the precious time they do have left.

I have a favorite patient with a disease that will eventually be fatal. One day his single mother said to me, "I wish it were all over now." She could not accept the pain of his eventual death, even though she still had a full six to eight years left with her son, who is a wonderful boy, bright and handsome. I had to talk almost harshly to make her understand that the time they still had could be a very special time. Counseling was arranged for her, and now they have a vital, fulfilling relationship with each other and the world.

Unless a cure is found, this boy will die in his early twenties.

I think, though, that his mother will look back over their last years together and be glad for the special times that they shared. She might easily have lost the gift of these years, had she not freed herself from the tyranny of her fears.

The inability to think about death or face the facts of death can make a parent put up walls. If, for example, you cannot make peace with the possibility of your child's death, you won't be able to open up for your child's questions. Your child will want to ask about his or her disease, and perhaps even about death. If this area is taboo to you, you can't "be there" for your child. You may need to have a counselor help you confront the possibility of death and learn to accept it as part of life.

If you notice that your child begins to be withdrawn or depressed as his disease progresses, you may need counseling for him. Depression is anger turned inward; a child needs to be given the opportunity to bring anger out into the open.

I had a teenage patient with a severe handicap who seemed very depressed. We discussed this, and I asked him if he felt a lot of anger. He said no, he didn't think so. Then I asked him to take a crayon and draw what anger he felt he did have. He took a red crayon and pressed so hard, with such defiant strokes, that he almost went through the paper! And he said he wasn't angry. Subsequent good counseling helped him a great deal.

If you can maintain open and close communication in the family, with an easy willingness to talk about anything, you will find that you can probably answer your child's questions by yourself.

Frequently, intelligent children or teenagers develop an attitude of why try, why go on learning and studying in school if my life is going to end? Learning to live just one day at a time and trying not to focus on tomorrow is a way to help them get through these low periods.

One boy with a progressive muscle disease said to me once, "I guess the most important thing I can do is to think just about today. Some special medicine may be found before too long, and if I keep myself in the best possible condition, maybe I will be okay. If a man can go to the moon, a cure for my disease surely can be found."

As a parent, you should know that children with fatal diseases often try to shield their parents, especially their mothers, from worrying about the disease and their eventual death. I have been privileged to read the diaries of some of the boys with muscular dystrophy I treated after they were gone, and it is very moving to realize how protective these boys were of their mothers. They tried to keep a great many things to themselves to spare their mothers more suffering. However, this kind of protectiveness can be carried too far. Children should feel free to talk about what is happening to them when they have a progressive disease. As a parent, you have to let your child know that this kind of discussion is okay and that you welcome close talk.

Living with Progressive Disease

The families I know that have been most successful with this hard task make each day count. I think living just one day at a time probably works best for us all.

If as a parent you start your mind spinning with all the terrible things that could happen to your child, you simply won't be able to go on functioning. None of us knows how long we may live, because sudden accidents or illnesses can always happen. Whether our lives last five years, twenty years, fifty years, or seventy years, we can practice the art of making each day a quality day.

If there is one prescription for doing the best you can as a parent of a child who is dying or who has serious disabilities, this is it: Make each day count.

I know this is not an easy prescription to fill when you are overtired and burdened with emotional strain, financial problems, work, frequent medical visits, and endless responsibilities. That's why an occasional day of forgetting your routine can be the best medicine. A little fun can make a big difference in the quality of your lives. Take your child out of school for a day and visit a park or the zoo. Take some time now and then just to enjoy being alive.

You also need to do some vigorous physical exercise and learn to release tension. Otherwise, you can create a pattern of internal stress that will continue to cause physical damage long after a child's death.

According to one mother, who lost her son to a chronic illness, the pressure constantly increases. Toward the end she kept wanting to ask the experts, How long? What will it be like for him? Will it hurt? You get overloaded emotionally and physically as death approaches, no matter what your support systems are.

Wonderful books have been written about the art of living, and almost all accent the value of delighting in simple things anyone can do, like listening to music, looking at art, enjoying nature. We can all have fun, cultivate love and laughter, give and get plenty of hugs if only we take the time. If you work to put some quality time into each day, each day will become what life is all about, and your fears about the future will fade.

You can build quality time into your life with your child in many, many ways. You don't have to take special vacations or trips or change anything in a big way. Just putting a note in your child's lunch or pocket with some special message or giving an extra hug or a little surprise can make moments that are special.

One of the things that I have done with my dystrophy boys is simply to ask them if there is anything else they need to do. I usually ask them as they are coming to the end of their lives. Often the boys will have a list of things they still want to accomplish before they die, and they are remarkably matter-of-fact about this. One of my patients said he wanted to become twenty-one so that he could go into a bar! Another one wanted to graduate from high school, and another one wanted to see Hawaii. Each seemed to have his own particular needs to fulfill.

By maintaining a day-to-day awareness of your child's wants and needs, you can find ways to give a quality of life that many, many so-called normal children never have.

After all, there are talented, beautiful whole people who wake up each morning not knowing what to do with their lives. A progressive disease can make life more vital because you and your child realize how precious the time you have is. You feel that you have to pack a lot of living into a few years, and there is no time to be wasted on regrets or hesitation. This can increase your energy and motivation to make each day count.

I found a letter on my desk one day when I came to work. It was left by the family of a very special patient with a progressive disease who died at the age of twenty-two—the same young man who wanted to be twenty-one so he could go into a bar! He had written the letter sometime before and left instructions that the letter be given to me after his death. His philosophy of life was wonderful, and he is missed by many. I would like to quote a paragraph from his letter:

"You'll understand when I say that I'm glad for the normal life I lived, and it was your guidance and assurance to my family that helped them treat me like I'm human instead of 4F. One of the best things that happened to me was staying in public school where I could meet people, make friends, and do things non-handicapped kids would do, like go to the movies until ungodly hours, go out to restaurants and have cocktails when they offered them and try to get away with everything other underaged kids do. These last two years have been really fantastic. A lot of people have given me the support to overcome my disabilities, and I want to thank you for all of your support all these years. It was always good to hear your cheerful voice coming down the hall towards me."

I would say that if you can talk with your child about death as a perfectly natural part of life, you will have accomplished something very special. Although death *is* a part of the cycle of life, we do not ordinarily think of it in this way. Children seem to understand more than we do about this, and we could learn from watching how they live when they know their lives will be short.

I have a poster that hangs in my house showing an ocean and shoreline, whose inscription reads, "An end is a beginning." This has helped me through some difficult times and has proven to be true. The end is the beginning of something new, something different. However, you have to eventually make peace with the past, to live with the day at hand, and be able to look forward to tomorrow—not an easy prescription.

I have a good friend whose son died of a progressive disease, and I was his doctor. I knew his mother only in this capacity until after his death, when we got together for a cup of coffee. Then the coffee became an occasional lunch, and finally our friendship began to deepen. She taught me a great deal about the aftershock of a child's death. Through her own experience and the reading she has done, she feels that the longer the period of pre-grief from the diagnosis to death, the longer the period of post-grief. Every single minute, she said, when she was awake, she was aware of the impending death. Her basic personality was colored by her son's constant downhill course, which was devastating. She felt as if she had run a marathon on awakening each morning.

She could not walk away, could not get a divorce, could not leave her son. There was no reasonable choice but to keep her son with her and slowly watch him die. Her husband was never very verbal and not really there for her when their son died. He never discussed any of the funeral arrangements, nor the son's death.

However, for five years after the young man died, the father went faithfully every Saturday to the cemetery and took flowers on his own initiative. His very understanding wife will now occasionally see him "lost in thought," and when she asks him what he is thinking, he will say that he is thinking about their son.

She notes that we insist that everyone be verbal, but we have to find other ways for some people to express their feelings. A partner must be really aware by subtle signs and body language of what may be troubling the nonverbal person and that it can't be brought up and talked about. A nonverbal parent must not be made to feel a failure; other ways can be found for that person to express hurt, sadness, or love.

She said that even though she was functional after her child's death, she doesn't really remember much for about three years. Her family can talk about things that happened, and she doesn't remember them at all. In her words, she had "total inertia." She had to learn to live all over again and feels that it has taken her almost fifteen years. It became very difficult for her to learn to let go of the past, and this is an important and real task for her. She went back to college, did wonderfully, decided on a postgraduate degree and eventually became a very successful social worker and administrator. She says that what helped the most to get out of her state of inertia was to become involved with other parents in my muscle-disease clinics. I sought her out to talk with parents who had sons dying of muscular dystrophy because I felt she had much to offer. Apparently this in turn brought some healing that allowed her to go on with life. So, for my friend, her son's death was the impetus for real growth, and the end was a beginning.

Catherine Marshall, in her book *To Live Again,* talks of how each day was a long, long journey after Peter Marshall's death. She put one foot in front of the other, survived, went on to be a successful author and to meet another man whom she loved very much. Sometimes just putting that one foot out a little ahead of the other one is all we can do. It helps to keep in mind that an end is also a beginning, and not to waste time on regrets and what cannot be. Celebrate what you do have.

Chapter 16

Success Stories

*Love is a seed from which only love can grow
. . . transforming a barren life into a garden of
loveliness.*

—DEAN WALLEY

It's wonderful to see someone who has overcome a special problem or has grown up to become a happy person against all odds. We've all heard about people who started out as stutterers and became great speakers, or athletes who had polio or another disease and who had to struggle to overcome limitations. I've been fortunate to work with some amazing handicapped children and teenagers who have made great successes out of their lives. Their stories are inspiring.

In our society, the word success often suggests money or fame or both. But this isn't what I'm talking about. The children I'm talking about are not rich or famous. Rather each has a beautiful, glowing force that draws people close. This is what I think means making a success of life. All of them have creative, loving qualities that push their handicaps to the background and make them seem unimportant. Although their bodies aren't whole, these children and teenagers are truly extraordinary human beings.

If there is some way you can help your child adjust to and accept being handicapped and go on to develop this open, loving quality that so attracts people, you will have accomplished something remarkable. In doing this, you will be giving your child a gift that can neither fail nor be taken away.

Too often we meet handicapped adults who have a chip on their shoulder, giving off such feelings of anger that they set themselves apart and become isolated from others. They may be so torn by bitterness that no one wants to be near them, and they end up adding severe emotional handicaps to the physical ones they already have. This doesn't have to happen.

I have some patients whose visits I look forward to, even if they come at the end of a long, hard day. Others, I frankly wish I didn't have to see. What makes the difference is something they carry inside themselves and the attitudes with which they approach life. All of us have vast untapped potential. It seems that any of us could become extraordinary human beings if we could fully use all our resources.

I've noticed that the way parents regard their children is almost a prediction of the future. For example, if you feel that your child or children are special and wonderful, they will truly grow and develop into special, exemplary human beings. Children who are just tolerated, or whose presence makes their parents angry or unhappy, reflect these emotions, too, as they develop. Children mirror what they see and hear in their homes. Loving, exceptional parents make for loving, extraordinary children.

A favorite teenager some years ago slowly lost her ability to walk due to a muscle disease. After a difficult period of searching, she finally ended up working in a college handicapped program. In due time she became director of the program, which attracted handicapped people from all over the United States. She eventually married a man, himself in a wheelchair, who had come there to work for an advanced degree. This woman is one of those rare people who is a delight. Whenever I spend time with her, I feel as if something quite magical has occurred. Others feel the same way.

Another special patient died several years ago at the age of twenty-two, but he left a mark on many lives, including mine. I still proudly carry the briefcase he had inscribed for me. He came in his wheelchair to bring it to me in the hospital when I was recovering from surgery. It was a nice turnabout for him to visit me there, since I had visited him in the hospital so many times before.

Even toward the end of his life, when he had almost no muscle strength, people did not think of him as handicapped. A teen-age friend was on an outing with him in his van once when he drove into a handicapped parking zone.

"Who's handicapped?" she asked.

It hadn't occurred to her that this young man was any different from her other friends, which is quite a statement about how he lived his life during the time he had.

Over three hundred people attended his funeral service, and many of us who knew him still miss him very much.

I have one young man as a patient who became deaf after an illness when he was just a little boy. We've known each other for several years because he has a slowly progressive muscle disease. He is not only pleasant, but he is also self-sufficient; he works, takes classes, travels, and goes about his life without complaint. When I moved from Southern to Northern California, he moved also, and drove up by himself to start a new life. His tenacity and ability to survive in the face of what would be overwhelming odds have always been amazing to me.

Another patient for whom I cared many years ago in New York had to spend two years as a teenager in the hospital with a severe muscle disease. He didn't allow this experience or the disease to ruin his chances for a full life, though. This man is now a professor of music. He is also skilled at reaching out with warmth to all those around him. It is always a pleasure to get a letter from him.

One of my other former patients, a teenage girl with rheumatoid arthritis, was in terrible pain at one time. Because of her intense suffering, she had become the angriest, most hostile youngster I had ever encountered. Yet this girl grew up to be a loving, outgoing, productive woman. She accomplished this through her own will to change and get well and the sure knowledge that we cared a great deal about her.

Most of us have heard of the DeBolts. They adopted many handicapped children and have made such adoption acceptable, by working very hard to help this cause.

I have known some other wonderful families who have adopted children with handicaps. Taking care of their own handicapped child has brought these families closer together. One family I know adopted a little girl with multiple problems several years ago. Recently they wanted to adopt a second handicapped child, and the adoption agency questioned me about the wisdom of this. I told them about the quality of care they gave the first little girl they had adopted.

Because of this first child's many physical problems, our medical team didn't think she would be able to do much in life. Yet with the loving care her new parents gave, she became a cute, perky little girl. She still has the same handicaps; they just aren't a barrier. It is always a high point for me when she comes with her mother for an office visit. My letter to the agency said that if all children could have this kind of parenting, the world would be a different and much happier place.

I know many stories like this. In most of the success stories, the handicapped child was valued and loved for who he or she was. Such children grow up developing unusual qualities of depth and human caring. They cherish other people as they were and are cherished, and because of this, people enjoy being with them. This is a wonderful legacy to give any child, especially a child who is handicapped.

Chapter 17

How to Go On

Courage expands with use.

—MERLE SHANE

I was recently asked what I would choose if I could give just three gifts to the parents of a handicapped child. First, I would certainly give patience, in abundance. The next would be the ability to accept whatever comes along and to work creatively with that. The last would be permission and support and encouragement for the parents to be themselves. By this, I mean for you to do the best you can as a person, not just as a parent. When you have good things going for you as an individual, it is good for the child or children in your life as well. Of course, I can't give these gifts to you no matter how much I'd like to. But you may be able to discover them for yourself.

I was also asked what three pieces of advice I would give to the parents of a handicapped child. This I can give based on what I have seen in over thirty years of working with handicapped children and their parents. First, I would say ignore your child's handicap as much as possible. Treat the child as much like a normal child as you realistically can. This doesn't mean to ignore the special medical, educational, and other requirements your child has. But it means to try working these needs into your routine rather than revolving your entire life around this one child.

My second suggestion is that you try to give everyone in your family equal time—including *yourself*. I know this is hard, but it really works for everyone's benefit, including the handicapped child's.

Third, establish mutual respect between all members of your family; between parents and children and vice versa. Without this respect, a family often consists of unpleasant children and overworked adults. Mutual respect is what keeps a healthy balance in any family.

Your child's birth, accident, or illness—whatever suddenly made you the parent of a handicapped child—may have felt like a death to you. In a real sense it was. Our lives from physical birth to physical death include many lesser deaths, times when we lose a cherished hope or something we treasure. We grieve at such times, just as we do when someone we love has died.

The other side of these deaths-in-life is the possibility of birth and rebirth. New strengths we didn't know we had can be born of our need and desperation. New interests and skills can spring up from the very burial place of a long-cherished dream. This is a testament to the basic goodness and creativity of human beings. We are able to renew and rekindle our love of life again and again.

Throughout this book, I have talked about the many situations you will be encountering with your child. The implication is that you will probably change as you adapt the details and activities of your daily life. With new demands, you develop new skills or strengthen old ones. You may, for example, become more organized, or you may find that you are becoming clearer and more assertive with medical professionals. Perhaps you will notice you are making more decisions, or the decisions seem to be easier to make with so many thrown at you so quickly. Undoubtedly you will uncover new parts of yourself—strengths and weaknesses, too, of which you were not aware. You may be fortunate enough to find an as-yet-untapped source of fun as you explore new ways to play with your child, or perhaps new depths of feeling and love.

Becoming the parent of a handicapped child is a time of stress and change. It also will inevitably be a process of personal transformation. In this sense, you will be starting life over from a new position, beginning a long and difficult journey of exploration and accomplishment, a journey into the human spirit and the very depths of your being.

Above all else, I wish you well.

Appendix A

Health Professionals You May Encounter

Anesthesiologist: An individual with a medical degree who has several years of additional special training giving anesthetics.

Cardiologist: A physician who has had specific training in diseases of the heart. There are pediatric cardiologists who have training specifically with children.

Dermatologist: A doctor who has had special training in diseases of the skin. There are now a few pediatric dermatologists, primarily in metropolitan areas.

Dietitian: An individual who has had special training in the planning of diets and specific nutritional needs of the body. Dietitians are generally connected with hospitals, but occasionally work independently.

Endocrinologist: A medical doctor who has had specific training in treating the endocrine diseases of children and adults. Endocrine glands are those concerned with hormones such as insulin, which relates to diabetes, and the production of thyroid hormones, which relate to growth and many other important functions.

Family Practitioner: A physician who has had training in many specialties and sees both children and adults. He or she has often had more years of training than a general practitioner.

Gastroenterologist: A medical doctor who has had special additional training in diseases of the gastrointestinal tract. There are now a few pediatric gastroenterologists usually found in large metropolitan areas.

Geneticist: A physician who generally has pediatric backgrounds with additional genetic training. There are also genetic counselors, who may be nurses or other paramedical people. When a genetic condition is suspected, it is important to establish it with certainty before seeking a genetic counselor, as counseling is difficult to give unless the exact disorders are known.

Hematologist: A medical doctor who may have either pediatric or internal-medicine backgrounds. Hematologists work with disorders of the blood and treat children with leukemia, anemias—such as sickle-cell disease—and any blood-related problems.

Internist: A medical doctor who has had the same type of training for adults that pediatricians have for children. Many internists have subspecialty training in gastroenterology, which concerns diseases of the stomach and intestines; rheumatology, which concerns diseases of the joints; and so on. They generally see adults, but some see teenagers.

Neurologist: A medical doctor who has had either pediatric or adult training specifically in disorders of the brain and nervous system.

Nurse practitioner: A registered nurse who has had additional training that allows her to do certain examinations and procedures that registered nurses are not licensed to do.

Obstetrician: A physician who sees women during pregnancy and is responsible for the delivery and immediate postnatal care. Obstetricians are also trained in gynecology, so that they provide ongoing care involving the female reproductive system.

Occupational therapist: An individual who has had specific training in the function of the musculoskeletal system, particularly in the upper extremities. Occupational therapists are involved in the developmental problems of children and also concerned with activities of daily living, such as dressing and eating, upper-extremity strength, and how to adapt the environment to make it more workable for a handicapped person.

Oncologist: A medical doctor who treats patients with tumors, both benign and malignant (cancers). Pediatric oncologists have had special training in working with children.

Ophthalmologist: A medical doctor who has had several years of additional training in examining and treating disorders of the eyes. An ophthalmologist is also a licensed surgeon who does eye surgery.

Optometrist: A doctor of optometry does not have a medical degree and is not licensed to issue or prescribe drugs. Optometrists can prescribe glasses, eye exercises, contact lenses, and so on.

Orthopedic surgeon: A physician who has had several years of postgraduate training in disorders of bones and joints. Such a surgeon performs surgical procedures on the back and extremities. There are many subspecialties of orthopedics, such as hand surgery, back surgery, children's orthopedics, and so on.

Osteopath: An individual who has graduated from a school of osteopathy. Some states now allow osteopaths to qualify for an M.D. degree. Their scope of treatment varies according to the school from which they graduated, but many are licensed to do almost the same things that medical doctors do.

Otolaryngologist: A medical doctor who has had additional training in treating diseases of the ears, nose, and throat. There are some who see only ear problems. Some see just children or a combination of children and adults.

Pathologist: A medical doctor who has had specific training in both gross and microscopic pathology and who diagnoses by looking at specific microscopic sections and studying tumors or tissues that have been removed surgically.

Pediatrician: A medical physician who has had additional training in the treatment of childhood disorders. There are now many subspecialties, such as pediatric gastroenterologists, cardiologists, allergists, neurologists, and so on.

Physiatrist: A medical doctor who has had additional training in rehabilitation or nonsurgical treatment of postaccident victims, back injuries, polio, and neuromuscular diseases.

Physical therapist: An individual who has had training in the structural function of joints and muscles. Physical therapists help evaluate and treat children and adults who have problems in the musculoskeletal system. They do this by teaching strengthening exercises, doing massage, or working with specific equipment to help strengthen muscles.

Psychiatrist: A medical doctor who has had specific additional training for mental and emotional disorders. There are both pediatric psychiatrists with background in child disorders and adult psychiatrists. Some psychiatrists see children just in hospitals; others practice only outpatient psychiatry.

Psychologist: An individual who has either a masters or a doctorate (Ph.D.) in psychology. Psychologists have had variable kinds of training in working with and testing children and adults. There are now many different schools of psychology, as well as specialties.

Radiologist: A radiologist is a licensed medical doctor who has had additional training in diagnosing conditions by X ray, CAT scan, and so on. Many radiologists also do therapy on cancer patients.

Registered nurses: An individual who has had nursing-school training and works under the supervision of a physician. There are now many nurses who are going on to get additional training so that they are equipped to do other types of procedures or examinations.

Rheumatologist: A physician who works with either children or adults. Rheumatologists have had additional training beyond pediatrics or internal medicine in diseases involving the joints, as for example, juvenile rheumatoid arthritis, and other collagen or connective-tissue diseases.

Social worker: An individual with special training in counseling and finding resources for different problems. Social workers have either a Medical Social Worker (M.S.W.) or Licensed Clinical Social Worker (L.C.S.W.) degree.

Urologist: A physician who has a medical degree and who has had specialized training in caring for conditions of the urinary tract and kidneys. Urologists are surgically trained, and there are both pediatric and adult specialists.

Appendix B

Definitions of Handicaps

Arthritis: The most common type in a child is juvenile rheumatoid arthritis. One or more jóints may swell and hurt, and special care is needed. The eyes must be watched closely in these children, too.

Arthrogryposis: This is a general or "wastebasket" term that really indicates fixed positions of the joints in a child. There are several reasons for this disorder, and a pediatrician, neurologist, or orthopedist who has had specific experience with the condition should be consulted. It is frequently necessary for these individuals to have a muscle biopsy to determine the underlying cause. However, the muscle biopsy can be misleading if not properly interpreted.

Blindness in childhood: This can be congenital in nature or develop after birth. It may be either hereditary or caused by prematurity, viruses, drugs, and so forth. Cataracts, glaucoma, or a detached retina may be the cause.

Cerebral palsy: There are several types of cerebral palsy, and the cause is often unknown. There is a higher incidence in infants who were premature or who had birth difficulties. Cerebral palsy affects the central nervous system so that speech, vision, hearing, and the function in the arms and legs may be impaired.

Congenital: A condition described as being congenital is evident at birth, and the cause may be unknown. This would be in contrast to a hereditary condition, although these terms are frequently used together.

Contracture: A shortening of the muscle or ligament so that normal joint movement is limited. It is seen in muscular dystrophy as it progresses, in cerebral palsy and postaccident, and in a variety of other situations.

Cystic fibrosis: A disease that affects not only the respiratory system but also the gastrointestinal tract. Children with this illness must have careful treatment and periodic review by someone knowledgeable in treating this disorder.

Cerebral vascular accident (CVA or stroke): A rare disorder that can occur in children and has a sudden onset. It is characterized by damage or loss of function to the central nervous system or brain so that a child becomes comatose, loses the use of arms, legs, speech, vision, and so on. Emergency care is of the utmost importance, and the postaccident problems depend on the amount of bleeding and the loss of nerve tissue that has occurred.

Colostomy: An opening created from the intestine to the abdomen that allows fecal material to go into an exterior bag. It may be necessary in a child who was not born with an anus, or opening for bowel movements. It may also be necessary in children who have had some kind of radical intestinal surgery.

Deafness: There are congenital and/or hereditary hearing problems that are present at birth. Deafness may also occur with repeated ear infections in small children. A child who is delayed in speech should always have his hearing checked to make sure he is hearing adequately.

Diabetes: A disorder in either children or adults in which there is not adequate utilization of sugar. Diabetes frequently recurs in families, and children with diabetes must be carefully monitored by someone who is knowledgeable in this field.

Encephalitis: An acute inflammation of the brain due to viruses or other agents. Many people recover completely from the initial attack, but some develop complications that include spasticity, loss of speech, and loss of the use of their extremities and general ability to function.

Epilepsy: There are many forms of epilepsy, and these are manifested by different types of seizures. There may be complete loss of consciousness with a grand mal seizure or almost unrecognizable so-called petit mal seizures. There are also other types of seizures. Medications are now available for the careful control of these different types of epilepsy.

Friedreich's ataxia: A progressive hereditary disease of the neuromuscular system that can affect the heart, nervous system, or bones. The cause is unknown, and patients should be followed closely.

Guillain-Barré syndrome: A disease of ascending paralysis (polyneuritis), which occurs usually one to three weeks after a respiratory infection. Complete recovery can occur.

Hemiplegia: This refers to the inability to use either one side of the body or one extremity. It may be caused at birth, by brain hemorrhage, or by accidents that happen later in life. A great deal can generally be done to help these individuals by means of physical therapy and occupational therapy.

Hydrocephalus (water on the brain): This is caused by blockage of the drainage system from the ventricles, or areas in the brain that contain fluid. It may be in association with spina bifida, or it may occur independently. It may also result from infection. Different types of shunts or tubes to relieve pressure that go from the ventricles to the abdomen are now being surgically inserted with very good results.

Incontinence: The inability to control the bladder or bowel. It may be due to spina bifida or paraplegia.

Meningitis: A condition caused either by viruses or bacteria that promote a disease or inflammation of the meninges, or brain membranes. Individuals may recover completely or may be left with retardation, spasticity, and so on.

Muscular dystrophy: A group of disorders that affect individuals in varying ways depending upon the type of onset. The principal type is Duchenne dystrophy, which occurs only in males and is first manifested by late walking. Two thirds of these chidren have a family history of the disease, and others in the family should be watched closely. There are also other disorders, such as myotonic dystrophy, which can occur in childhood and may also be progressive. Children with congenital muscular dystrophy should in general get stronger from birth.

Myasthenia gravis: A disease in which the child or adult becomes gradually weaker as the day progresses. The children generally have weakness of the eye muscles. Infants born of mothers with this disease may have a temporary form of the disorder. There is good medication available, though it must be monitored carefully.

Osteoporosis: A loss of calcium in bones such as can occur in bedridden or wheelchair-bound patients. Aggressive physical therapy and maintaining an upright position as best as possible may help make the disorder less severe.

Paraplegia: A loss in the use of the lower extremities. The level of loss depends on the area of involvement in the spinal cord. Generally, bowel and bladder function are affected, and this condition can either exist from birth or be due to trauma or infection.

Polyneuritis: A disorder caused, in some cases, by infection or toxins. Loss of strength in the extremities may occur, and nerves in and around the face may be affected.

Progressive spinal atrophy: A group of disorders that can affect infants, children, or adults. There is an infantile form called Werdnig-Hoffmann, which generally begins at birth and may be very severe. However, there is also a somewhat milder form, which is now recognized to become either arrested or nonprogressive. An intermediate childhood form is called Kugelberg-Welander disease, which has a slow progressive course, and there is also the adult type of spinal atrophy.

Quadriplegia: Loss of movement in all four extremities, due either to injury, infection, or hemorrhage. The level of the spinal-cord injury determines the extent of the involvement.

Spina bifida: A congenital abnormality in the vertebrae of the spine. The vertebral bodies do not close in certain areas, and the spinal cord and layers may herniate through. Varying forms occur, and the level of lower-extremity involvement depends on the level at which the abnormality occurs. Hydrocephalus and urinary and orthopedic anomalies are common accompanying features.

Appendix C

Agencies That Can Give You Information

Abused children
Parents Anonymous
7120 Franklin Ave.
Los Angeles, CA 90046
(800) 352-0386 (in Calif.)
(800) 421-0353

Amputees
National Amputation Foundation
12-45 150th St.
Whitestone, NY 11357
(212) 767-0596

Parents of Amputee Children
Together (PACT)
c/o Kessler Institute of Rehabilitation
Pleasant Valley Way
West Orange, NJ 07052
(201) 731-3600, Ext. 291

Arthritis
Arthritis Foundation
1314 Spring St., N.W.
Atlanta, GA 30309
(404) 872-7100

Arthrogryposis
National Support Group for Arthrogryposis
1311 N. 169th St.
Seattle, WA 98123
(206) 871-5057 / (206) 542-7021

Ataxia
Friedreich's Ataxia Group in
America, Inc.
P.O. Box 1116
Oakland, CA 94611
(415) 655-0833

National Ataxia Foundation
600 Twelve Oaks Ctr.
15500 Wayzata Blvd.
Wayzata, MN 55391
(612) 473-7666

Autism
National Society for Children and
Adults with Autism
1234 Massachusetts Ave., N.W.,
Suite 1017
Washington, DC 20005
(202) 783-0125

Birth defects
Association of Birth Defect Children
3526 Emerywood Lane
Orlando, FL 32806
(305) 859-2821

March of Dimes
P.O. Box 2000
White Plains, NY 10605
(941) 428-7100

National Easter Seal Society for Crippled Children and Adults
2023 W. Ogden Ave.
Chicago, IL 60612
(312) 243-8400

Blindness
American Blind Bowling Association,
Inc.
150 N. Bellaire Ave.
Louisville, KY 40206
(804) 857-7267

Helen Keller National Center for
Deaf-Blind Youths and Adults
111 Middle Neck Rd.
Sands Point, NY 11050
(516) 944-8900 (TTY and voice)

National Association for Parents of
Visually Impaired, Inc.
P.O. Box 180806
Austin, TX 78718
(512) 459-6651

Cancer
The Candlelighters Childhood Cancer
Foundation
2025 Eye St., N.W., Suite 1011
Washington, DC 20003
(202) 659-5136

Cerebral palsy
United Cerebral Palsy Association
122 E. 23rd St.
New York, NY 10010
(212) 677-7400

Chronically ill children
Pediatric Projects, Inc.
(For chronically ill, disabled or hospi-
talized children and their families)
P.O. Box 1880
Santa Monica, CA 90406
(213) 459-7710

Cleft lip and palate
Prescription Parents, Inc.
P.O. Box 426
Quincy, MA 02269
(617) 479-2463

Cystic fibrosis
Cystic Fibrosis Foundation
6000 Executive Blvd.
Rockville, MD 20852
(301) 881-9130

Deafness
American Society for Deaf Children
814 Thayer Ave.
Silver Spring, MD 20910
(301) 585-5400

Dentistry
National Foundation of Dentistry for
the Handicapped
1250 14th St., Suite 610
Denver, CO 80202
(303) 573-0264

Diabetes
Juvenile Diabetes Foundation International
60 Madison Ave.
New York, NY 10010-1550
(212) 889-7575

Down syndrome
National Down Syndrome Congress
1800 Dempster
Parkridge, IL 60068
(312) 226-0416
(800) 232-6372

Dysautonomia
Dysautonomia Foundation
370 Lexington Ave.
New York, NY 10017
(212) 889-5222

Epilepsy
Epilepsy Foundation of America
4351 Garden City Dr.
Landover, MD 20785
(301) 459-3200

Glycogen-storage diseases
The Association for Glycogen Storage
Disease
Box 896
Durant, IA 52747
(319) 785-6038

Growth disorders
Little People of America
P.O. Box 633
San Bruno, CA 94066
(415) 589-0695

Guillain-Barré syndrome
Guillain-Barré Syndrome Support
Group
P.O. Box 262
Wynnewood, PA 91096
(215) 896-6372 / (215) 649-7837

Hemophilia
National Hemophilia Foundation
The SoHo Bldg.
110 Greene St., Room 406
New York, NY 10012
(212) 219-8180

Huntington's disease
Huntington's Disease Foundation of
America, Inc.
440 W. 22nd St., 6th fl.
New York, NY 10011
(212) 242-1968

Hydrocephalus
Hydrocephalus Parent Support Group
UCSD Medical Center
255 Dickinson St.
H-893
San Diego, CA 92103
(619) 695-3139 / 726-0507

Kidney disease
National Kidney Foundation
2 Park Ave.
New York, NY 10016
(212) 889-2210

Learning disabilities
Foundation for Children with Learning Disabilities
99 Park Ave., 6th floor
New York, NY 10011
(212) 687-7211

Marfan syndrome
National Marfan Foundation
54 Irma Street
Port Washington, NY 11050
(516) 883-8712

Mental retardation
American Association on Mental De-
ficiencies
1719 Kalorama Rd., N.W.
Washington, DC 20009
(202) 387-1968

Multiple sclerosis
National Multiple Sclerosis Society
205 E. 42nd St.
New York, NY 10017
(212) 986-3240

Muscular dystrophy
Muscular Dystrophy Association of
America
810 Seventh Ave.
New York, NY 10019
(212) 568-0808

Neurofibromatosis
National Neurofibromatosis Foundation, Inc.
141 Fifth Ave., Suite 7S
New York, NY 10010
(212) 460-8980

Osteogenesis imperfecta
American Brittle Bone Society
1256 Merrill Dr.
West Chester, PA 19380
(215) 692-6248

Osteogenesis Imperfecta Foundation
P.O. Box 245
Eastport, NY 11941
(516) 325-8992

Ostomies
United Ostomy Association, Inc.
2001 W. Beverly Blvd.
Los Angeles, CA 90057
(213) 413-5510

Premature and high-risk infants
Parent Care
University of Utah Medical Center
2A210
Salt Lake City, UT 84132
(801) 581-5323

Prader-Willi syndrome
Prader-Willi Syndrome Association
5515 Malibu Dr.
Edina, MN 55436
(612) 933-0113

Retinitis pigmentosa
Retinitis Pigmentosa Foundation
1401 Mt. Royal Ave.
Baltimore, MD 21217
(800) 638-2300 / TDD (301) 225-9409

Scoliosis
Scoliosis Research Society
Orange County Medical Center
101 S. Manchester

Orange, CA 92668
(714) 997-3000

Sickle cell
National Association for Sickle Cell
Anemia
4221 Wilshire Blvd., Suite 360
Los Angeles, CA 90010-3503
(800) 421-8453 / (213) 936-7205

Special agencies
Home Care for Medically Fragile
Children
Sick Kids (Need) Involved People
(SKIP)
216 Newport Dr.
Severna Park, MD 21146
(301) 647-0164

Scouting for the Handicapped
1325 Walnut Hill Lane
Irving, TX 75062-1296
(214) 659-2127

Girl Scouts of the USA
830 Third Ave.
New York, NY 10022
(212) 940-7500

The Association for Persons with Severe Handicaps (TASH)
7010 Roosevelt Way, N.E.
Seattle, WA 98115
(206) 523-8446

National Library for the Blind and
Physically Handicapped
The Library of Congress
Washington, DC 20542
(202) 287-5100

Special Olympics
1350 New York Ave., N.E.
Suite 500
Washington, DC 20005
(302) 628-3630

Spina bifida
Spina Bifida Association of America
343 South Deerborn, Suite 317

Chicago, IL 60604
(800) 621-3141 (except Illinois)
(312) 663-1562 (in Illinois)

Spinal-cord injuries
American Paralysis Association
650 California St.
San Francisco, CA 94108
(415) 434-1514

National Spinal Cord Injury Association
149 California St.
Newton, MA 02158
(617) 964-0521

Sudden infant death syndrome
SIDS Foundation
2 Metro Plaza, Suite 205

8240 Professional Pl.
Landover, MD 20785
(800) 221-SIDS

Turner's syndrome
Turner's Syndrome Society
York University
Administrative Studies Bldg.
4700 Keele St.
Downsview, Ontario M3J 1P3
(416) 665-3773

Tourette syndrome
Tourette Syndrome Association
41-02 Bell Blvd.
Bayside, NY 11361
(718) 224-2999

Where to Have Fun

This is a representative sampling of the kinds of facilities available for the handicapped. Check your own city for what's available for your child, and the level
of accessibility.

California
Berkeley
    Lawrence Hall of Science .... (415) 642-5132
San Francisco
    Exploratorium .... (415) 563-7337
    Maritime Historic Park .... (415) 556-7337
    Josephine D. Randall
      Junior Museum .... (415) 863-1399
    Fort Point .... (415) 556-1693
    Golden Gate Park .... (415) 558-3706
Oakland
    Hall of Science Museum .... (415) 273-3401
    Rotary Natural Science Center .... (415) 273-3739
Walnut Creek
    Alexander Lindsay Junior Museum .... (415) 935-1978
San Diego
    Convention and Visitors Bureau .... (619) 232-3101
    Mission Bay Park .... (619) 276-8200

Old Town Plaza .... (619) 237-6770
Sea World.. (619) 224-3901
San Diego Zoo .... (619) 234-3153
Balboa Park .... (619) 239-0512
   Museum of Man .... (619) 239-2001
   Natural History Museum............................. (619) 232-3821
   Fine Arts Gallery .... (619) 232-7931
Anaheim
   Disneyland .... (714) 999-4565
      Send for or obtain at park:
      Disneyland Handicapped Guest Guide
      Steve Birnbaum's Guide to Disneyland
California PG&E Recreation Areas:
Call (415) 972-5697 for additional information regarding accessibility.
   Pit River Area
      Hawkins Landing
      North Battle Creek
   Feather River Area
      Belden (picnic sites not accessible)
      De Sabla Forebay
      Hutchins Meadow Group Camp
      Lake Almanor Campgrounds (not all campsites accessible)
      Philbrook
      Shady Rest
   Interstate 80–Donner Summit Area
      Lake Spaulding
      Lodgepole
   Kings River Area
      Lilly Pad
      Trapper Springs
      Upper Kings River
   Eel River Area
      Rivers Edge

Colorado
Call Tourist Bureau (303) 892-1112 if wheelchair accessibility needed.
Denver
   Denver Botanic Gardens .... (303) 575-2547
   Denver Zoo .... (303) 575-2754
   Heritage Square .... (303) 277-0040
   Buffalo Bill's Grave and Museum .... (303) 526-0747
   The Children's Museum .... (303) 433-7444
   Colorado Railroad Museum .... (303) 279-4590
   Denver Firefighters Museum and Restaurant .... (303) 892-1436
   Denver Museum of Natural History .... (303) 370-6300
   Forney Transportation Museum......................... (303) 433-3643

Washington, D.C.
Books

Going Places with Children in Washington, Susan E. Parsons and Katherine S. Tippett.

Washington! Adventure for Kids, Florri DeCell, Heidi Simmons, and Mari Weston.

Convention and Visitors Association..................... (202) 789-7000
National Zoo .... (202) 673-4800
National Aquarium.................................... (202) 377-2826
U.S. Capitol.. (202) 224-3121
Bureau of Engraving and Printing .... (202) 447-1380
Tourmobile tram (available with wheelchair lift) .... (202) 554-7020
Federal Bureau of Investigation .... (202) 324-3447
Lincoln Memorial .... (202) 426-6841
Washington Monument .... (202) 426-6839
The White House .... (202) 456-2200
Rock Creek Park and Nature Center..................... (202) 426-6829
Capital Children's Museum............................. (202) 543-8600
Washington Doll's House and Toy Museum .... (202) 244-0024
London Brass Rubbing Centre .... (202) 364-9303
Saturday Morning at the National:
"It's a theater just for children" .... (202) 783-3370
Dial-A-Park .... TTY (202) 472-5265
                                          Voice (202) 426-6975
To receive a copy of the Smithsonian's publication A Guide for Disabled Visitors... (TDD) (202) 357-1729
                                      (Voice) (202) 357-2700
D.C. Center for Independent Living .... (202) 383-0033
For additional information regarding accessibility at sites operated by the National Capital Park Service............................... (202) 426-6770

Idaho
Boise

Boise Little Theater (limited
   accessibility) .... (208) 342-5104
Meridian Bowling Lanes .... (208) 888-2048
Lake Hazel Lanes (bowling alley with limited
   accessibility) .... (208) 362-2695
Bronco Stadium/Lyle Smith Field .... (208) 385-1253
BSU Pavilion... (208) 385-1900
Western Idaho Fairgrounds .... (208) 376-3247
Boise Gun Club....................................... (208) 342-0892
Owyhee Motorcycle Club, Inc. (limited accessibility) ..... (208) 377-0409
Morrison Center for the Performing Arts .... (208) 385-1577
Firebird International Raceway .... (208) 344-0411
Meridian Speedway.................................... (208) 888-2813

Super Oval Speedway .... (208) 344-1593
BSU Swimming Pool................................ (208) 385-1570
Borah Swimming Pool............................... (208) 384-4256
Fairmont Swimming Pool .... (208) 384-4256

Massachusettes
Boston
Convention and Visitors Bureau .... (617) 563-4100
Children's Museum........................... Voice (617) 426-6500
TDD (617) 426-6501
John Hancock Observatory .... (617) 247-1976
Freedom Trail .... (617) 242-5642
Museum of Science................................... (617) 723-2501
New England Aquarium .... (617) 742-8870
Christian Science Center
  Of special interest unique "walk-in" globe
  of the world....................................... (617) 262-2300

Minnesota
Office of Tourism
240 Bremer Bldg.
419 N. Robert St.
St. Paul, MN 55101
Travel Information .... (800) 238-1461 (outside Minnesota)
(800) 652-9747 (in Minnesota)
Excellent brochure on places to visit and information about accessibility.

Missouri
Kansas City
Convention and Visitors Bureau .... (800) 523-5953
Visitor Information Phone............................. (913) 474-9600
City Market .... (913) 274-1341
Hallmark Visitors Center............................. (913) 274-3613
  Kaleidoscope .... (913) 274-8301
Missouri River Queen .... (913) 842-0027
Kansas City Zoo .... (913) 333-7405
Clay County Historical Museum .... (913) 781-8062
Hispanic Cultural Museum .... (913) 556-0773
Fort Leavenworth Museum............................ (913) 684-4051
Jesse James Bank Museum............................ (913) 781-4458
Heritage Village...................................... (913) 444-4363
Miniature Museum .... (913) 333-2055
Shawnee Mission Indian Museum .... (913) 262-0867
St. Louis
Visitors Information Center .... (901) 526-4880
For information call Paraquad.................... Voice (314) 531-3050

```
4397 Laclede Ave. ...............................TTY (314) 531-3048
St. Louis, MO 63108
Busch Stadium.......................................(314) 241-3900
Magic House .........................................(314) 822-8900
Laumeier Sculpture Park ..............................(314) 821-1209
Museum of Transport .................................(314) 965-8007
Sports Hall of Fame ..................................(314) 421-6790
Grants Farm .........................................(314) 843-1700
St. Louis Zoo.........................................(314) 781-0900
St. Louis Art Museum .................................(314) 721-0072
St. Louis Science Center ..............................(314) 652-5500
Missouri Botanical Gardens............................(314) 557-5100
```

New York
New York City
```
American Museum of Natural History ..................(212) 496-0900
    Planetarium .......................................(212) 863-8828
The Big Apple Circus .................................(212) 860-7320
Bronx Zoo Children's Zoo ............................(212) 367-1010
Brooklyn Children's Museum...........................(212) 735-4432
Children's Museum of Manhattan ......................(212) 765-5904
Dance Theatre of Harlem .............................(212) 977-7751
                                                     (212) 582-9810
Magic Towne House ...................................(212) 752-1165
The Market at Citicorp Center.........................(212) 559-2330
Metropolitan Museum of Art ................ (212) 879-5500, Ext. 3932
Museum of the City of New York ......................(212) 534-1672
New York Historical Society ...........................(212) 873-3400
Off Center Theatre....................................(212) 929-8299
Mt. Morris/Marcus Garvey Park .......................(212) 397-3139
Staten Island Children's Museum.......................(212) 273-2060
Hans Christian Andersen Statue, Storytelling,
    Central Park.......................................(212) 397-3183
```

Ohio
```
Historical sites .............................................(800) BUCKEYE
                                                     or (614) 466-1500
```
List is available of wheelchair accessibility.

Pennsylvania
Philadelphia
```
Convention and Visitors Bureau .......................(215) 636-3300
Mayor's Office for the Handicapped ...................(215) 686-2798
Library for the Blind and Physically
    Handicapped....................... (in Pennsylvania) (800) 222-1754
                                                     (215) 925-3213
```

Afro-American History Museum .... (215) 574-0380
Franklin Institute and Fels Planetarium .... (215) 448-1200
Historical Society of Pennsylvania .... (215) 732-6200
National Museum of American Jewish History .... (215) 923-3811
Philadelphia Museum of Art .... (215) 763-8100
Rodin Museum .... (215) 787-5476
Independence National Historical Park ... (Voice or TDD) (215) 597-8974
Congress Hall .... (215) 597-8974
Independence Hall .... (215) 597-8974
Liberty Bell Pavilion................................. (212) 597-8974
Old City Hall... (212) 597-8974
The Philadelphia Zoo .... (215) 243-1100
Please Touch Museum .... (215) 963-0666

Tennessee
Memphis
For information regarding accessibility to the following institutions, call the Visitors Information Center at (901) 526-4880.
Tours for the blind offered by Brooks Museum of Art.
Victorian Village—Braille guidebooks available, only ground floors are wheelchair-accessible.
Mud Island
Memphis Queen
Libertyland
The Memphis Zoo
Pink Palace Museum and Planetarium
Botanic Gardens
Chucalissa Indian Museum
Lichterman Nature Center
Nashville
Tourist Information .... (615) 741-2158

Texas
Dallas
Books and publications:
The Handicapped Book Access Dallas/Texas and
The Handicapped Travel Request: Access Dallas '82
Easter Seal Society .... (214) 934-9104
4300 Beltway Dr.
Dallas, TX 75234
Bachman Recreation Center .... (214) 351-0101
Houston
Astrodome .... (713) 799-9544
Astroworld... (713) 799-1234
Houston Zoological Gardens.......................... (713) 520-3257
The Museum of Fine Arts .... (713) 526-1361

Museum of Medical Science .... (713) 529-3766
Museum of Natural Science .... (713) 526-4271
La Porte
     Battleship Texas Historical Park....................... (713) 479-2411
     San Jacinto Monument and Museum of History .... (713) 479-2421
Livingston
     Alabama-Coushatta Indian Reservation................. (409) 563-4391
                                                       (800) 393-4794

Books on Tape

Recorded Books .... (800) 638-1304
     (in Maryland).. (301) 868-7856
"Books on Tape" .... (800) 626-3333
     (in California)....................................... (714) 548-5525
Caedmon "Spoken-Word Audio" specializing in fiction .... (800) 223-0420
     (in New York)....................................... (212) 580-3400
Listening Library.. (800) 243-4504
     (in Connecticut)..................................... (203) 637-3616

Appendix E

Resource Directory for Handicapped Children and Youth

ALABAMA

GOVERNMENT AGENCIES

General Disabilities
Program for Exceptional Children
and Youth
868 State Office Bldg.
Montgomery, AL 36130
(205) 261-5099
(800) 392-8020 (in Alabama)

Division of Rehabilitation and
Crippled Children's Services
Department of Education
2129 E. South Blvd.
P.O. Box 11586
Montgomery, AL 36111-0586
(205) 281-8780

Special Needs Programs
Division of Vocational Educational
Services
Department of Education
806 State Office Bldg.
Montgomery, AL 36130
(205) 261-5224

Division of Rehabilitation and
Crippled Children's Services
Department of Education
2129 E. South Blvd.
Montgomery, AL 36111-0586
(205) 281-8780

Developmental Disabilities
Developmental Disabilities Planning
Council
Department of Mental Health and
Mental Retardation
200 Interstate Park Dr.
P.O. Box 3710
Montgomery, AL 36193-5001
(205) 271-9278

PRIVATE AGENCIES

General Disabilities
Alabama Society for Crippled
Children and Adults, Inc.
P.O. Box 6130
2125 E. South Blvd.
Montgomery, AL 36194
(205) 288-8382

Cerebral Palsy
UCP Association of Alabama
2430 11th Avenue
Birmingham, AL 35234
(205) 251-0165

Mental Retardation
Alabama Association for Retarded
Citizens
4301 Norman Bridge Road
Montgomery, AL 36105
(205) 288-9434

ALASKA

GOVERNMENT AGENCIES

General Disabilities
Exceptional Children and Youth
Department of Education
Pouch F
Juneau, AK 99811
(907) 465-2970

Office of Vocational Rehabilitation
Department of Education
Pouch F
State Office Bldg.
Juneau, AK 99811
(907) 465-2814

Special Needs, Career and Vocational
Education
Pouch F
Juneau, AK 99811
(907) 465-2980

Crippled Children's Services
Department of Health and Social
Services
Pouch H-06B
Juneau, AK 99801
(907) 465-3101/3100

Developmental Disabilities
Developmental Disabilities Section
Department of Health and Social
Services
Pouch H-04

Juneau, AK 99811
(907) 465-3372

PRIVATE AGENCIES
General Disabilities
Easter Seal Society of Alaska
620 E. 10th Avenue
Anchorage, AK 99510
(907) 277-2451

Governor's Council for the
Handicapped and Gifted
600 University Ave., Suite C
Fairbanks, AK 99701
(907) 479-6507

AMERICAN SAMOA

GOVERNMENT AGENCIES
General Disabilities
Division of Special Education
State Department of Education
Pago Pago, American Samoa 96799
011 (684) 623-1323

Maternal and Child Health and
Crippled Children's Program
LBJ Tropical Medical Center
Division of Public Health
Pago Pago, American Samoa 96799
011 (684) 633-4590

Maternal and Child Health and
Crippled Children's Program
LBJ Tropical Medical Center
Government of American Samoa
Pago Pago, American Samoa 96799
011 (684) 633-4590

ARIZONA

GOVERNMENT AGENCIES
General Disabilities
Division of Special Education
State Department of Education
1535 W. Jefferson

Phoenix, AZ 85007
(602) 255-3183

Division of Special Education
1535 W. Jefferson
Phoenix, AZ 85007
(602) 255-3183

Bureau of Crippled Children's
Services
Department of Health Services
1740 W. Adams
Phoenix, AZ 85007
(602) 255-1860

State Library for Blind and
Physically Handicapped
1030 N. 32nd St.
Phoenix, AZ 85008
(602) 255-5578
(800) 255-5578 (in Arizona)

Developmental Disabilities
Governor's Council on
Developmental Disabilities
1717 W. Jefferson
P.O. Box 6123
Phoenix, AZ 85007
(602) 255-4049

PRIVATE AGENCIES

Cerebral Palsy
UCP Association of Central Arizona
7337 N. 19th Ave.
Phoenix, AZ 85021
(602) 864-1300

ARKANSAS

GOVERNMENT AGENCIES

General Disabilities
Special Education
Department of Education
Arch Ford Education Bldg.
Room 105-C
Little Rock, AR 72201
(501) 371-2161

Crippled Children's Section of Social
Services
Department of Human Services
P.O. Box 1437
Little Rock, AR 72203
(501) 371-2277
(800) 482-5850 (in Arkansas)

Developmental Disabilities
Governor's Developmental
Disabilities Planning Council
4815 W. Markham St.
Little Rock, AR 72201
(501) 661-2399

PRIVATE AGENCIES

General Disabilities
Arkansas Easter Seal Society
2801 Lee Ave.
P.O. Box 5148
Little Rock, AR 72205
(501) 663-8331

Cerebral Palsy
UCP of Central Arkansas
10400 W. 36th St.
Little Rock, AR 72204-6616
(501) 663-9478

Mental Retardation
Association of Retarded
Citizens/Arkansas
6115 W. Markham, Room 107
Little Rock, AR 72205
(501) 661-9992

CALIFORNIA

GOVERNMENT AGENCIES

General Diabilities
Special Education Division
Department of Education
721 Capitol Mall, Room 614
Sacramento, CA 95814
(916) 445-4036

Developmental Disabilities
California State Council on
Developmental Disabilities
1507 21st. St., Suite 320
Sacramento, CA 95814
(916) 322-8481

California Children's Service Branch
(formerly Crippled Children's
Services)
Department of Health Services
714 P St., Room 323
Sacramento, CA 95814
(916) 322-2090

PRIVATE AGENCIES

Cerebral Palsy
UCP of California
120 N. El Camino Real
San Mateo, CA 94401
(415) 348-1641

Mental Retardation
California Association for Retarded
Citizens
1414 K St., 3rd floor
Sacramento, CA 95814
(916) 441-3322

COLORADO

GOVERNMENT AGENCIES

General Disabilities
Special Education
State Department of Education
303 W. Colfax Ave.
Denver, CO 80204
(303) 573-3232

Crippled Children's Services
Family Health Services Division
Colorado Department of Health
4210 E. 11th Ave.
Denver, CO 80220
(303) 320-6137

Handicapped Children's Program
Colorado Department of Health
4210 E. 11th Ave.
Denver, Colorado 80220
(303) 320-6137

Developmental Disabilities
Developmental Disabilities Planning
Council
4126 S. Knox Court
Denver, CO 80236
(303) 761-0220, Ext 332

PRIVATE AGENCIES

General Disabilities
Easter Seal Society for Crippled
Children and Adults
609 W. Littleton Blvd.
Littleton, CO 80120
(303) 795-2016

Mental Retardation
Colorado Association for Retarded
Citizens
2727 Bryant St., L-3
Denver, CO 80211
(303) 455-4411
(800) 332-7690

Cerebral Palsy
UCP of Denver
2727 Columbine St.
Denver, CO 80205
(303) 355-7337

CONNECTICUT

GOVERNMENT AGENCIES

General Disabilities
Bureau of Student Services
Department of Education
P.O. Box 2219
Hartford, CT 06145
(203) 566-4383

Early Childhood Unit
Department of Education
P.O. Box 2219
Hartford, CT 06145
(203) 566-5225

Health Services for Handicapped
Children's Section
Department of Health
150 Washington St.
Hartford, CT 06106
(203) 566-2057

Developmental Disabilities
Connecticut Developmental
Disabilities Council
90 Pitkin St.
East Hartford, CT 06108
(203) 725-3829

Visual Impairments
Board of Education and Services for
the Blind
170 Ridge Rd.
Wethersfield, CT 06109
(203) 566-5800
(800) 842-4510 (in Connecticut)

PRIVATE AGENCIES

General Disabilities
Special Education Resource Center
275 Windsor St.
Hartford, CT 06120
(203) 246-8514

Cerebral Palsy
UCP Association of Connecticut
P.O. Box 83
New Britain, CT 06050
(203) 229-3351

Epilepsy
Epilepsy Foundation of Connecticut
165 Ocean Terrace
Bridgeport, CT 06605
(203) 334-0854

Mental Retardation
Connecticut Association for Retarded
Citizens
15 High St., Room 237
Hartford, CT 06103
(203) 522-1179

DELAWARE

GOVERNMENT AGENCIES

General Disabilities
Exceptional Children/Special
Programs Division
Department of Public Instruction
P.O. Box 1402
Dover, DE 19903
(302) 736-5471

Handicapped Children's Services
Jesse S. Cooper Memorial Bldg.
Capitol Square
Dover, DE 19901
(302) 736-4768

Bureau of Personal Health Services
Division of Public Health
Jesse Cooper Memorial Bldg.
P.O. Box 637
Dover, DE 19903
(302) 736-4768

Developmental Disabilities
State Developmental Disabilities
Program
156 S. State St.
P.O. Box 1401
Dover, DE 19901
(302) 736-4456

Mental Retardation
Division of Mental Retardation
449 N. duPont Highway
Dover, DE 19901
(302) 736-4386

PRIVATE AGENCIES

General Disabilities
Easter Seal Society of Del-Mar
2705 Baynard Blvd.
Wilmington, DE 19802
(302) 658-6417

Cerebral Palsy
UCP Association of Delaware, Inc.
701 Shipley St.
Wilmington, DE 19801
(302) 656-8131

Mental Retardation
Delaware Association for Retarded
Citizens
P.O. Box 1896
Wilmington, DE 19899
(302) 764-3662

Visual Impairments
Division of Social Services
305 W. Eighth St.
Wilmington, DE 19801
(302) 571-3570

DISTRICT OF COLUMBIA

GOVERNMENT AGENCIES

General Disabilities
Division of Special Education and
Pupil Personnel Services
District of Columbia Public Schools
10th & H Sts., N.W.
Washington, DC 20001
(202) 724-4018

Maternal and Child Health and
Crippled Children's Services
Department of Human Services
1875 Connecticut Ave., N.W.
Washington, DC 20009
(202) 673-6665

Developmental Disabilities
Mayor's Developmental Disabilities
Planning Council

Randall Bldg., Room 224
First & I Sts., S.W.
Washington, DC 20024
(202) 727-5930

PRIVATE AGENCIES

General Disabilities
Easter Seal Society for Crippled
Children
2800 13th St., N.W.
Washington, DC 20009
(202) 232-2342

Cerebral Palsy
United Cerebral Palsy
1522 K St., N.W., 1112
Washington, DC 20005-1202
(202) 842-1268

Muscular Dystrophy
Muscular Dystrophy Association
5249 Duke St.
Alexandria, VA 22304
(703) 823-1115

FLORIDA

GOVERNMENT AGENCIES

General Disabilities
Bureau of Education for Exceptional
Students
Department of Education
Knott Bldg.
Tallahassee, FL 32301
(904) 488-1570

Children's Medical Services Program
Department of Health and
Rehabilitation Services
1323 Winewood Blvd.
Bldg. 5, Room 127
Tallahassee, FL 32301
(904) 487-2690

Developmental Disabilities
Developmental Services Program
Department of Health and
Rehabilitation Services

1311 Winewood Blvd.
Bldg. 5, Room 215
Tallahassee, FL 32301
(904) 488-4257

Developmental Disabilities Council
1311 Winewood Blvd.
Bldg. 1, Room 308
Tallahassee, FL 32301
(904) 488-4180

Visual Impairments
Department of Education
Division of Blind Services
2540 Executive Center Circle, West
203 Douglas Bldg.
Tallahassee, FL 23201
(904) 488-1330

PRIVATE AGENCIES

General Disabilities
Florida Easter Seal Society
1010 Executive Center Drive,
Suite 101
Orlando, FL 32803
(305) 896-7881

Cerebral Palsy
UCP of Florida
P.O. Box 6476
Tallahassee, FL 32301
(904) 878-2141

Mental Retardation
Association of Retarded
Citizens/Florida
106 N. Bronough St.
Tallahassee, FL 32301
(904) 681-1931

GEORGIA

GOVERNMENT AGENCIES

General Disabilities
State Department of Education
1970 Twin Towers East

205 Butler St.
Atlanta, GA 30334
(404) 656-2425

Crippled Children's Services
Children's Medical Services
Department of Human Resources
878 Peachtree St., N.E., Room 214
Atlanta, GA 30309
(404) 894-6608

Developmental Disabilities
Georgia Council on Developmental
Disabilities
878 Peachtree St., N.E., Room 620
Atlanta, GA 30309
(404) 894-5790

Emotional Disturbance
Child and Adolescent Mental Health
Services
Division of Mental Health
Department of Human Resources
878 Peachtree St., N.E., Room 315
Atlanta, GA 80309
(404) 894-6559

Mental Retardation
Division of Mental Health and Mental
Retardation
Departmemt of Human Resources
878 Peachtree St., N.E., Room 306
Atlanta, GA 30309
(404) 894-6311

PRIVATE AGENCIES

General Disabilities
Georgia Easter Seal Society
1900 Emery St., N.W., Suite 106
Atlanta GA 30318
(404) 351-6551

Cerebral Palsy
UCP of Greater Atlanta Georgia, Inc.
1815 Ponce St.
Atlanta, GA 30305
(4040) 377-3836

GUAM

GOVERNMENT AGENCIES

General Disabilities
Special Education Section
Department of Education
P.O. Box DE
Agana, Guam 96910
011 (671) 472-8906

Crippled Children's Services
Bureau of Public Health and Social
Services
Government of Guam
P.O. Box 2816
Agana, Guam 96910
011 (671) 734-4192

Developmental Disabilities
State Developmental Disabilities
Program
Department of Vocational
Rehabilitation
GCIC Bldg., 9th floor
414 W. Soledad Ave.
Agana, Guam 96910
011 (809) 472-8806

HAWAII

GOVERNMENT AGENCIES

General Disabilities
Special Needs Branch
State Department of Education
3430 Leahi Ave.
Honolulu, HI 96815
(808) 737-3720

Crippled Children's Services
State of Hawaii Department of Health
741 Sunset Ave.
Honolulu, HI 96816
(808) 732-3197

Crippled Children's Services Branch
State of Hawaii Department of Health

3652 Kilauea Ave.
Honolulu, HI 96816
(808) 548-6574

Developmental Disabilities
State Planning Council on
Developmental Disabilities
Programming
Department of Health
P.O. Box 3378
Honolulu, HI 96801
(808) 548-5994/8482/8483

Emotional Disturbance
Division of Mental Health
Department of Health
P.O. Box 3378
Honolulu, HI 96801
(808) 548-6505

PRIVATE AGENCIES

Mental Retardation
Hawaii Association for Retarded
Citizens
245 N. Kukui St.
Honolulu, HI 96817
(808) 536-2274

Cerebral Palsy
UCP Association of Hawaii
2545 N. Kukui St., Suite 207
Honolulu, HI 96817
(808) 538-6789

IDAHO

GOVERNMENT AGENCIES

General Disabilities
State Department of Education
Special Education Division
Len B. Jordan Bldg.
650 W. State St.
Boise, ID 83720
(208) 334-3940

Crippled Children's Program
Department of Health and Welfare
450 W. State, 4th floor
Boise, ID 83720
(208) 334-4136

Bureau of Child Health
Department of Health and Welfare
Statehouse
450 W. State
Boise, ID 83720
(208) 334-4139

Developmental Disabilities
Idaho State Council on
Developmental Disabilities
450 W. State, 10th floor
Boise, ID 83720
(208) 334-4408

Emotional Disturbance
Bureau of Community Mental Health
Division of Community
Rehabilitation
Department of Health and Welfare
450 W. State, 10th floor
Boise, ID 83720
(208) 334-4181

Mental Retardation
Bureau of Developmental
Disabilities
Division of Community
Rehabilitation
Department of Health and Welfare
450 W. State, 10th floor
Boise, ID 83720
(208) 334-4181

Visual Impairments
Commission for the Blind
State House
Boise, ID 83720
(208) 334-3220

PRIVATE AGENCIES

General Disabilities
Easter Seal Society for Crippled
Children and Adults of Idaho

7905 Ustick Rd., Unit E
Boise, ID 83704
(208) 377-1910

Cerebral Palsy
UCP Association of Idaho
5530 Emerald
Boise, ID 83706
(208) 377-8070

Epilepsy
Idaho Epilepsy League
1020 W. Franklin St.
Boise, ID 83702
(208) 344-4340

Speech and Hearing Impairments
Allen D. Renshaw, President
Idaho Speech, Language, and Hearing
Association
1207 Forst St.
Boise, ID 83702
(208) 338-3655

ILLINOIS

GOVERNMENT AGENCIES

General Disabilities
Department of Specialized
Educational Services
State Department of Education
100 N. First St.
Springfield, IL 62777
(217) 782-6601

Division of Services for Crippled
Children
2040 Hill Meadow Dr.
Springfield, IL 62718
(217) 793-2350

Hearing and Visual Impairments
Illinois Deaf/Blind School and Service
Center
818 DuPage Blvd.
Glen Ellyn, IL 60137
(312) 790-2470

Services for the Visually Impaired
Springfield School District #186
444 W. Reynolds
Springfield, IL 62702
(217) 525-3000

PRIVATE AGENCIES

General Disabilities
Coordinating Council for
Handicapped Children
220 S. State St.
Chicago, IL 60604
(312) 939-3513

Illinois Alliance for Exceptional
Children and Adults
515 W. Giles Ave.
Peoria, IL 61614

Down Syndrome
National Down Syndrome Congress
1800 Dempster
Parkridge, IL 60068
(800) 232-6372

INDIANA

GOVERNMENT AGENCIES

General Disabilities
Division of Special Education
Department of Education
Room 229, State House
Indianapolis, IN 46204
(317) 927-0216

Early Childhood Special Education
Department of Education
Division of Special Education
Room 229, State House
Indianapolis, IN 46204
(317) 927-0216

Division of Services for Crippled
Children
Department of Public Welfare
141 S. Meridian St., 6th floor
Indianapolis, IN 46225
(317) 232-4283

Developmental Disabilities
Developmental Disabilities Advisory
Council
Department of Mental Health
429 N. Pennsylvania St.
Indianapolis, IN 46204
(317) 232-7885

PRIVATE AGENCIES

General Disabilities
Indiana Easter Seal Society for
Crippled Children and Adults
3816 E. 96th St.
Indianapolis, IN 46240
(317) 844-7919

Task Force on Education for the
Handicapped
(Parent Advocacy Group)
812 E. Jefferson Blvd.
South Bend, IN 46617
(219) 234-7101

Cerebral Palsy
UCP Association of Indiana
445 N. Pennsylvania St., Room 303
Indianapolis, IN 46204
(317) 634-7134

Mental Retardation
Association for Retarded Citizens of
Indiana
110 E. Washington St., 9th floor
Indianapolis, IN 46204
(317) 632-4387
(800) 383-9100 (in Indiana)

IOWA

GOVERNMENT AGENCIES

General Disabilities
Crippled Children's Services
Child Health Specialty Clinic
University of Iowa
Iowa City, IA 52242
(319) 353-4431

Division of Special Education
Department of Public Instruction
Grimes State Office Bldg.
510 E. 12th St.
Des Moines, IA 50319
(515) 281-3176

Developmental Disabilities
Governor's Planning Council for
Developmental Disabilities
Division of MH/MR/DD
Departm   of Human Services
Hoover State Office Bldg.
Des Moines, IA 50319
(515) 281-7632

Hearing Impairments
Deaf Services of Iowa
Department of Health
Lucas State Office Bldg.
Des Moines, IA 50319
(515) 281-3164

Visual Impairments
State Commission for the Blind
524 Fourth St.
Des Moines, IA 50309
(515) 281-7999

PRIVATE AGENCIES

General Disabilities
Easter Seal Society of Iowa
P.O. Box 4002
Des Moines, IA 50333
(515) 289-1933

March of Dimes Birth Defects
Foundation
554 28th St.
Des Moines, IA 50313
(515) 280-7750

Iowa Federation, Council for
Exceptional Children
240 Pickardy Lane
Council Bluffs, IA 51501
(712) 322-8336

Cerebral Palsy
UCP Association of Iowa
3705 Washington Ave.
Des Moines, IA 50310-4433
(515) 255-7679

Epilepsy
Epilepsy Foundation of America—
Iowa
2915 47th St.
Des Moines, IA 50313
(515) 277-1872

Mental Retardation
Iowa Association for Retarded
Citizens
1707 High St.
Des Moines, IA 50309
(515) 283-2358
(800) 367-2927

Severe and Profound Handicaps
The Association for Persons with
Severe Handicaps (TASH)
NTAEA
Box M
Clear Lake, IA 50428
(206) 523-8446

Speech and Hearing Impairments
Iowa Speech, Language and Hearing
Association
1200 Pleasant St.
Des Moines, IA 50308
(515) 283-6344

KANSAS

GOVERNMENT AGENCIES

General Disabilities
Division of Special Education
State Department of Education
120 E. 10th St.
Topeka, KS 66612
(913) 296-7454

Crippled Children's Services
State Department of Health and
Environment
Forbes Field #740
Topeka, KS 66620
(913) 862-9360, Ext. 576

Developmental Disabilities
Planning Council for Developmental
Disabilities
State Office Bldg., 5th floor
Topeka, KS 66612
(913) 296-2608

Emotional Disturbance
Education Program Specialist for
Mental Health and Youth Services
Youth Center at Topeka
1440 N.W. 25th St.
Topeka, KS 66617
(913) 296-7711

Mental Retardation
Division of Mental Health and
Retardation Services
State Office Bldg., 5th floor
Topeka, KS 66612
(913) 296-3471

PRIVATE AGENCIES

General Disabilities
Goodwill Industries—Easter Seal
Society of Kansas
3636 N. Oliver
Wichita, KS 67220
(316) 744-0483

Cerebral Palsy
UCP Association of Kansas, Inc.
P.O. Box 8217
Wichita, KS 67208
(316) 688-1888

Mental Retardation
Kansas Association for Retarded
Citizens
11111 W. 59th Terrace

Shawnee, KS 66203
(913) 268-8200

Speech and Hearing Impairments
400 N. Woodlawn, Suite 18
Wichita, KS 67208
(316) 683-7831

KENTUCKY

GOVERNMENT AGENCIES

General Disabilities
Office of Education for Exceptional
Children
State Department of Education
Capital Plaza Tower, 8th floor
Frankfort, KY 40601
(502) 564-4970

Department for Health Services
Cabinet for Human Resources
275 E. Main St.
Frankfort, KY 40621
(502) 564-3970

Crippled Children's Services
Division of Maternal and Child
Health
Department for Health Services
Cabinet for Human Resources
275 E. Main St.
Frankfort, KY 40621
(502) 564-4830

Kentucky Commission for
Handicapped Conditions
1405 E. Burnette Ave.
Louisville, KY 40217
(502) 588-4459

Developmental Disabilities
Department of Mental Health/Mental
Retardation Services
Cabinet for Human Resources
275 E. Main St.
Frankfort, KY 40621
(502) 564-7842

Emotional Disturbance
Department for Mental
Health/Mental Retardation
Cabinet for Human Resources
275 E. Main St.
Frankfort, KY 40621
(502) 564-4527

Visual Impairments
Department for the Blind
Education and Humanities Cabinet
427 Versailles Rd.
Frankfort, KY 40601
(502) 564-4754

Hearing Impairments
Commission on Deaf and Hearing
Impaired
Capitol Plaza Tower, 12th floor
Frankfort, KY 40601
(502) 564-2604

PRIVATE AGENCIES

General Disabilities
Kentucky Easter Seal Society for
Crippled Children and Adults
233 E. Broadway
Louisville, KY 40202
(502) 584-9781

Cerebral Palsy
UCP Association of Kentucky
465 Spring Hill
Lexington, KY 40555
(606) 278-6851

LOUISIANA

GOVERNMENT AGENCIES

General Disabilities
Special Educational Services
State Department of Education
P.O. Box 94064
Baton Rouge, LA 70804-9064
(504) 342-3631

Handicapped Children Program
Office of Preventive and Public
Health Services
P.O. Box 60630, Room 607
New Orleans, LA 70160
(504) 568-5055

Handicapped Children's Service and
Environmental Quality
Department of Health and Human
Resources
P.O. Box 60630
New Orleans, LA 70160
(504) 568-5055

Developmental Disabilities
Louisiana State Planning Council on
Developmental Disabilities
721 Government St., Room 202
Baton Rouge, LA 70802
(504) 342-6804

Emotional Disturbance
Office of Mental Health
Department of Health and Human
Resources
P.O. Box 4049
Baton Rouge, LA 70821
(504) 342-2544

Mental Retardation
Office of Mental Retardation
Department of Health and Human
Resources
721 Government St., Room 308
Baton Rouge, LA 70802
(504) 342-6811

Visual Impairments
Blind Services Program
Office of Human Development
P.O. Box 28
Baton Rouge, LA 70821
(504) 342-5282

PRIVATE AGENCIES

General Disabilities
Easter Seal Society
4631 W. Napoleon Ave.
Metairie, LA 70011
(504) 885-0480

Cerebral Palsy
UCP of Louisiana
1500 Edwards Ave., Suite M
Harahan, LA 70123
(504) 733-6851

Mental Retardation
Louisiana Association for Retarded
Citizens
658 St. Louis St.
Baton Rouge, LA 70802
(504) 383-0742

Speech and Hearing Impairments
Louisiana Speech-Language-Hearing
Association
815 Desire St.
New Orleans, LA 70117
(504) 483-7690

MAINE

GOVERNMENT AGENCIES

General Disabilities
Division of Special Education
State Department of Educational and
Cultural Services
State House, Station #23
157 Capital St.
Augusta, ME 04333
(207) 289-3451

Crippled Children's Services
Division of Maternal and Child
Health
Department of Human Services
State House, Station #11
157 Capital St.

Augusta, ME 04333
(207) 289-3311

Developmental Disabilities
Developmental Disabilities Council
State Office Bldg., Room 411
Statoin #40
Augusta, ME 04330
(207) 289-3161

Mental Retardation
Bureau of Mental Retardation
Department of Mental Health and
Mental Retardation
State Office Bldg., Room 411
Station #40
Augusta, ME 04330
(207) 289-3161

PRIVATE AGENCIES

General Disabilities
Pine Tree Society of Handicapped
Children and Adults
84 Front St.
P.O. Box 518
Bath, ME 04530
(207) 443-3341

Advisory Panel on the Education of
Exceptional Children
Hancock County Education
Cooperative
P.O. Box 37
Ellsworth, ME 04605
(207) 667-5388

Cerebral Palsy
UCP of Northeastern Maine
103 Texas Ave.
Bangor, ME 04401
(207) 947-6771

Speech and Hearing Impairments
Maine Speech-Language-Hearing
Association
RFD 2, Box 304
Gorham, ME 04038
(207) 892-3574

Parent Organization
Special-Needs Parent Information
Network (SPIN)
P.O. Box 2067
Augusta, ME 04330
(207) 582-2504

MARIANA ISLANDS

GOVERNMENT AGENCIES

General Disabilities
Office of Special Education Programs
Headquarters, Office of Education
Office of the High Commissioner
Trust Territory of the Pacific Islands
Saipan, Mariana Islands 96950
(670) 322-9956

Vocational Rehabilitation Service
Dr. Torres Memorial Hospital
Commonwealth of the Northern
Marianas
Saipan, Mariana Islands 96950
(670) 234-6538

Maternal and Child Health and
Crippled Children's Services
Department of Health Services
Office of the High Commissioner
Trust Territory of the Pacific Islands
Saipan, Mariana Islands 96950
(670) 322-9355

Maternal and Child Health and
Family Planning
Department of Public Health and
Environmental Services
Dr. Torres Memorial Hospital
Saipan, Mariana Islands 96950
011 (160) 671-6110

MARYLAND

GOVERNMENT AGENCIES

General Disabilities
Division of Special Education
State Department of Education
200 W. Baltimore St.
Baltimore, MD 21201
(301) 659-2489

Information and Referral for
Handicapped
Department of Education
200 W. Baltimore St.
Baltimore, MD 21201
(301) 385-6523 (call collect)

Developmental Disabilities
Developmental Disabilities Council
201 W. Preston St., 4th floor
Baltimore, MD 21201
(301) 383-3358

Crippled Children's Programs
Department of Mental Health
201 W. Preston St., 4th floor
Baltimore, MD 21201
(301) 383-2821

Emotional Disturbance
Child and Adolescent Services Unit
Mental Hygiene Administration
Department of Health & Mental
Hygiene
201 W. Preston St., 4th floor
Baltimore, MD 21201
(301) 659-2099

Mental Retardation
Mental Retardation/Development
Disabilities Administration
Department of Health and Mental
Hygiene
201 W. Preston St.
Baltimore, MD 21201
(301) 383-3354

PRIVATE AGENCIES

General Disabilities
Central Maryland Chapter of the
National Easter Seal Society
3700 Fourth St.
Baltimore, MD 21225
(301) 355-0100

Cerebral Palsy
UCP of Maryland
1416 Forest Dr.
Annapolis, MD 21403
(301) 263-9600

Learning Disabilities
Maryland Association for Children
with Learning Disabilities
1747 Wentworth Ave.
Baltimore, MD 21234
(301) 665-3309

Mental Retardation
Maryland Association for Retarded
Citizens
5602 Baltimore National Pike
Baltimore, MD 21228
(301) 744-0255

MASSACHUSETTS

GOVERNMENT AGENCIES

General Disabilities
Division of Special Education
State Department of Education
Quincy Center Plaza
1385 Hancock St.
Quincy, MA 0216?
(617) 770-7468

State Office of Handicapped Affairs
1 Ashburton Pl., Room 303
Boston, MA 02108
(617) 727-7440

Services for Handicapped Children,
Division of FHS
Department of Public Health
150 Tremont St.
Boston, MA 02111
(617) 727-3372
(800) 882-1435 (Massachusetts only)

Developmental Disabilities
Massachusetts Developmental
Disabilities Council
One Ashburton Pl.

Boston, MA 02108
(617) 727-6374

Emotional Disturbance
Department of Mental Health
160 N. Washington St.
Boston, MA 02114
(617) 727-5603

Mental Retardation
State Mental Retardation Program
Department of Mental Health
160 N. Washington St.
Boston, MA 02114
(617) 727-5608

PRIVATE AGENCIES

General Disabilities
Massachusetts Easter Seal Society
Denholm Bldg.
484 Main St.
Worcester, MA 01608
(617) 757-2756
(800) 922-8290 (in Massachusetts)

Federation for Children with Special
Needs
313 Stuart St., 2nd floor
Boston, MA 02116
(617) 482-2915

Information Center for Individuals
with Disabilities
20 Park Plaza, Room 330
Boston, MA 02116
(617) 727-5540 (Voice)
(617) 727-5236 (TTY)
(800) 462-5015 (in Massachusetts)

Cerebral Palsy
UCP Association of Metropolitan
Area
71 Arsenal St.
Watertown, MA 02172
(617) 926-5480

Learning Disabilities
Massachusetts Association for Children with Learning Disabilities

P.O. Box 28
West Newton, MA 02165
(617) 891-5009

Mental Retardation
Massachusetts Association for Retarded Citizens
217 South St.
Waltham, MA 02154
(617) 891-6270

Eunice Kennedy Shriver Center for Mental Retardation
Walter E. Fernald School
200 Trapelo Rd.
Waltham, MA 02254
(617) 893-3500

Visual Impairments
Vision Foundation, Inc.
2 Mt. Auburn St.
Watertown, MA 02172
(617) 926-4232
(800) 852-3029 (Massachusetts only)

MICHIGAN

GOVERNMENT AGENCIES

General Disabilities
Special Education Services
Department of Education
P.O. Box 30008
Lansing, MI 48909
(517) 373-1695

Services to Crippled Children
Department of Public Health
3500 North Logan St.
P.O. Box 30035
Lansing, MI 48909
(517) 373-3416

Developmental Disabilities
Developmental Disabilities Council
Department of Mental Health
Lewis Cass Bldg., 6th floor

Lansing, MI 48926
(517) 373-6443

Emotional Disturbance
Department of Mental Health
Lewis Cass Bldg.
Lansing, MI 48926
(517) 373-3500

Mental Retardation
State Mental Retardation Program
Program Development and Support Systems
Department of Mental Health
Lewis Cass Bldg., 6th floor
Lansing, MI 48926
(517) 373-2900

Visual Impairments
Commission for the Blind
Department of Labor
309 N. Washington St.
P.O. Box 30015
Lansing, MI 48909
(517) 373-2062

PRIVATE AGENCIES

General Disabilities
Easter Seal Society of Michigan
4065 Saladin Dr., S.E.
Grand Rapids, MI 49506
(616) 942-2081

Cerebral Palsy
UCP Association of Michigan, Inc.
202 E. Boulevard Dr.
Flint, MI 48503
(313) 239-9459

Mental Retardation
Michigan Association for Retarded Citizens
313 S. Washington St., Suite 310
(517) 487-5426
(800) 292-7851 (in Michigan)

MINNESOTA

GOVERNMENT AGENCIES

General Disabilities
Special Education Section
State Department of Education
Capitol Square Bldg.
550 Cedar St.
St. Paul, MN 55101
(612) 296-4163

Division of Maternal and Child
Health and Crippled Children's
Services
Department of Health
717 Delaware St., S.E.
P.O. Box 9441
Minneapolis, MN 55440
(612) 623-5150

Services for Children with Handicaps
Department of Health
717 Delaware St., S.E.
Minneapolis, MN 55440
(612) 623-5150

Minnesota State Council for the
Handicapped
208 Metro Square Bldg.
St. Paul, MN 55101
(612) 296-6785
(800) 652-9747 (in Minnesota)

Developmental Disabilities
Governor's Planning Council on
Development Disabilities
201 Capitol Square Bldg.
550 Cedar St.
St. Paul, MN 55101
(612) 296-4018

Mental Retardation
Division of Retardation Services
Department of Human Services
Centennial Office Bldg., 4th floor
St. Paul, MN 55155
(612) 296-2160

Visual Impairments
Services for the Blind and Visually
Handicapped
Department of Human Services
1745 University Ave.
St. Paul, MN 55104
(612) 296-6080

Hearing Impairments
Regional Service Center for Hearing
Impaired
390 N. Roberts St., 5th floor
St. Paul, MN 55101
(612) 297-1872

PRIVATE AGENCIES

Cerebral Palsy
UCP of Minnesota
Giggs Midway Bldg., S-233
1821 University Ave.
St. Paul, MN 55104
(612) 646-7588

Mental Retardation
Minnesota Association for Retarded
Citizens
3225 Lydale Ave., South
Minneapolis, MN 55408-3699
(612) 827-5641
(800) 582-5256 (in Minnesota only)

PARENT ORGANIZATION

Parent Advocate Coalition for
Education Rights (PACER)
PACER Center, Inc.
4826 Chicago Ave., South
Minneapolis, MN 55417-1055
(612) 827-2966

MISSISSIPPI

GOVERNMENT AGENCIES

General Disabilities
Bureau of Special Services
Department of Education

P.O. Box 771
Jackson, MS 39205
(601) 359-3490

Children's Medical Program
State Board of Health
P.O. Box 1700
Jackson, MS
(601) 982-6571

Developmental Disabilities
Developmental Disabilities Program
Department of Mental Health
1100 Robert E. Lee Bldg.
Jackson, MS 39201
(601) 359-1290

Emotional Disturbance
Department of Mental Health
1100 Robert E. Lee Bldg.
Jackson, MS 39201
(601) 359-1288

Mental Retardation
Bureau of Mental Retardation
Department of Mental Health
1100 Robert E. Lee Bldg.
Jackson, MS 39201
(601) 359-1290

PRIVATE AGENCIES

Cerebral Palsy
United Cerebral Palsy of Mississippi
P.O. Box 16924
Jackson, MS 39236
(601) 362-5607

MISSOURI

GOVERNMENT AGENCIES

General Disabilities
Division of Special Education
Department of Elementary and
Secondary Education
P.O. Box 480

Jefferson City, MO 65102
(314) 751-2965

Crippled Children's Services
P.O. Box 570
Jefferson City, MO 65102
(314) 751-2407

Developmental Disabilities
Division of Mental
Retardation/Development Disabilities
Department of Mental Health
P.O. Box 687
Jefferson City, MO 65102
(314) 751-4054

Emotional Disturbance
Department of Mental Health
P.O. Box 687
Jefferson City, MO 65102
(314) 751-3070

Visual Impairments
Bureau for the Blind
Division of Family Services
619 E. Capitol Ave.
Jefferson City, MO 65101
(314) 751-4249

PRIVATE AGENCIES

Cerebral Palsy
UCP of Missouri
125 W. Dunklin St.
Jefferson City, MO 65101-2937
(314) 636-5334

Mental Retardation
Missouri Association for Retarded
Citizens
P.O. Box 1705
Jefferson City, MO 65102
(314) 634-2220

Speech and Hearing Impairments
Missouri Speech-Language-Hearing
Association
Central Missouri State University

Department of Speech Pathology and
Audiology
Warrensburg, MO 65093
(816) 429-4993

MONTANA

GOVERNMENT AGENCIES

General Disabilities
Special Education Unit
Office of Public Instruction
State Capitol
Helena, MT 59620
(406) 444-5661

Crippled Children's Services
Bureau of Maternal and Child Health
Cogswell Bldg.
Helena, MT 59620
(406) 444-4740

Mental Retardation
Developmental Disabilities
Division of Social and Rehabilitative
Services
P.O. Box 4210
Helena, MT 59604
(406) 444-2995

PRIVATE AGENCIES

Mental Retardation
Montana Association for Retarded
Children
1443 Jackson
Missoula, MT 59801
(406) 549-3064

NEBRASKA

GOVERNMENT AGENCIES

General Disabilities
Special Education Branch
State Department of Education

301 Centennial Mall
P.O. Box 94987
Lincoln, NB 68509
(402) 471-2471

Crippled Children's Services
Department of Public Welfare
301 Centennial Mall South
Lincoln, NB 68509
(402) 471-3121

Hotline for the Handicapped/
Nebraska Childfind
Nebraska Department of Education
6th Floor
301 Centennial Mall South
Lincoln, NB 68509
(402) 471-3656

Developmental Disabilities
Department of Health/Developmental
Disabilities
301 Centennial Mall South
P.O. Box 95007
Lincoln, NB 68509
(402) 471-2981

Emotional Disturbance
State Mental Health Agency
Lincoln Regional Center
P.O. Box 80499
Lincoln, NB 68501
(402) 471-4444

Mental Retardation
Office of Mental Retardation
Department of Public Institutions
P.O. Box 94728
Lincoln, NB 68509
(402) 471-2851, Ext. 457

NEVADA

GOVERNMENT AGENCIES

General Disabilities
Special Education Branch
Nevada Department of Education

400 W. King St.
Capitol Complex
Carson City, NV 89710
(702) 885-3140

Crippled Children's Services
Bureau of Maternal, Child, and
School Health
Department of Human Services
505 E. King St., Room 205
Carson City, NV 89710
(702) 885-4885

Developmental Disabilities
Developmental Disabilities Council
505 E. King St., Room 502
Capitol Complex
Carson City, NV 89710
(702) 885-4440

Mental Retardation
Division of Mental Health/Mental
Retardation
Department of Human Resources
1001 N. Mountain St., Suite 2-A
Capitol Complex
Carson City, NV 89710
(702) 885-5943

PRIVATE AGENCIES

General Disabilities
Easter Seal Society for Crippled
Children and Adults of Nevada
1455 E. Tropicana Ave., Suite 660
Las Vegas, NV 89119
(702) 739-7771

Nevada Association for the
Handicapped (parent advocacy group)
P.O. Box 28458
Las Vegas, NV 89126
(702) 870-7050

Coalition for Handicapped Children's
Education (CHANCE)
5124 Casco Way
Las Vegas, NV 89107
(702) 870-8221

Cerebral Palsy
UCP of Southern Nevada
3101 S. Maryland Pky., Suite 209
Las Vegas, NV 89109
(702) 731-3895

Mental Retardation
Association for Retarded Citizens
1520 Maine St.
Fallon, NV 89046
(702) 432-4760

Speech and Hearing Impairments
Nevada Speech and Hearing
Association
505 S. Arlington Ave., B2
Reno, NV 89509
(702) 329-5108

NEW HAMPSHIRE

GOVERNMENT AGENCIES

General Disabilities
Special Education Section
State Department of Education
101 Pleasant St.
Concord, NH 03301
(603) 271-3741

Bureau for Handicapped Children
Office of Family and Community
Health
Division of Public Health Services
Hazen Dr.
Concord, NH 03301
(603) 271-4499
(800) 852-3345 (in New Hampshire)

Developmental Disabilities
New Hampshire Developmental
Disabilities Council
One Eagle Square, Suite 510
Concord, NH 03301
(603) 271-3236

Emotional Disturbance
Adolescent Services
New Hampshire Hospital

Concord, NH 03301
(603) 224-6531, Ext. 2407

Mental Retardation
Mental Retardation and
Developmental Services Program
Division for Community
Developmental Services
Health and Welfare Bldg.
Hazen Dr.
Concord, NH 03301
(603) 271-4706

PRIVATE AGENCIES

General Disabilities
Easter Seal Society—Goodwill
Industries of New Hampshire
555 Auburn St.
Manchester, NH 03103
(603) 623-8863

Parent Information Center (PIC)
P.O. Box 1422
Concord, NH 03301
(603) 224-7005

Mental Retardation
Association for Retarded Citizens of
New Hampshire
244 N. Main St.
Carrigan Commons
Concord, NH 03301
(603) 228-9092

NEW JERSEY

GOVERNMENT AGENCIES

General Disabilities
Crippled Children's Services
Special Child Health Services
Department of Health
CN 364
Trenton, NJ 08625
(609) 292-5676

Division of Special Education
Department of Education
225 W. State St., CN 500
Trenton, NJ 08625
(609) 292-0147

Developmental Disabilities
Developmental Disabilities Council
108-110 N. Broad St., CN 700
Trenton, NJ 08625
(609) 292-3745

Emotional Disturbance
Division of Mental Health and
Hospitals
Department of Human Services
CN 700
Trenton, NJ 08625
(609) 987-0886

Mental Retardation
Division of Mental Retardation
Department of Human Services
222 S. Warren St.
Capitol Place One
Trenton, NJ 08625
(609) 292-3742

Visual Impairments
Commission for the Blind
State Board of Control
Department of Human Services
Newark Center Bldg.
100 Raymond Blvd.
Newark, NJ 07102
(201) 648-3333
(800) 962-1233 (in New Jersey)

PRIVATE AGENCIES

Cerebral Palsy
UCP Association of New Jersey
956 S. Broad St.
Trenton, NJ 08611
(609) 392-4004

Epilepsy
Epilepsy Foundation of New Jersey
206 W. State St.
Trenton, NJ 08608
(609) 392-4900

Mental Retardation
Association for Retarded Citizens
99 Bayard St.
New Brunswick, NJ 08901
(201) 246-2525

NEW MEXICO

GOVERNMENT AGENCIES

General Disabilities
Division of Special Education
State Department of Education
300 Don Gaspar Ave.
Santa Fe, NM 87503
(505) 827-6541

Crippled Children's Services
Children's Medical Services
Health and Environment Department
P.O. Box 968
Santa Fe, NM 87503
(505) 827-3201

Developmental Disabilities
DDPC
440-B Cerrillos Rd.
Santa Fe, NM 87503
(505) 827-7371

Emotional Disturbance
Mental Health Bureau
P.O. Box 968
Santa Fe, NM 87504-0968
(505) 984-0020

Mental Retardation
Developmental Disabilities Bureau
HED-Behavioral Health Services
Division

P.O. Box 968
Santa Fe, NM 87504-0968
(505) 984-0020

PRIVATE AGENCIES

General Disabilities
Easter Seal Society of New Mexico
4805 Menaul, N.E.
Albuquerque, NM 87110
(505) 888-3811

Mental Retardation
New Mexico Association for
Retarded Citizens
8200½ Menaul Blvd., No. 3
Albuquerque, NM 87110
(505) 298-6796

NEW YORK

GOVERNMENT AGENCIES

General Disabilities
Office for Education of Children with
Handicapping Conditions
State Department of Education
Education Bldg. Annex, Room 1073
Albany, NY 12234
(518) 474-5548

Crippled Children's Services
Special Children Services
Bureau of Maternal and Child Health
Corning Tower Bldg., Room 821
Empire State Plaza
Albany, NY 12237
(518) 474-1912

Developmental Disabilities
New York State Developmental
Disabilities Planning Council
1 Empire State Plaza, 10th floor
Albany, NY 12223
(518) 474-3655

Emotional Disturbance
Office of Mental Health
44 Holland Ave.
Albany, NY 12229
(518) 474-4403

Mental Retardation
Office of Mental Retarda-
tion/Developmental Disabilities
44 Holland Ave.
Albany, NY 12229
(518) 473-1997

Visual Impairments
Commission for the Blind and
Visually Handicapped
State Department of Social Services
40 N. Pearl St.
Albany, NY 12243
(518) 473-1801
(800) 342-3715, Ext. 46812 (in New
York)

PRIVATE AGENCIES

General Disabilities
New York Easter Seal Society for
Crippled Children and Adults
194 Washington Ave.
Albany, NY 12210
(518) 434-4103

Cerebral Palsy
UCP Association of New York State
330 W. 34th St.
New York, NY 10001
(212) 947-5770

Mental Retardation
New York State Association for
Retarded Children, Inc.
393 Delaware Ave.
Delmar, NY 12054
(518) 439-8311

Spina Bifida
Spina Bifida Association
86-07 134th St.

Richmond Hill, NY 11460
(212) 526-4708

NORTH CAROLINA

GOVERNMENT AGENCIES

General Disabilities
Division of Exceptional Children
Department of Public Instruction
114 E. Edenton St.
Raleigh, NC 27611
(919) 733-3921

Crippled Children's Program
Division of Health Services
Department of Human Resources
P.O. Box 2091
Raleigh, NC 27602
(919) 733-7437

Developmental Disabilities
Council on Developmental
Disabilities
Department of Human Resources
325 N. Salisbury St., Suite 616
(919) 733-6566

Emotional Disturbance
Division of Mental Health, Mental
Retardation and Substance Abuse
Services
Department of Human Resources
325 N. Salisbury St.
Raleigh, NC 27611
(919) 733-7011

Mental Retardation
Mental Retardation Services
Division of Mental Health, Mental
Retardation and Substance Abuse
Services
Department of Human Resources
325 N. Salisbury St.
Raleigh, NC 27611
(919) 733-3654

Visual Impairments
Division of Services for the Blind
Department of Human Resources
309 Ashe Ave.
Raleigh, NC 27606
(919) 733-9822

PRIVATE AGENCIES

General Disabilities
Easter Seal Society of North Carolina
832 Wake Forest Rd.
Raleigh, NC 27604
(919) 834-1191

Cerebral Palsy
UCP of North Carolina
P.O. Box 12728
Raleigh, NC 27605
(919) 832-3787

Mental Retardation
North Carolina Association for
Retarded Citizens
P.O. Box 18551
Raleigh, NC 27619
(919) 782-4632

NORTH DAKOTA

GOVERNMENT AGENCIES

General Disabilities
Special Education Division
Department of Public Instruction
State Capitol
Bismarck, ND 58505
(701) 224-2277
(800) 932-8974 (in North Dakota)

Crippled Children's Services
Department of Human Services
State Capitol
Bismarck, ND 58505
(701) 224-2436

Developmental Disabilities
Developmental Disabilities Division
Department of Human Services
State Capitol Bldg.
Bismarck, ND 58505
(701) 224-2768

ND Developmental Disabilities
Council
ND Department of Human Services
State Capitol Bldg.
Bismarck, ND 58505
(701) 224-2970

Emotional Disturbance
Mental Health and Retardation
Services
State Department of Health
909 Basin Ave.
Bismarck, ND 58505
(701) 253-2964

PRIVATE AGENCIES

General Disabilities
Easter Seal Society of North Dakota
Box 490
Bismarck, ND 58501
(701) 223-8730

Mental Retardation
North Dakota Association for
Retarded Citizens
418 E. Broadway
Bismarck, ND 58501
(701) 223-5349

OHIO

GOVERNMENT AGENCIES

General Disabilities
Division of Special Education
State Department of Education
933 High St.
Worthington, OH 43085
(614) 466-2650

Crippled Children's Services
Division of Maternal and Child
Health
P.O. Box 118
Columbus, OH 43216
(614) 466-3263

Governor's Office of Advocacy for
Disabled Persons
State Office Tower, Suite 1376
30 E. Broad St.
Columbus, OH 43215
(614) 466-9956

Developmental Disabilities
Office of Developmental Disabilities
Council
Department of Mental Retardation/
Developmental Disabilities
State Office Tower, Suite 1020
30 E. Broad St.
Columbus, OH 43215
(614) 466-5205

Emotional Disturbance
Department of Mental Health
State Office Tower, Suite 1180
30 E. Broad St.
Columbus, OH 43215
(614) 466-2337

Mental Retardation
Department of Mental Retarda-
tion/Developmental Disabilities
State Office Tower, Suite 1280
30 E. Broad St.
Columbus, OH 43215
(614) 466-5214

PRIVATE AGENCIES

General Disabilities
Ohio Easter Seal Society, Inc.
2204 S. Hamilton Rd.
P.O. Box 32462
Columbus, OH 43232
(614) 868-9126

Cerebral Palsy
UCP of Ohio
P.O. Box 2643
Lakewood, OH 44107
(216) 228-5133

Learning Disabilities
Ohio Association for Children with
Learning Disabilities
4601 N. High St.
Columbus, OH 43214
(614) 891-1167

Mental Retardation
Ohio Association for Retarded
Citizens
360 S. 3rd St., Suite 101
Columbus, OH 43215
(614) 228-4412

Speech and Hearing Impairments
Ohio Speech and Hearing Association
9331 Union Rd. South
Miamisburg, OH 45342
(513) 866-4972

OKLAHOMA

GOVERNMENT AGENCIES

General Disabilities
Exceptional Children's Services
State Department of Education
2500 N. Lincoln, Suite 263
Oklahoma City, OK 73105
(405) 521-3351

Crippled Children's Services
Department of Human Services
P.O. Box 25352
Oklahoma City, OK 73125
(405) 557-2525

Oklahoma Office for Handicapped
Concerns
4300 N. Lincoln Blvd., Suite 200
Oklahoma City, OK 73105
(405) 521-3756

Developmental Disabilities
Mental Retardation/Developmental
Disabilities Community Services
Department of Human Resources
P.O. Box 25352
Oklahoma City, OK 73125
(405) 521-2988

Emotional Disturbance
Department of Mental Health
P.O. Box 53277
Capitol Station
Oklahoma City, OK 73152
(405) 521-0044

Mental Retardation
Developmental Disabilities Services
Department of Human Resources
P.O. Box 25352
Oklahoma City, OK 73125
(405) 521-3571

PRIVATE AGENCIES

General Disabilities
Easter Seal Society, Inc.
2100 N.W. 63rd St.
Oklahoma City, OK 73116
(405) 848-7603

Cerebral Palsy
UCP of Oklahoma
3428 N.W. 20th St.
Oklahoma City, OK 73107
(405) 947-7641

Speech and Hearing Impairments
Oklahoma Speech-Language-Hearing
Association
Box 53217
State Capitol Station
Oklahoma City, OK 73105
(405) 624-6020

OREGON

GOVERNMENT AGENCIES

General Disabilities
Special Education and Student
Services Division

Department of Education
700 Pringle Pky., S.E.
Salem, OR 97310-0290
(503) 378-3598

Crippled Children's Services
P.O. Box 574
Portland, OR 97207
(503) 225-8095

Developmental Disabilities
Oregon Developmental Disabilities
Council
2575 Bittern St., N.E.
Salem, OR 97310-0520
(503) 378-2429

Emotional Disturbance
Mental Health Division
Department of Human Resources
2575 Bittern St., N.E.
Salem, OR 97310-0520
(503) 378-2671

Mental Retardation
Program for Mental Retardation/
Developmental Disabilities
Mental Health Division
Department of Human Resources
2575 Bittern St., N.E.
Salem, OR 97310-0520
(503) 378-2429

Visual Impairments
Commission for the Blind
535 S.E. 12th St.
Portland, OR 97214
(503) 238-8380

PRIVATE AGENCIES

Cerebral Palsy
UCP of Oregon
7830 S.E. Foster Rd.
Portland, OR 97206
(503) 777-4166

Mental Retardation
Oregon Association for Retarded
Citizens

1745 State St., N.E.
Salem, OR 97301
(503) 581-2726
(800) 452-0313 (in Oregon)

Speech and Hearing Impairments
Oregon Speech and Hearing
Association
3734 N.E. Alameda
Portland, OR 97212
(503) 232-4424

PENNSYLVANIA

GOVERNMENT AGENCIES

General Disabilities
Bureau of Special Education
State Department of Education
333 Market St.
Harrisburg, PA 17126-0333
(717) 783-6913

Children's Rehabilitative Services
Bureau of Professional Health
Services
State Department of Health
P.O. Box 90, Room 714
Harrisburg, PA 17108
(717) 783-5436

Developmental Disabilities
Developmental Disabilities Planning
Council
569 Forum Bldg.
Harrisburg, PA 17120
(717) 787-6057

Mental Retardation
State Mental Retardation Program
302 Health and Welfare Bldg.
P.O. Box 2675
Harrisburg, PA 17105
(717) 787-3700

Emotional Disturbance
State Mental Health Agency
308 Health and Welfare Bldg.

Harrisburg, PA 17120
(717) 787-6443

PRIVATE AGENCIES
Cerebral Palsy
UCP of Pennsylvania
925 Linda Lane
Camp Hill, PA 17011
(717) 761-5656

Mental Retardation
Pennsylvania Association for
Retarded Citizens
1500 N. 2nd St.
Harrisburg, PA 17102
(717) 234-2621

Visual Impairments
Blindness and Visual Services
Department of Public Welfare
902 N. 7th St.
P.O. Box 2675
Harrisburg, PA 17105
(717) 787-6176

PUERTO RICO

GOVERNMENT AGENCIES
General Disabilities
Special Education Program for
Handicapped Children
Department of Education
Box 759
Hato Rey, PR 00919
(809) 764-8059

Crippled Children's Services
Box CH-11321
Caparra Heights Station
San Juan, PR 00922
(809) 781-2728

Developmental Disabilities
Developmental Disabilities Council
Box 9543
Santurce, PR 00908
(809) 722-0590/0595

Mental Retardation
State Mental Retardation Program
Family Services
Department of Social Services
P.O. Box 11398
Santurce, PR 00910
(809) 723-2127

RHODE ISLAND

GOVERNMENT AGENCIES

General Disabilities
Special Education Unit
Department of Education
Roger Williams Bldg., Room 200
22 Hayes St.
Providence, RI 02908
(401) 277-3505

Crippled Children's Services
Division of Family Health
Department of Health
75 Davis St., Room 302
Providence, RI 02908
(401) 277-2312

Developmental Disabilities
Developmental Disabilities Council
600 New London Ave.
Cranston, RI 02920
(401) 464-3191

Emotional Disturbance
Department of Mental Health,
Retardation and Hospitals
600 New London Ave.
Cranston, RI 02920
(401) 464-3201

Mental Retardation
Division of Retardation
Department of Mental Health,
Retardation and Hospitals
600 New London Ave.
Cranston, RI 02920
(401) 464-3234

PRIVATE AGENCIES

General Disabilities
Easter Seal Society of Rhode Island
667 Waterman Ave.
East Providence, RI 02914
(401) 438-9500

Cerebral Palsy
UCP of Rhode Island
500 Prospect St.
Pawtucket, RI 02860
(401) 728-7800

Mental Retardation
Association for Retarded Citizens
Craik Bldg.
2845 Post Rd.
Warwick, RI 02886
(401) 738-5550

Visual Impairments
Services for the Blind and Visually
Impaired
Social and Rehabilitation Services
46 Aborn St.
Providence, RI 02903
(401) 277-2300

SOUTH CAROLINA

GOVERNMENT AGENCIES

General Disabilities
Office of Programs for the
Handicapped
Koger Executive Center
100 Executive Center Dr.
Santee Bldg., Suite A-24
Columbia, SC 29210
(803) 758-6122

Crippled Children's Services
Division of Children's Health
Department of Health and
Environmental Control
2600 Bull St.
Columbia, SC 29201
(803) 758-5491

Developmental Disabilities
Developmental Disabilities Council
1205 Pendleton St., Room 404
Columbia, SC 29201
(803) 758-8016

Emotional Disturbance
Department of Mental Health
2414 Bull St., P.O. Box 485
Columbia, SC 29202
(803) 758-7701

Mental Retardation
Department of Mental Retardation
2712 Middleburg Dr.
P.O. Box 4706
Columbia, SC 29240
(803) 758-3671

Visual Impairments
Commission for the Blind
1430 Confederate Ave.
Columbia, SC 29201
(803) 758-2595

PRIVATE AGENCIES

General Disabilities
Easter Seal Society of South Carolina
3020 Farrow Rd.
Columbia, SC 29203
(803) 256-0735

Mental Retardation
South Carolina Association for
Retarded Citizens
7412 Fairfield Rd.
Columbia, SC 29202
(803) 754-4763

SOUTH DAKOTA

GOVERNMENT AGENCIES

General Disabilities
Section for Special Education
Division of Education
700 N. Illinois St.

Pierre, SD 57501-2293
(605) 733-3315

Crippled Children's Services
Children's Comprehensive Health
Care Services Program
Division of Health Services
Department of Health
Joe Foss Bldg., Room 313
523 E. Capital
Pierre, SD 57501
(605) 773-3737

Developmental Disabilities
Office of Developmental Disabilities
and Mental Health
Department of Social Services
700 N. Illinois St.
Pierre, SD 57501
(605) 773-3438

PRIVATE AGENCIES

General Disabilities
Easter Seal Society of South Dakota
106 W. Capitol
Pierre, SD 57501
(605) 224-5879

Cerebral Palsy
UCP of South Dakota
3600 S. Duluth
Sioux Falls, SD 57105
(605) 334-4220

Mental Retardation
South Dakota Association for
Retarded Citizens
222 W. Pleasant Dr.
P.O. Box 502
Pierre, SD 57501
(605) 224-8211

Speech and Hearing Impairments
South Dakota Speech-Language-
Hearing Association
R.R. #1, Box 94
Canistota, SD 57012
(605) 296-3544

TENNESSEE

GOVERNMENT AGENCIES

General Disabilities
Division of Special Programs
132 Cordell Hull Bldg.
Nashville, TN 37219
(615) 741-2851

Crippled Children's Services
Department of Public Health
100 Ninth Ave., N.
Nashville, TN 37219-5405
(615) 741-7353

Developmental Disabilities
Developmental Disabilities Council
James K. Polk Bldg., 4th floor
Nashville, TN 37219-5393
(615) 741-1742

Emotional Disturbance
Department of Mental Health and
Mental Retardation
James K. Polk Bldg., 3rd floor
505 Deaderick St.
Nashville, TN 37219
(615) 741-3107

Mental Retardation
Department of Mental Health and
Retardation
James K. Polk Bldg., 4th floor
505 Deaderick St.
Nashville, TN 37219
(615) 741-3803

Visual Impairments
Services for the Blind
Department of Human Services
1808 West End Bldg., 9th floor
Nashville, TN 37203
(615) 741-2919

PRIVATE AGENCIES

General Disabilities
Easter Seal Society of Tennessee
2001 Woodmont Blvd.

P.O. Box 158145
Nashville, TN 37215
(615) 292-6639

Cerebral Palsy
UCP of the Mid-South, Inc.
2670 Union Ave., Extended,
Suite 500
Memphis, TN 38112
(901) 323-0190

Mental Retardation
Tennessee Association for Retarded
Citizens
1700 Hayes St., Suite 200
Nashville, TN 37203
(615) 327-0294

TEXAS

GOVERNMENT AGENCIES

General Disabilities
Department of Special Education
201 E. 11th St.
Austin, TX 78701
(512) 834-4494
(800) 252-9968 (in Texas)

Crippled Children's Services
Texas Department of Health
1100 W. 49th St.
Austin, TX 78756
(512) 465-2666

Developmental Disabilities
Texas Planning Council for the
Developmentally Disabled
118 E. Riverside
Austin, TX 78704
(512) 445-8867

Emotional Disturbance
Department of Mental Health and
Retardation
Box 12668
Austin, TX 78711
(512) 454-3761

Mental Retardation
Department of Mental
Health/Developmental Disabilities
Box 12668
Austin, TX 78711
(512) 465-4520

PRIVATE AGENCIES

General Disabilities
Texas Easter Seal Society
4429 N. Central Expressway
Dallas, TX 75205
(214) 934-9104

Mental Retardation
Association for Retarded Citizens,
Texas
833 Houston St.
Austin, TX 78756
(512) 454-6694

Cerebral Palsy
UCP of Texas
7801 N. Lamar St., Suite F39
Austin, TX 78752
(512) 458-8161

Visual Impairments
State Commission for the Blind
314 W. 11th St.
P.O. Box 12866
Austin, TX 78711
(512) 475-6036

UTAH

GOVERNMENT AGENCIES

General Disabilities
Special Education Section
State Office of Education
250 E. 5th South
Salt Lake City, UT 84111
(801) 533-5982

Handicapped Children Services
Bureau

Family Health Services Division
Department of Health
2738 South, 2000 East
Salt Lake City, UT 84109
(801) 533-4173/6165

Developmental Disabilities
Utah Council for Handicapped and
Developmentally Disabled Persons
P.O. Box 11356
Salt Lake City, UT 84147
(801) 533-6770

Emotional Disturbance
Division of Mental Health
Department of Social Services
P.O. Box 45500
Salt Lake City, UT 84145-0500
(801) 533-5783

Mental Retardation
Division of Services to the
Handicapped
Department of Social Services
P.O. Box 45500
Salt Lake City, UT 84145-0500
(801) 533-7146

Visual Impairments
Services for the Visually Handicapped
Division of Adult Education and
Training
309 East 1st South
Salt Lake City, UT 84111
(801) 533-9393

PRIVATE AGENCIES

Cerebral Palsy
UCP of Utah
2500 Emigration Canyon
Salt Lake City, UT 84108
(801) 582-0700

Speech and Hearing Impairments
Utah Speech-Language-Hearing
Association
247 North, 400 East

Spanish Fork, UT 84660
(801) 798-8651

PARENT ORGANIZATIONS

General Disabilities
Utah Parent Information and Training
Center
4984 South, 300 West
Murray, UT 84107
(801) 265-9883
(800) 468-1160

Spina Bifida
Spina Bifida Association of Utah
8705 Brian Head Circle
Sandy, UT 84092
(801) 942-4097

VERMONT

GOVERNMENT AGENCIES

General Disabilities
Special Education Unit
Department of Education
120 State St.
Montpelier, VT 05602
(802) 828-3141

Crippled Children's Services
Medical Services Division
Department of Health
1193 North Ave.
P.O. Box 70
Burlington, VT 05401
(802) 863-7338

Developmental Disabilities
Vermont Developmental Disabilities
Council
103 S. Main St.
Waterbury, VT 05676
(802) 241-2612

Emotional Disturbance
Department of Mental Health
103 S. Main St.

Montpelier, VT 05602
(802) 241-2610

Mental Retardation
Community Mental Retardation
Programs
Department of Mental Health
103 S. Main St.
Waterbury, VT 05676
(802) 241-2636

Visual Impairments
Division for the Blind and Visually
Impaired
Department of Social and
Rehabilitation Services
103 S. Main St.
Waterbury, VT 05676
(802) 241-2210

PRIVATE AGENCIES

General Disabilities
Vermont Coalition of the
Handicapped
73 Main St.
Montpelier, VT 05602
(802) 223-6149

Cerebral Palsy
UCP of Vermont
73 Main St., Room 402
Montpelier, Vt 05602
(802) 223-5161

Mental Retardation
Vermont Association for Retarded
Citizens
Champlain Mall, #37
Winooski, VT 05404
(802) 655-4014

VIRGINIA

GOVERNMENT AGENCIES

General Disabilities
Special and Compensatory Education
Department of Education

P.O. Box 6-Q
Richmond, VA 23216
(804) 225-2402

Bureau of Crippled Children's
Services
Department of Health
109 Governor St.
Richmond, VA 23219
(804) 786-3691

State Mental Health Agency
Department of Mental Health and
Mental Retardation
P.O. Box 1797
Richmond, VA 23214
(804) 786-3921

Developmental Disabilities
Developmental Disabilities Program
Department of Mental Health and
Mental Retardation
P.O. Box 1797
Richmond, VA 23214
(804) 786-5313

Mental Retardation
Mental Retardation Program
Department of Mental Health and
Mental Retardation
P.O. Box 1797
Richmond, VA 23214
(804) 786-1746

Visual Impairments
Department for the Visually
Handicapped
397 Azalea Ave.
Richmond, VA 23227
(804) 264-3140

PRIVATE AGENCIES

General Disabilities
Easter Seal Society of Virginia, Inc.
4841 Williamson Rd.
P.O. Box 5496
Roanoke, VA 24012
(703) 362-1656

Mental Retardation
Association for Retarded Citizens
6 North 6th St., Suite 102
Richmond, VA 23219
(804) 649-8481

VIRGIN ISLANDS

GOVERNMENT AGENCIES

General Disabilities
Division of Special Education
Department of Education
P.O. Box 6640
Charlotte Amalie
St. Thomas, VI 00801
(809) 774-0100

Division of Maternal and Child
Health
Services for Crippled Children
Department of Health
P.O. Box 7309
Charlotte Amalie
St. Thomas, VI 00801
(809) 774-9000

Crippled Children's Services
Virgin Islands Department of Health
P.O. Box 520
Christiansted
St. Croix, VI 00802
(809) 778-6311

Developmental Disabilities
Virgin Islands Commission on
Handicaps
Windward Passage Hotel Plaza
P.O. Box 11179
St. Thomas, VI 00801
(809) 776-2043

Mental Retardation
Mental Retardation Program
Mental Health, Alcoholism, and Drug
Dependency Services
Department of Health

P.O. Box 7309
St. Thomas, VI 00801
(809) 774-4888

WASHINGTON

GOVERNMENT AGENCIES

General Disabilities
Special Education Programs
Office of Public Instruction
Old Capitol Bldg., F-G 11
Olympia, WA 98504
(206) 753-6733

Crippled Children's Services
Office of Community Health Services
Airport Bldg. 3, MS-LC-12D
Olympia, WA 98504
(206) 753-5853

Child Health Program Section
Office of Community Health Services
Airport Bldg. 3, MC-LC-12A
Olympia, WA 98504
(206) 753-9619

Developmental Disabilities
Developmental Disabilities Planning
Council
Mail Stop GH-52
Olympia, WA 98504
(206) 753-3908

Emotional Disturbance
Division of Mental Health
Department of Social and Health
Services
Mail Stop OB-425
Olympia, WA 98504
(206) 753-5414

Mental Retardation
Mental Retardation Program
Division of Developmental
Disabilities
Department of Social and Health
Services

Mail Stop OB-42C
Olympia, WA 98504
(206) 753-3900

PRIVATE AGENCIES

General Disabilities
Easter Seal Society for Crippled
Children and Adults of Washington
521 Second Avenue, West
Seattle, WA 98119
(206) 281-5700

Cerebral Palsy
UCPA of Washington
4409 Interlake Ave., North
P.O. Box C 30300
Wallingford Branch
Seattle, WA 98103
(206) 632-6191

Mental Retardation
Washington Association for Retarded
Citizens
1703 E. State Ave.
Olympia, WA 98506
(206) 357-5596

WEST VIRGINIA

GOVERNMENT AGENCIES

General Disabilities
Office of Special Education
Administration
Capitol Complex
Bldg. 6, Room B-309
Charleston, WV 25305
(304) 349-8830
(800) 642-8541 (in West Virginia)

Division of Handicapped Children
Department of Human Services
1356 Hansford St.
Charleston, WV 25301
(304) 348-3071

Developmental Disabilities
Developmental Disabilities Planning
Council
1800 Washington St.
Charleston, WV 25305
(304) 348-2276

Mental Retardation
Mental Retardation Program
Developmental Disabilities Services
Division of Behavioral Health
Department of Health
1800 Washington St.
Charleston, WV 25305
(304) 348-2276

PRIVATE AGENCIES

General Disabilities
Easter Seal Society of West Virginia
1210 Virginia St. East
Charleston, WV 25301
(304) 346-3508

Cerebral Palsy
UCP of West Virginia
P.O. Box 4012
St. Albans, WV 25177
(304) 727-6677

Mental Retardation
Association for Retarded Citizens in
West Virginia
70 Market St.
Union Trust Bldg., Room 400
Parkersburg, WV 26101
(304) 485-5283

WISCONSIN

GOVERNMENT AGENCIES

General Disabilities
Division of Handicapped Children
and Pupil Services
125 S. Webster St.
P.O. Box 7841

Madison, WI 53707
(608) 266-1649

Bureau for Children with Physical
Needs
Department of Public Instruction
125 S. Webster St.
P.O. Box 7841
Madison, WI 53707
(608) 266-3886

Developmental Disabilities
Wisconsin Council on Developmental
Disabilities
P.O. Box 7851
Madison, WI 53707
(608) 266-7826

Mental Health
TRY Adolescent Unit
Mendota Mental Health Institute
301 Troy Dr.
Madison, WI 53704
(608) 244-2411

Mental Retardation
Mental Retardation Program
Developmental Disabilities Office
Bureau of Community Programs
Division of Community Services
P.O. Box 7851
Madison, WI 53707
(608) 266-2862

PRIVATE AGENCIES

General Disabilities
Easter Seal Society of Wisconsin, Inc.
2702 Monroe St.
Madison, WI 53711
(608) 231-3411

Cerebral Palsy
UCP of Wisconsin
121 S. Hancock St.
Madison, WI 53703-3461
(608) 251-6533

Mental Retardation
Association for Retarded Citizens
5522 University Ave.
Madison, WI 53705
(608) 231-3335

WYOMING

GOVERNMENT AGENCIES

General Disabilities
Program Services Unit
State Department of Education
Hathaway Office Bldg.
Cheyenne, WY 82002
(307) 777-7417

Children's Health Services
Hathaway Office Bldg.
Cheyenne, WY 82002
(307) 777-7941

Developmental Disabilities
State Planning Council on
Developmental Disabilities
P.O. Box 265
Cheyenne, WY 82003
(307) 632-0775

Emotional Disturbances
Division of Community Programs
Department of Health and Social
Services
Hathaway Office Bldg.
Cheyenne, WY 82002
(307) 777-7094

Adapted from information furnished by the National Information Center for Handicapped Children and Youth (NICHCY). Updates are available by writing
    NICHCY
    P.O. Box 1492
    Washington, D.C. 20013.

National Toll-free Numbers

Toll-free Directory Assistance............................. (800) 555-1212
Acquired Immune Deficiency Syndrome (AIDS) .... (800) 221-7044
AMC Cancer Information Center .... (800) 525-3777
American Council of the Blind............................ (800) 424-8666
American Kidney Fund .... (800) 638-8299
Amtrak .... (TTY) (800) 523-6590
                                    (800) 562-6960 (in Pennsylvania)
                                                    (800) 872-7245
Better Hearing Institute Hearing Helpline .... (800) 424-8576
Cancer Information Service National Line ....(800) 4-CANCER
Center for Special Education Technology.................. (800) 345-TECH
Epilepsy Information Line .... (800) 426-0660
HeartLife (limited information for parents) .... (800) 241-6993
International Shriners Headquarters .... (800) 237-5055
                                        (800) 282-9161 (in Florida)

Juvenile Diabetes Foundation International Hotline .... (800) 223-1138
National Association for Hearing and Speech Action Line ..... (800) 638-8255
National Asthma Center at the National Jewish Hospital
   and Research Center .... (800) 222-5864
National Center for Stuttering .... (800) 221-2483
National Committee for Citizens in Education .... (800) NETWORK
National Crisis Center for the Deaf......................... (800) 446-9876
                                        (800) 552-3723 (in Virginia)
National Cystic Fibrosis Foundation .... (800) 344-4823
National Down Syndrome Society .... (800) 221-4602
National Down Syndrome Congress......................... (800) 232-6372
National Easter Seal Society .... (800) 221-6827
National Health Information Clearinghouse.................. (800) 336-4797
National Hearing Aid Society................................ (800) 521-5247
National Information Center for Educational Media .... (800) 421-8711
Library of Congress—
National Library Services for the Blind and
   Physically Handicapped .... (800) 424-8567
National Organization on Disability .... (800) 248-ABLE
National Rehabilitation Information Center .... (800) 34-NARIC
National Retinitis Pigmentosa Foundation .... (800) 638-2300
National Society to Prevent Blindness....................... (800) 221-3004
National Special Needs Center .... (800) 233-1222
                                        (TDD) (800) 833-3232
National Spinal Cord Injury Hotline .... (800) 526-3456
National SIDS Foundation.................................. (800) 221-SIDS
Orton Dyslexia Society .... (800) 222-3123
Parents Without Partners .... (800) 638-8078
RP Foundation Fighting Blindness........................... (800) 638-2300
Spina Bifida Hotline ....(800) 621-3141 (except Illinois)
Spinal Cord Society .... (800) 328-8253
                                        (800) 862-0179 (in Minnesota)
Tripod—Service for Hearing Impaired .... (800) 352-8888
U.S. Consumer Product Safety Commission.................. (800) 638-2772
                                        (TTY) (800) 836-8270

Bibliography

Arthritis

Williams, Gordon F. *Children with Chronic Arthritis, A Primer for Patients and Parents.* Littleton, MA: PSG Publishing Co., 1981.

We Can: A Guide for Parents of Children with Arthritis. Atlanta: Arthritis Foundation, 1982.

Art

Anderson, F. E., J. D. Calchado, and P. McNally. *Art for the Handicapped.* Normal, IL: Illinois State University Press, 1979.

Atack, Sally. *Art Activities for the Handicapped.* Englewood Cliffs, NJ: Prentice-Hall, 1982.

Gault, E., and S. Sykes. *Crafts for the Disabled: A New Kind of Crafts Book for People with Special Needs.* New York: Thomas Y. Crowell, 1979.

Gould, E., and L. Gould. *Arts and Crafts for Physically and Mentally Disabled.* Springfield, IL: Charles C. Thomas, 1978.

Pfeuffer, D. B., and R. F. Kingsley. *Enhancing Learning for the Handicapped Through the Arts.* Columbus: Ohio Department of Education, 1982.

Sherrill, Claudine. *Creative Arts for the Severely Handicapped.* Springfield, IL: Charles C. Thomas, 1979.

Silver, R. *Developing Cognitive and Creative Skills Through Art.* Baltimore: University Park Press, 1982.

Autism

Balow, B., S. Raison, and G. Reid. *Revised Autism Sourcebook for Parents and Professionals.* Minneapolis: Special Education Programs, University of Minnesota, 1980.

DeMyer, M. *Parents and Children in Autism.* New York: John Wiley and Sons, 1979.

National Society for Autistic Children. *How They Grow: A Handbook for Parents of Young Children With Autism.* 1980. Available from National Society for Autistic Children, 1234 Massachusetts Ave., N.W., Washington, DC 20005; also available in Spanish.

Paluszny, M. *Autism, a Practical Guide for Parents and Professionals.* Syracuse: Syracuse University Press, 1979.

Blindness

Ferrell, Kay A. *Parenting Preschoolers: Suggestions for Raising Young Blind and Visually Impaired Children.* 1984. Available from The American Foundation for the Blind, 15 W. 16th St., New York, NY 10011.

Kastein, S., I. Spaulding, and B. Scarf. *Raising the Young Blind Child: A Guide for Parents and Educators.* New York: Human Sciences Press, 1980.

Bowel and Bladder

Chapman, Warren, Margaret Hill, and David Shurlett. *Management of the Neurogenic Bowel and Bladder.* Oak Brook, IL: Eterna Press, 1979.

Cerebral Palsy

Finnie, Nancie R. *Handling the Young Cerebral Palsied Child at Home.* Second edition. New York: E. P. Dutton, 1975.

Clothing

Laurel Designs
5 Laurel Ave., #6
Belvedere, CA 94920
(415) 435-1891

Akcess
P.O. Box 15891
San Diego, CA 92115

Death and Dying

Bordow, Joan. *The Ultimate Loss: Coping with the Death of a Child.* New York: Beaufort Books, 1982.

Grollman, Earl A., ed. *Explaining Death to Children.* Boston: Beacon Press, 1967.

Kübler-Ross, Elisabeth. *On Death and Dying.* London: Macmillan Co., 1969.

Kushner, Harold S. *When Bad Things Happen to Good People.* New York: Avon, 1981.

Middleton, A. H., A. A. Attwell, and G. O. Walsh. *Epilepsy: A Handbook for Patients, Parents, Families, Teachers, Health and Social Workers*. Boston: Little Brown and Co., 1981.

Prensky, A. L. and H. S. Pulkes. *Care of the Neurologically Handicapped Child: A Book for Parents and Professionals*. New York: Oxford University Press, 1982.

Equipment

Gaston, D. *It's Easy to Make Aides for Your Handicapped Child*. Englewood Cliffs, NJ: Prentice-Hall, 1981.

Dental Care

National Easter Seal Society for Crippled Children and Adults, Chicago: *Toothbrushing and Flossing: A Manual of Home Dental Care for Persons Who Are Handicapped*. 1978.

Schey, Linda S. *Home Dental Care for the Handicapped Child*. 1974. Available from Boston Children's Hospital Medical Center, 300 Longwood Ave., Boston, MA 02115.

Weyman, Joan. *The Dental Care of Handicapped Children*. Baltimore: Williams and Wilkins, 1971.

Diabetes

Little, Billie. *Recipes for Diabetes*. New York: Bantam, 1981.

Travis, Luther. *Instructional Aid on Juvenile Diabetes Mellitus*. Available from South Texas Diabetes Association, 6201 Middle Fisk Ville Rd., Austin, TX 75784.

Discipline

Dobson, James. *Dare to Discipline*. Wheaton, IL: Tyndale House Publishers, 1970.

Gordon, Thomas. *Parent Effectiveness Training*. New York: New American Library, 1975.

Silberman, Melvin and Susan Wheelan. *How to Discipline Without Feeling Guilty*. New York: Hawthorne Books, 1980.

Epilepsy

Epilepsy: You and Your Child, A Guide for Parents. 1983. Available free from Epilepsy Foundation of America (EFA), 4351 Garden City Dr., Landover, MD 20785.

Jan, J. E., R. G. Ziegler, and G. Erba. *Does Your Child Have Epilepsy?* Baltimore: University Park Press, 1983.

Hofmann, Ruth. *How to Build Special Furniture and Equipment for Handicapped Children*. Springfield, IL: Charles C. Thomas, 1970.

Hutt, J. K. *Equipment for Physically Handicapped Children in Rattan and Bamboo*. Amberley, England: Disabilities Study Unit, 1979.

General

Bigge, June. *Teaching Individuals with Physical and Multiple Disabilities*. Columbus: Charles E. Merrill, 1982.

Blakeslee, Mary E. *The Wheelchair Gourmet*. New York: Beaufort Books, 1981.

Clark, Bettina. *Going to the Hospital*. New York: Random House, 1971.

Cohen, Sara Kay. *Whoever Said Life Is Fair?* New York: Charles Scribner's Sons, 1977.

Cruzic, Kathleen. *Disabled? Yes. Defeated? No*. Englewood Cliffs, NJ: Prentice-Hall, 1982.

Downey, John, and Neils Low. *The Child with the Disabling Illness*. Philadelphia: W. B. Saunders Co., 1982.

Dudale, A. E. "Is Human Life Precious?" In *Clinical Pediatrics VII*. p. 379. Philadelphia: J. B. Lippincott Co., 1968.

Hale, Glorya. *The Source Book for the Disabled*. New York and London: Paddington Press, Ltd., 1979.

Martin, Patricia. "Marital Breakdown in Families with Patients with Spina Bifida Cystica." *Developmental Medicine and Child Neurology*, 17:757–64, 1975.

Porter, Sylvia. *Your Own Money*. New York: Avon, 1983.

Potts, William J. "The Heart of a Child." *Journal of the American Medical Association*, 161:6, 1956.

Rainer, Tristine. *The New Diary*. Los Angeles: J. P. Tarcher, 1978.

Rusk, Howard, and Eugene Taylor. *Living with a Disability*. Garden City, NJ: Balliston Co., 1953.

Hearing Disabilities

Does My Infant Hear? Testing Your Baby's Hearing at Home. Available from House Ear Institute, 256 S. Lake St., Los Angeles, CA 90057.

Seligman, Milton. *The Family with a Handicapped Child*. New York: Grune and Stratton, 1983.

Spock, Benjamin, and Marion Lenigo. *Caring for Your Disabled Child*. Greenwich, CT: Fawcett Publications, 1965.

Vignos, Paul, George Spencer, and Kenneth Archibald. "Management of Progressive Muscular Dystrophy of Childhood." *Journal of the American Medical Association*, 184:39–96, 1963.

Wickes, Frances. *The Inner World of Childhood*. Englewood, NJ: Prentice-Hall, 1966.

Learning Disabilities

Brutten, M., et al. *Something's Wrong with My Child*. New York: Harcourt Brace Janovich, 1973.

D'Antoni, Alice C., et al. *A Parent's Guide to Learning Disabilities*. Elizabethtown, PA: Continental Press, 1978.

A Directory of Summer Camps for Children with Learning Disabilities. Available from ACLD, 4156 Library Rd., Pittsburgh, PA 15234.

Melton, David. *Promises to Keep: A Handbook for Parents of Learning Disabled, Handicapped and Brain-Injured Children*. Danbury, CT: Franklin Watts, 1984.

Osman, Betty B., with Henriette Blinder. *No One to Play with: The Social Side of Learning Disabilities*. New York: Random House, 1982.

Rowan, Ruth Dinkins. *Helping Children with Learning Disabilities: In the Home, Church and Community*. Nashville: Abingdon Press, 1977.

Schoonover, R. J. *Handbook for Parents of Children with Learning Disabilities*. Danville, IL: Interstate Printers and Publishers, 1976.

Smith, S. *No Easy Answers—The Learning Disabled Child*. New York: Bantam, 1980.

Typing for People with Learning Disabilities. Available from Jack Heller, % Teaching Institute for Special Education, 2947 Bayside Ct., Wantagh, NY 11793.

Mental Retardation

Blodgett, H. E. *Mentally Retarded Children: What Parents and Others Should Know*. Minneapolis: University of Minnesota Press, 1974.

Brehm, S. *Help for Your Child: A Parent's Guide to Mental Health Services*. Englewood Cliffs, NJ: Prentice-Hall, 1978.

Cunningham, C., and P. Sloper. *Helping Your Exceptional Baby: A Practical and Honest Approach to Raising a Mentally Handicapped Child*. New York: Pantheon Books, 1980.

Stabler, E. *Primer for Parents of a Mentally Retarded Child*. Available from Association for Retarded Citizens, P.O. Box 6109, 2501 Avenue J, Arlington, TX 76011.

Music Therapy

Nordoff, Paul. *Therapy in Music for Handicapped Children*. London: Gollancz, 1981.

Ostomies

Hamilton, Susan. *My Child Has an Ostomy*. 1974. Available from United Ostomy Association, Inc., 2001 W. Beverly Blvd., Los Angeles, CA 90057.

Held, Doris, and Arlene Klostermann. *Chris Has an Ostomy*. Available from United Ostomy Association, Inc., 2001 W. Beverly Blvd., Los Angeles, CA 90057.

Jeter, Katherine F. *These Special Children: The Ostomy Ostomy Book for Parents of Children with Colostomies, Ileostomies and Urostomies*. Palo Alto: Bull Publishing, 1982.

Parenting

Heisler, Verda. *A Handicapped Child in the Family*. New York: Grune and Stratton, 1972.

Klein, Carole. *The Single Parent Experience*. New York: Avon, 1973.

Play

Alkerna, Chester J. *Puppet Making*. New York: Sterling Publishing, 1971.

Bergstrom, Joan M. *School's Out—Now What?* Berkeley, CA: Ten Speed Press, 1984.

Eckstein, Joan, and Joyce Gleit. *Fun with Making Things*. New York: Avon, 1979.

Gregg, Elizabeth. *What to Do When There's Nothing to Do*. New York: Dell Publishing, 1968.

Johnson, June. *Home Play for the Pre-School Child*. New York: Harper & Bros., 1957.

Kauffman, C., and P. Farrell. *If You Live with Little Children*. New York: G. P. Putnam & Sons, 1957.

McConkey, Roy, and Dorothy Jeffree. *Making Toys for Handicapped Children*. Englewood Cliffs, NJ: Prentice-Hall, 1983.

Respiratory Problems

Barr, Anne. *At Home with a Monitor*. 1980. Available from the National Sudden Infant Death Syndrome Foundation, Two Metro Plaza, Suite 205, 8240 Professional Pl., Landover, MD 20785.

Filipek, Judith. *Caring for Your Baby with a Trach Tube*. Available from the American Lung Association of Alameda County, 295 27th St., Oakland, CA 94612.

Putman, Margaret, Thomas R. Harris, and Mary M. Payne. *Handbook for Parents of Children with Bronchopulmonary Dysplasia*. Available from Larry Olsen, Biomedical Communications Department, University of Arizona Health Sciences Center, University of Arizona, Tucson, AZ 85724.

Spina Bifida

Swinyard, C. A., *The Child with Spina Bifida*. 1977. Available from Spina Bifida Association, 343 S. Dearborn St., Chicago, IL 60604; also available in Spanish.

Stoma Care

Lund, C., and V. Atterescu. "Stoma Care." *Neonatal Network,* Dec. 1984, pp. 28–33.

Travel

Barish, Frances. *Frommer's Guide for the Disabled Traveler*. New York: Simon & Schuster, 1985.

Visual Impairments

Maloney, Patricia L. *Practical Guidance for Parents of the Visually Handicapped Pre-Schooler*. Springfield, IL: Charles C. Thomas, 1981.

By Parents of Handicapped Children

Ayauet, Evelyn. *Living with the Handicapped Child*. New York: G. P. Putnam, 1964.

Dickman, Irving R., and Sol Gordon. *One Miracle at a Time: How to Get Help for Your Disabled Child—From the Experiences of Other Parents*. New York: Simon & Schuster, 1986.

Featherstone, Helen. *A Difference in the Family—Living with a Disabled Child*. New York: Penguin Books, 1981.

Jones, Monica. *Home Care for the Chronically Ill or Disabled Child*. New York: Harper & Row, 1985.

McNamara, John, and B. McNamara. *The Special Child Handbook*. New York: Hawthorn Books, 1977.

Ross, Bette M. *Our Special Child*. Springfield, IL: Charles E. Merrill, 1981.

Russell, Philippa. *The Wheelchair Child*. Englewood Cliffs, NJ: Prentice-Hall, 1985.

RESOURCE LIST

* **BABYSITTERS**

Name	Address	Phone
_____	_____	_____
_____	_____	_____
	_____	_____

* *Places for our weekly dates*

_____ _____ _____

_____ _____ _____

* **DOCTORS**

Name	Address	Phone
_____	_____	_____
_____	_____	_____

* *Drugstore* _____
* *Hospital* _____
* *Ambulance* _____
* *Physical Therapists* _____
* *Schoolteachers/Counselors* _____
* *Support Group/Supportive Friends*

Name	Address	Phone
_____	_____	_____
_____	_____	_____

* **BOOKS**

Author	Title
_____	_____
_____	_____
_____	_____

* *Adaptive Equipment*

_____

_____

_____

* *Agencies that can help with:*
Medical Expenses

_____

Emotional Needs

_____

Equipment _____

WEEKLY CALENDAR

	7–12 A.M.		1–6 P.M.	7–12 P.M.
MONDAY Date				
	Rx			
TUESDAY Date				
	Rx			
WEDNESDAY Date				
	Rx			
THURSDAY Date				
	Rx			
FRIDAY Date				
	Rx			
SATURDAY Date				
	Rx			
SUNDAY Date				
	Rx			

Index

Bathroom aids, 163. *See also* Bladder
    controls and aids; Bowel
    programs
Big Brother programs, 80
Bigge, June, 117, 118
Big Sister programs, 80
Birth defects, agencies concerned
    with, 206
Bladder controls and aids, 164–66
Blindness, 202
    agencies, 206, 208
Blocks, toy, 78
Body awareness, 78
Books, children's, 122–23
    about hospitals, 178
Bowel programs, 167–69
Boys' Clubs, 80
Braces, 158–60
Brainstem audiometry, 104
Buscaglia, Leo, 137
Buttons, 171
Byram Public Pressure Urinary de-
    vice, 164

California, agencies in, 219–20
California Children's Services (CCS),
    58
Cancer, agencies concerned with, 206
Candlelighters Childhood Cancer
    Foundation, The, 206
Cardiologists, 199
Cardiopulmonary resuscitation
    (CPR), 174
Cataracts, 202
Catheters, 164
Catholic Social Services, 79
Cerebral palsy, 202, 206
Cerebral vascular accident (CVA or
    stroke), 203
Child care. *See also* Day care
    financial assistance for, 58
    shared among mothers, 108–9
    support networks for, 62
Chores, 82–83, 138–40
Chronically ill children, agencies con-
    cerned with, 206

Clark, Bettina, 178
Clay modeling, 125
Cleft lip and palate, agencies con-
    cerned with, 206
Clinics, large, 93–95. *See also* Hospitals
Clothing, 58, 156, 171–72
Cluck, Amy, 77–79
Cohen, Sara Kay, 21–22, 60
Collages, 125
Colorado, agencies in, 221
Colostomy, 166–67, 203, 208
Communication
    between parents and relatives or family
        friends, 41–43
    between parents and siblings of handi-
        capped child, 67–71
    with teenagers, 142–44
Communication disorders, education
    of children with, 117–19
Community recreation centers, 80
Confidence. *See* Self-esteem
Congenital, definition of, 202
Connecticut, agencies in, 220–21
Constipation, 170
Contracture, 202
Control. *See* Discipline
Coordination, 78, 125, 126
Coping mechanisms. *See* Emotional
    responses
Counseling for parents, 14–16, 19,
    33, 35, 36, 41, 59, 80
    by friends of the family, 28
    at neonatal intensive-care nurseries,
        22, 24
    by religious or spiritual advisers,
        28, 29
Counseling for the handicapped
    child, 81
    teenagers, 130, 134, 135
CPR (cardiopulmonary resuscitation),
    174
Crafts, 121, 125
Crayons, 179
Creativity, 77, 125, 126
Cribs, 173
Crippled Children's Services, 93

About the Author

Raising a Handicapped Child stems from Dr. Thompson's thirty years of experience in diagnosing and treating children with neuromuscular diseases and handicapping physical conditions. She is currently director of the Center for Handicapped Children and Teenagers in San Francisco and has served as director of six other neuromuscular programs. She is a Fellow of the American Academy of Pediatrics, an assistant clinical professor of pediatrics at the University of California Medical School in San Diego, and a consultant at the San Diego U.S. Naval Hospital. She treats patients not only from California but from other states and foreign countries and is a recognized authority in her field.